Shifting Boundaries

Shifting Boundaries

Immigrant Youth Negotiating National,
State, and Small-Town Politics

Alexis M. Silver

Stanford University Press
Stanford, California

Stanford University Press
Stanford, California

Printed in the United States of America on acid-free, archival-quality paper

Library of Congress Cataloging-in-Publication Data

Names: Silver, Alexis M., author.
Title: Shifting boundaries : immigrant youth negotiating national, state, and small town politics / Alexis M. Silver.
Description: Stanford, California : Stanford University Press, 2018. | Includes bibliographical references and index.
Identifiers: LCCN 2017043707 (print) | LCCN 2017046089 (ebook) | ISBN 9781503605756 | ISBN 9781503604988 (cloth : alk. paper) | ISBN 9781503605749 (pbk. : alk. paper)
Subjects: LCSH: Immigrant youth—North Carolina. | Illegal aliens—North Carolina. | Children of immigrants—North Carolina. | Latin Americans—North Carolina. | Hispanic American youth—North Carolina. | North Carolina—Emigration and immigration—Government policy. | United States—Emigration and immigration—Government policy.
Classification: LCC JV7053 (ebook) | LCC JV7053 .S55 2018 (print) | DDC 323.3/508691209776—dc23
LC record available at https://lccn.loc.gov/2017043707

To all of the youth who shared their stories, and to all of the teachers and mentors who helped them fight for a brighter future

Contents

Acknowledgments

This book would not have been possible without the extensive support of many people. I express my deepest gratitude to all of the young adults, teachers, parents, and mentors who shared their time, experiences, reflections, frustrations, and hopes. It has been an amazing experience to watch the youth I interviewed for this book grow up into productive and self-assured adults and, in some cases, become parents. I thank them for their honesty and friendship, and I feel incredibly privileged that they trusted me with their stories.

I began research on this book over a decade ago and learned so much about fieldwork, writing, and analysis in the process. I am indebted to Jacqueline Hagan and Ted Mouw for guiding me along the way. Their extensive and thoughtful critiques in earlier stages of this project strengthened my research and writing considerably, and I will never be able to repay them for their intellectual and emotional support. Jackie opened up her heart and her home to me. She helped me build professional connections and offered invaluable feedback on my research and analysis—all while making me laugh. I continue to rely on her support and friendship, and I am so grateful to have her in my corner. Ted ignited my love for immigration research and social demography, deepened my intellectual curiosity by challenging me to think about my research from new angles, and was often the only person who could calm me down when stress got the better of me. Their guidance nurtured my professional and intellectual development, and I cannot thank them enough.

I also thank and acknowledge Paul Cuadros, who has been an amazing example of an engaged professor. I continue to be inspired by him and have learned so much from him about how to do thoughtful, caring, and impactful research. I am so thankful for his friendship.

I am grateful for the support of the intellectual community of scholars who have challenged and pushed me. In particular, I acknowledge Kara Cebulko, who has helped me develop many of the ideas in this book and whose friendship and writing support have been invaluable to me. Helen Marrow also provided critical feedback that helped me deepen the theory and analysis presented in this book. Robert Smith has provided advice and feedback since the early stages of this project, and I am so thankful for his insight and support. Bernadette Ludwig and Stephen Ruszczyk were extremely helpful in keeping me on task and offering suggestions to help develop my ideas. I thank Sergio Chavez and Vanesa Ribas for their friendship and guidance about the book-publishing process. My dear friends, Ria Van Ryn and Mairead Moloney, helped me both emotionally and intellectually on this journey, and I am so grateful for their endless encouragement and editing help. I also thank Roberto Gonzales, whose work has inspired and pushed mine. I am grateful to Cedric de Leon, whose insight on the proposal was so generous and amazingly helpful. I am also thankful to Jessica Cobb, whose editing and insight helped me think about ways to develop my analysis and organize the book. I am lucky to be surrounded by supportive and intellectually challenging colleagues at Purchase College. I thank Linda Bastone, Leandro Benmergui, Paula Halperin, Matthew Immergut, Chrys Ingraham, Kristin Karlberg, Suzanne Kessler, Mary Kossut, Lisa Jean Moore, and Liza Steele for listening to me talk through this project for years and for providing comic relief when I needed it. Lisa Jean, especially, was incredibly helpful in offering feedback and guiding me through the book proposal process. Finally, I acknowledge Amada Armenta, Elizabeth Aranda, Jennifer Bickham Mendez, Philip Cohen, Heather Edelblute, Barbara Entwisle, René Flores, Hannah Gill, Tanya Golsh-Boza, Shannon Gleeson, Emilio Parrado, Lisa Pearce, Beatriz Riefkohl Muñiz, Leah Schmalzbauer, Michael Shanahan, and Elizabeth Vaquera, who have all provided advice, insight, and feedback in various stages of this research.

I am grateful to all of the people at Stanford University Press. In particular, Marcela Maxfield supported the project from the beginning and provided extremely helpful feedback, and Olivia Bartz worked tirelessly to answer all of my questions and bring this project to fruition. I also thank the anonymous reviewers. Their critiques strengthened the manuscript considerably.

I am thankful for the financial support of the Center for the Study of the American South and the sociology department at the University of North Carolina at Chapel Hill as well as the faculty support from the State University of New York—Purchase College.

Finally, I thank my family for their endless support. I am incredibly fortunate to come from a family that has always believed in my education. As I spoke with youth who struggled against closed doors and limited opportunities, I frequently reflected on my own good fortune. I am grateful to have parents who were willing and able to help open so many doors for me. My father and sister also helped edit various chapters and helped me talk through my ideas. My mother made me the proud daughter of an immigrant. My wonderful husband somehow endured living with me through the book-writing process and pregnancy, neither of which brought out the best in me. I could not imagine a more patient, supportive, or loving partner. I am so grateful to have him by my side. My daughter managed to wait inside me while I finished this book and even gave me three days to prepare for her arrival after I sent it out for review. I am so thankful for the joy that she has brought into our lives.

Shifting Boundaries

Introduction: Navigating Exclusion

In 2008 Diana, age eighteen, was sitting in class when a voice over the intercom requested that she report to the main office.[1] Two months later, she recalled that August afternoon:

> Oh my god . . . I felt something really [she pauses, struggling to find the right words]. Inside of me, like, something bad was going to happen. I told myself that something bad was about to happen, and I got there [to the office], and that lady said, "I'm sorry but you can't keep coming to school anymore." They told me that I couldn't study there anymore because I didn't have a Social Security number or a green card. And after, I cried because all of my dreams and everything, they just disappeared.

The administration caught their mistake the week that Diana began community college. Less than a month after Diana enrolled, the North Carolina Community College System (NCCCS) passed a resolution barring undocumented students from attending community colleges throughout the state (North Carolina Community College System 2008). Relying on a strict interpretation of the federal Illegal Immigration Reform and Immigrant Responsibility Act of 1996, the NCCCS board had determined postsecondary education to be a state benefit and had thus deemed unauthorized immigrants ineligible to enroll.[2] Diana knew about the ban on undocumented students, but because no one mentioned her status when she registered for classes, she thought she was safe. After her admission was revoked, Diana returned home, ashamed and heartbroken.

She withdrew into her room and barely spoke to anyone for a week. Gradually, Diana emerged from her state of shock, and from her bedroom, and began making plans to apply to four-year colleges. Four-year colleges were not affected by the ban, but they were far more expensive and she had already missed the deadline to apply. She did not find her way back to school that year, or the year after, even after the ban on undocumented immigrants was overturned. Instead, she joined her mother and older sisters at a paper factory, where she worked from seven in the morning until five in the evening. The factory was over an hour's drive from their home, and the early mornings left her exhausted. She abandoned her plans to return to college, deciding instead to focus on work.

I got to know Diana during the seven years of fieldwork and interview research I conducted in the town that I call Allen Creek, North Carolina. In the following pages, I tell the stories of 1.5-generation youth like Diana to illustrate how individual lives become entangled in institutional-, state-, and federal-level policies that alternately define immigrant youth and young adults as incorporated members or unwanted outsiders. The 1.5 generation are immigrants who were brought to the United States as children, while the second generation are the US-born children of immigrants. Because both 1.5- and second-generation immigrants have largely grown up in the United States, they have similar access to cultural and linguistic capital and often have similar experiences in primary and secondary school. While not all within the 1.5 generation lack immigration authorization, many do. As they attempt to apply for college and enter the labor market, the nearly two million 1.5-generation unauthorized immigrants in the country face extensive obstacles that their second-generation peers do not. In new-destination states, or states that have recently experienced demographic shifts as a result of new immigration flows, unauthorized 1.5-generation youth like Diana faced particularly hostile political climates as they aged into the early stages of adulthood.

Though this book focuses primarily on 1.5-generation unauthorized youth, I also incorporate stories from their second-generation citizen peers to distinguish the impacts that shifting policies had on each group. They too faced racism, expectations of illegality, and threats to their safety and security as they feared the deportation of their unauthorized parents and siblings. In small-town settings with recent in-flows of immigrants, Latinos were conspicuous and anti-immigrant hostility spilled over to affect the entire Latino community, regardless of immigration status. As communities throughout North Carolina grappled with how to respond to growing Latino immigration, proposed anti-immigrant legislation became a recurring feature in the state's General Assembly.

Frustrated by the political bravado but limited action at the federal level, state governments increasingly enacted policies aimed at immigrants in the first decade of the 2000s. Research has shown that the devolution of immigration enforcement from the federal to state level has created more exclusionary living environments for immigrants, particularly in conservative states and localities with less immigration experience (Bada et al. 2010; Brettle and Nibbs 2011; Coleman 2012; Coleman and Kocher 2011; Flores 2014; Furuseth and Smith 2010; Hagan, Rodriguez, and Castro 2011; Olivas 2007; Ramakrishnan and Wong 2010; Varsanyi et al. 2012; Wishnie 2001). Exclusionary laws and ordinances have been particularly prevalent in new-destination areas, such as the South (Leerkes, Leach, and Bachmeier 2012), where large percentages of Latino populations comprise unauthorized immigrants. As new immigrant populations came into contact with communities that had very little experience with immigration, tensions flared and new-destination sites became hotbeds for growing anti-immigrant legislation. Yet, even within hostile contexts, research has repeatedly shown that immigrants establish connections to their communities of residence, often as a result of local interactions (Marrow 2011; Silver 2012).

Immigration policies catapulted to the top of the political agenda in North Carolina as the state witnessed unprecedented growth in its Latino population in the 1990s and early 2000s. According to the US Census, the foreign-born population in North Carolina grew at a rate of 273.7 percent between 1990 and 2000, the fastest rate of growth in the country. Among children of immigrants, the growth was even faster at a 508 percent rate of increase between 1990 and 2008 (Fortuny 2010). The vast majority of this population growth was fueled by Latino immigrants. Between 1990 and 2000, the Latino population in the state increased by 394 percent (Kochhar, Suro, and Tofoya 2005), and by 2010, the total Latino population had reached eight hundred thousand, comprising 8.4 percent of the state's population (Passel, Cohn, and Lopez 2011). As the state's demographic profile shifted, politicians and school administrators grappled with how to respond effectively to the new and largely unauthorized population. As institutional policies became more restrictive and local immigration enforcement increased, youth like Diana became increasingly aware of the anti-immigrant climate in their home state. For Diana and many of her peers, this realization was heartbreaking, as they had come to embrace North Carolina as their home.

Diana had moved to the United States from Guatemala when she was eleven years old. She crossed the border with her younger sister and older brother and twenty-one other immigrants. When I asked Diana if she was scared crossing over at such a young age, she said that she remembered feeling hot and exhausted under the scorching sun, but not scared. She focused on the excitement of seeing her parents. Diana's father had left Guatemala when she was just six years old, followed three years later by her mother. The children missed their parents terribly and were ecstatic when, two years later, their parents arranged for a *coyote* (human smuggler) to bring the three youngest children to North Carolina. Three years later, after saving enough money, they sent for the two eldest sisters as well.

Diana was thrilled to be reunited with her parents, but her adjustment to North Carolina was bumpy. She remembers seeing her mobile home on arrival and feeling shocked because she had assumed that their house in the United States would be bigger than their home in Guatemala. Moreover, communication in school was difficult, until a bilingual Mexican girl in her class befriended her and helped translate. After school, Diana's mother brought her to the house of an older white woman in town, where she had been working as a part-time domestic worker for over a year when Diana arrived. Michelle, her employer, took an immediate liking to Diana and her siblings and tutored them in English. When Diana graduated from high school in 2008, Michelle offered to pay Diana's community college tuition, which amounted to about thirty-five hundred dollars per semester at out-of-state rates. Diana leapt at the opportunity, but when the NCCCS banned unauthorized immigrant students, Diana's plans crumbled around her. When the community college ban was overturned in 2009, Diana did not reenroll in college. She explained her decision to work full-time: "I didn't have a choice." Diana's mother was sick, and the dust from the paper factory exacerbated her lung problems. Eventually, her health issues became so severe that she had to stop working. Compounding their difficulties, Diana's father had an accident that caused him to drastically reduce his hours at his construction job. Diana could not justify going to school when she felt that her family was relying on her to help pay the bills.

Diana shifted her ambitions for college onto her younger sister, Nuria. In 2011, Nuria had already secured a partial college scholarship with the help of her high school AVID adviser.[3] Michelle promised to pay the remainder of Nuria's tuition, and Diana and her siblings would help pay for books and supplies. Diana decided that once she helped put Nuria through college in the United States, she would return to Guatemala to complete her own education. She had misgivings about returning to a place that she could scarcely remember, but she saw no other way to avoid the hardships that her parents had endured for so long. She laid out her options:

> I'll probably go back to Guatemala. . . . Right now, I'll be working to help
> Nuria until she's through college. . . . But after that, I think I'll go back to
> Guatemala. I have cousins and land and a house there. I don't remember too
> much about Guatemala, but I'll probably go to school there. That's what I'm
> planning to do. It's an advantage to know English and Spanish over there, and
> I have my diploma from here from high school, so I think that will help me a
> lot. It's going to feel weird though. It's been a long time since I've been there,
> but if I have to go, I will go. I would have a better life. I probably would go to
> college there since I couldn't go here, and graduate and have a better job. And
> be legal.

The idea of separating from her family again saddened Diana deeply. Nonetheless, she believed she would have better work opportunities without the constraints of her unauthorized immigration status.

Diana's opportunities changed suddenly when President Obama announced Deferred Action for Childhood Arrivals (DACA) on June 15, 2012. An action of prosecutorial discretion, DACA provided protection from deportation and work permits to unauthorized immigrants under the age of thirty-one who were brought to the United States before their sixteenth birthday, were educated in US schools, had no criminal history, and were enrolled in school or had earned high school diplomas or GEDs or served in the military. Though it was not a cure-all policy, DACA aimed to address some of the unequal opportunities between eligible unauthorized 1.5-generation immigrants and their authorized immigrant and second-generation peers.

DACA gave Diana a reason to stay in the United States, and it motivated her to return to college. Yet out-of-state tuition remained a barrier to enrolling in college, and her plans of obtaining a driver's license were delayed when the North Carolina Department of Motor Vehicles (DMV) temporarily ceased issuing licenses to DACA beneficiaries in response to public backlash against the federal policy. Although Diana viewed DACA as a step toward inclusion, pushback from state legislators and institutional administrators quickly reminded her that her opportunities remained obstructed. Moreover, because DACA was implemented through prosecutorial discretion, it did not offer Diana or other beneficiaries permanent protection. Nonetheless, Diana leveraged her new work permit to apply for a job working as an assistant in a nearby realty office owned by a friend of her godmother's. And while the high cost of tuition delayed her path back to college, after saving money for a year, she enrolled part-time in community college. She hoped to eventually graduate with an associate's degree, but she knew that her time line to completion would be slow given the high cost of out-of-state tuition. Though Diana was acutely aware of the limitations of DACA, she was relieved that it allowed her to remain with her family and friends in the place that she considered home.

Allen Creek, Diana's hometown and the site of this study, was a small town of approximately eight thousand people, of whom about four thousand were Latino, primarily of Mexican and Guatemalan origin. Thanks in part to a proportionately large coethnic community, caring teachers and coaches, and a church that she attended regularly, Diana found a place of belonging in North Carolina even as she became increasingly aware that she was considered an outsider in the United States. When she began to face exclusionary policies at the state level, however, Diana realized that her home state was not a shelter in an unwelcoming country. Instead, North Carolina became a hostile state in a nation that, at the time of the study, moved to grant more opportunities to young immigrants who had arrived in the country as children.

North Carolina: A New Immigrant Destination in the New US South

North Carolina was among a handful of states implementing aggressive anti-immigration enforcement measures and limiting resources for unauthorized immigrants during the first two decades of the 2000s. Immigration policies catapulted to the top of the political agenda as North Carolina witnessed a rapid growth in its Latino population in the 1990s and early 2000s. During the 1990s, immigrants were dispersing into new-destination areas at unprecedented rates. Migration to nontraditional destinations resulted from selective border fortification along traditional routes of entry, as well as growing labor demands in states with laxer labor laws and simultaneous dwindling labor demands in traditional urban industrial centers (Massey and Capoferro 2008). New-destination states were largely concentrated in the South, where labor demands in manufacturing and food processing outpaced supply.

For immigrant youth who grew up in North Carolina, the president's announcement of DACA was the first time that they had seen policies shift toward inclusion. For years prior to DACA, both state and federal policies had trended toward more restrictions. As efforts to pass comprehensive immigration reform stalled in the US Congress, new-destination states and states with more conservative governments led the charge in increasing local-level enforcement policies and surveillance of immigrants (Bada et al. 2010; Capps et al. 2011; Coleman 2012; Olivas 2007; Pham 2004; Ramakrishnan and Wong 2010; Rodríguez, Chisti, and Nortman 2010; Varsanyi 2010; Varsanyi et al. 2012; Wishnie 2001). Given the rapid influx of immigrants to a region that previously had very few immigrants outside its metropolitan areas, it was not entirely surprising that the political atmosphere in the Southeast became charged as the population reacted. Hispanic population growth was higher in the South than in any other region of the country (Ennis, Ríos-Vargas, and Albert 2011; Passel, Cohn, and Lopez 2011), and the demographic shift prompted many scholars to term the region the "New (Nuevo) South" (Mohl 2003; B. Smith 2001; Smith and Furuseth 2006). The New South, however, approached issues of race and ethnicity in ways highly reminiscent of those of the Old South.

Anti-immigrant legislation in the region climaxed in 2011, when Alabama passed the most severe anti-immigration bill in the nation. Alabama's HB 56 included provisions allowing local police to check immigration status at all police stops and arrests, penalizing people who transported or knowingly employed undocumented immigrants, barring undocumented immigrants from receiving public benefits or attending public colleges and universities, and requiring all public elementary and secondary schools to collect information about students' immigration status.[4] Only Arizona, a border state, came close to enacting such a strict policy with its SB 1070, which gained national attention for its provision allowing police officers to request proof of identification from all persons suspected of being in the country without legal documentation. Although Arizona was the first state to enact a policy allowing police officers to request official documentation from people who had not been apprehended for criminal activity, communities throughout the South had been patrolling and setting up routine traffic stops strategically targeting Latino neighborhoods for years (American Civil Liberties Union and Rights Working Group 2009; Coleman 2012; Shahshahani 2010, 5). Moreover, formal partnerships with Immigration and Customs Enforcement (ICE) allowing local police forces to begin deportation proceedings were, and continue to be, largely concentrated in the Southeast (Capps et al. 2011).

The devolution of immigration law to the state level reached new heights during the first decade of the 2000s (Bada et al. 2010; Coleman 2009, 2012; Gilbert 2009; Rodríguez, Chisti, and Nortman 2010; Varsanyi 2010; Varsanyi et al. 2012; Wishnie 2001). Targeting young immigrants specifically, South Carolina, Georgia, and Alabama passed bills between 2008 and 2011 prohibiting undocumented students from enrolling in public institutions of higher education. Sixteen other states (California, Colorado, Connecticut, Florida, Illinois, Kansas, Maryland, Minnesota, Nebraska, New Jersey, New Mexico, New York, Oregon, Texas, Utah, and Washington) passed laws granting in-state tuition to undocumented students who attended high schools in the same state, and state university systems in Hawaii, Michigan, Oklahoma, and Rhode Island established policies to offer in-state tuition to unauthorized students (National Conference of State Legislatures 2015). In less welcoming states, such as North Carolina, reactive policies emerged as legislators and political pundits treated state and national membership as statuses to be protected from an immigrant or "Latino threat" (Chavez 2008). The resultant political landscape was a "multilayered jurisdictional patchwork" of confusing and even conflicting policies at the institutional, local, state, and federal levels (Varsanyi et al. 2012). DACA and the subsequent state-level responses provided fertile ground for the growth of conflicting messages in this multilayered environment.

When DACA was announced, eligible youth in North Carolina hoped that the policy would facilitate pathways to higher education, upwardly mobile jobs, and permanent residence. Many linked the temporary policy to the proposed Development, Relief, and Education for Alien Minors (or DREAM) Act and expected it to benefit them in the same way.[5] First introduced in 2001, the DREAM Act was intended to offer undocumented youth a pathway to citizenship, provided that they met certain age, educational, and moral requirements. Despite several failed attempts to pass the act in the Senate and Congress, the DREAM Act remains a hope for the approximately 1.8 million eligible youth and young adults who yearn for secure futures in the United States where they grew up.

DACA was not as comprehensive as the DREAM Act, and it did not provide the long-term certainty of legislation. Yet the policy had measurable impacts on the lives of its beneficiaries who were able to obtain new jobs, increase their earnings, open up bank accounts, acquire credit cards, enroll in school, obtain driver's licenses, and, in some cases, travel abroad as a result of their authorized presence (Gonzales and Terriquez 2013; Gonzales, Terriquez, and Ruszczyk 2014; Hipsman, Gómez-Aguiñaga, and Capps 2016). Nonetheless, DACA beneficiaries in North Carolina continued to struggle against a hostile state climate even as their opportunities increased with DACA.

DACA beneficiaries in North Carolina were not granted in-state tuition rates as a result of their newly acquired legal presence. Moreover, although beneficiaries in the state were thrilled to get driver's licenses and the independence that came with being able to drive, they were disheartened that the licenses were

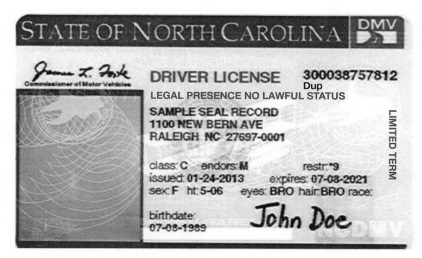

Figure I.1. Sample of a North Carolina driver's license for DACA beneficiaries. Source: North Carolina Department of Transportation (2013).

marked with the phrase, "LEGAL PRESENCE NO LAWFUL STATUS" (see Figure I.1). Thus, even with the temporary authorization granted by DACA, official documentation from North Carolina reminded beneficiaries in bright red letters of their outsider status in their home state.

For youth like Diana, DACA offered protection from deportation and greater access to more stable jobs, but it did nothing to ensure that mixed-status families would remain intact, nor did it facilitate a clear pathway to membership or an easy route to upward mobility.

Tectonic Incorporation: Argument and Contribution to Theory

Diana's story illustrates what I call "tectonic incorporation" (see Figure I.2). As Diana traversed her path from high school to her first full-time job, she was forced to navigate political and institutional structures that moved unpredictably around her. Teachers, family friends, and a mostly welcoming high school offered her spaces of inclusion, but her journey to adulthood was marked with bitter disappointments as she struggled to gain access to college and the workforce. These contexts—families and friends, primary and secondary schools, nonprofit institutions and activist groups, local policies and law enforcement, colleges and university policies, and state and federal policies—all interact with one another to form a layered and unstable context of reception for unauthor-

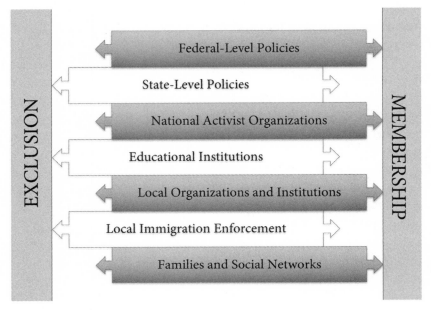

Figure I.2. Tectonic incorporation model.

ized immigrant youth. Diana found herself constantly adapting her plans, ambitions, and identity as she responded to legislative and institutional shifts that often conflicted.

Like tectonic plates, the structures on which Diana stood moved underneath her feet. As policies shifted and one plate slid in one direction or the other, Diana was forced to regain her footing and change her plans to accommodate to the new landscape. Political and institutional shifts at times felt like earthquakes, pitching Diana into chasms of near helplessness. But when policies became more accommodating and plates at institutional and political levels converged, they could also act like mountains, propelling Diana upward and closer to her goals. Unlike tectonic shifts, however, political and institutional shifts are not slow moving and are often unpredictable. For example, the community college policy on undocumented students shifted back and forth five times between 2000 and 2008, illustrating how figurative tectonic shifts caused immigrant youth in North Carolina to scramble for secure footing as they attempted to further their educations and gain necessary skills and credentials for their first adult jobs.

This book highlights the important and interactive influences of federal, state, and local policies in shaping a very complex context of reception for immigrant youth coming of age in the early twenty-first century. Focusing on the instability of institutional and governmental policies, I argue that young unauthorized immigrants do not, and cannot, follow a linear path to incorporation because they do not stand on solid ground. Rather, the social institutions in which they are involved, and the institutional, local, state, and federal policies that determine their access to resources, all act as tectonic plates, sometimes moving them toward incorporation and other times shifting them farther toward the margins. When the plates move in concert with one another toward membership, the foundation on which unauthorized immigrant youth navigate their pathways to adulthood can feel sturdy. When state and federal policies move in opposite directions, these movements reveal fault lines and destabilize youth. Unauthorized youth who experience backslides in their trajectories may retreat from their ambitions out of fear of repeated disappointment. Consequently, many will be poorly positioned to take full advantage of programs like DACA that emerge unexpectedly. In contrast, when policies like DACA disappear, youth are left at the edge of the precipice, unsure whether they will be able to reach the summits of the mountains they began to climb or tumble backward, watching their dreams slip from their grasp.

Like Diana, most unauthorized immigrant youth growing up in North Carolina during the early 2000s struggled to achieve upward mobility and gain a full sense of membership. Although previous research has highlighted the importance of acknowledging complex local contexts (Cebulko and Silver 2016; Ellis and Almgren 2009; Marrow 2011; Schmalzbauer 2014; R. Smith 2014) and unique "historical conjunctures" (R. Smith 2014; Wimmer 2008, 2013), literature about immigrant youth has typically underemphasized the overlapping influences of institutional, local, state, and federal immigration policies. Youth in different states and localities face very different contexts of reception. Thus, as youth in hostile states may feel state-level policies sliding them toward the margins even as federal-level contexts offer them more protections, youth in more welcoming states may benefit from protective state and institutional policies even when federal policies shift onto less secure terrain. However, youth in more hostile states may feel magnified impacts of hostile federal policies.

In North Carolina, the increasing hostility at the state level marked a harsh introduction to early adulthood for unauthorized immigrants in Allen Creek. In spite of their unauthorized immigration status, many had felt nurtured and supported while growing up in their small-town community. As in other new-destination areas (Marrow 2011; Schmalzbauer 2014), the unauthorized immigrant youth in Allen Creek expressed a love for the bucolic surroundings, peacefulness, and intimacy of their community. Moreover, many expressed deep gratitude for their teachers, coaches, and neighbors who supported them and helped them persevere through high school. This small-town support helped shelter youth from the harsh political climate in the state, and teachers did a remarkable job of encouraging students to remain in high school despite the uncertain payoff at the end. Especially as community colleges shut their doors to unauthorized youth and state colleges continued to charge out-of-state tuition, social network support was crucial to helping youth maintain feelings of membership in their community and school.

Upon high school graduation, however, the impact of exclusionary policies at the state level amplified, and unauthorized youth began to lament their exclusion from institutions of higher education and fear for their safety as police checkpoints proliferated throughout the region. Though eligible youth found that their anxiety was partially tempered by a more hospitable federal environment after the implementation of DACA, it was far from a comprehensive antidote. Though DACA increased access to resources for beneficiaries throughout the nation, without a pathway to lawful status, beneficiaries remained second-class residents (Gonzales, Terriquez, and Ruszczyk 2014). Moreover, DACA did not erase the fears about deportation for beneficiaries who remained connected to unauthorized family members (Aranda and Vaquera 2015; Gonzales and Terriquez 2013), nor did it protect beneficiaries from racial profiling (Aranda and Vaquera 2015).

Particularly in states with high barriers to resources such as postsecondary education, DACA beneficiaries could not reap the full benefits of the policy in the way that their peers in more welcoming states could (Cebulko and Silver 2016). When the political landscape moved again with the election of Donald Trump in 2016, the federal climate threatened to further magnify the influences of hostile state policies in North Carolina. When DACA was rescinded in 2017, beneficiaries knew that state policies would do little to protect them if Congress did not pass legislation to maintain the protections and opportunities DACA provided.

Though US-born, second-generation youth did not face the same barriers to advancement as their unauthorized peers, they nonetheless felt the impacts of the hostile political climate in North Carolina. Like other research in non-traditional destinations has shown (Romero 2006; Schmalzbauer 2014), Latino citizens in North Carolina frequently faced assumptions of foreign origin and illegality by people in their community. Consequently, Latino citizens in North Carolina worried about harassment and judgment from police, DMV workers, store clerks, and other citizens who viewed them with suspicion. Moreover, they feared family separation, as many had parents, siblings, or other close relatives who lacked immigration authorization and were therefore vulnerable to deportation. Thus, as other research has found (Aranda, Menjívar, and Donato 2014; Ebert and Ovink 2014; Esbenshade and Ozburt 2008; Szkupinski Quiroga, Medina, and Glick 2014; Valdez 2016), the repercussions of immigration enforcement tended to spill over to affect Latinos in general. While unauthorized immigrants are of course the most structurally vulnerable to exclusionary policies, the impacts of these policies extend beyond their immediate targets to affect documented and US-born Latinos as well.

Though existing theories of immigrant and second-generation incorporation acknowledge complex contexts of reception, they underemphasize the impacts of rapidly shifting policies at various layers (Alba and Nee 2003; Portes and Rumbaut 2001; Portes and Zhou 1993). Thus, established theories do not easily map onto the unauthorized youth transitioning to adulthood in the first and second decade of the 2000s in new immigrant destinations. The unauthorized youth who grew up in Allen Creek did not gradually gain access to mainstream institutions and, in the process, "remake the mainstream" (Alba and Nee 2003). But neither did they downwardly assimilate into the margins of society in response to pervasive racism and destructive social pressures (Portes and Rumbaut 2001; Portes and Zhou 1993; Rumbaut 2005). Instead, they followed "bumpy-line" pathways to incorporation (Gans 1992) as they responded to overlapping and constantly changing policies that interacted with one another in unpredictable ways. And though Herbert Gans vaguely theorized more disjointed pathways to immigrant incorporation, "bumpy-line" assimilation theory does not account for local contexts embedded within multilayered environments, nor does it detail how these contexts move and shift, affecting immigrants' feelings of membership and belonging in various settings simultaneously and within one generation.

The immigrant youth in North Carolina described fragmented incorporation experiences as they traversed constantly shifting landscapes in various settings. Their experiences more closely aligned with pluralistic models of incorporation that describe how immigrants assimilate across various social dimensions at different rates (Bean, Brown, and Bachmeier 2015; Marrow 2011; Telles and Ortiz 2008). For example, immigrants may become more economically or educationally integrated before becoming residentially integrated.

However, previous models of multidimensional incorporation have down-played the constantly shifting nature of these overlapping contexts of reception. I argue that incongruent and unstable governmental and institutional polices in the early 2000s and 2010s created a disjointed process of incorporation for unauthorized immigrant youth. And while barriers to membership were of course the highest for unauthorized immigrant youth, second-generation Latino citizens also confronted challenges because of racial profiling as well as intimate connections to unauthorized immigrants.

Data, Methods, and Research Site

By the time I initiated my research in 2007, immigration to the South was no longer a new phenomenon. Nonetheless, immigrants continued to struggle against a hostile reception. In the following chapters, I tell the stories of youth growing up in immigrant families in a town that I call Allen Creek. At the time of the study, Allen Creek had a population of just over eight thousand residents, and was approximately 50 percent Latino, 30 percent white, and 20 percent black. The town witnessed a vast increase in its Latino population during the 1990s, as immigrants were drawn to the region to fill jobs in poultry plants and manufacturing. Prior to this in-migration, the town's population was approximately five thousand people and was made up almost exclusively of black and white residents.

Southern communities like Allen Creek were a world apart from the traditional immigrant destinations of New York City, Chicago, and Los Angeles, and youth who had moved from other states noted and (mostly) welcomed the difference. As Armando, an eighteen-year-old Mexican American who moved from Bakersfield, California, stated, "I'd never seen like a lot of animals, farms, and stuff. That was surprising. And also, the people I guess. I was used to having classes with, like, full of Hispanic students, and then I came here and it was a mixture, so that was different . . . [but] I wouldn't like to live in a big city. I like the small city where kinda everyone knows everyone around here and they know where every place is at, and the diversity I guess." Armando felt comfortable in North Carolina, and he appreciated Allen Creek's pastoral surroundings and the diversity of the small-town community.

But the Allen Creek community was far from idyllic. If the close-knit relationships and farmlands conjured up romantic images of small-town America, the odor of the chicken plant quickly shattered any picture of bucolic tranquility. Allen Creek embodied all of the complexity of real small-town America. McDonalds, Taco Bell, and AutoZone stores interrupted the strawberry fields and cow pastures. The quaint churches, with signs in both English and Spanish, looked out of place next to the two strip malls on either side of the highway. A low-flying aircraft occasionally passed overhead searching for illegal marijuana fields, and the town's liveliest attraction was the large Walmart that stood off the highway leading into town. Selene, an eighteen-year-old US-born child of Mexican and Guatemalan parents, described Allen Creek as "small, and there's nothing to do. There's no mall and nowhere to go to the movies. Usually what people do is go to the Walmart and walk around. Or people go to McDonalds and hang out. But I was born here, so I like it. It's small and calm."

Selene's comments were echoed by most of the youth I spoke to in Allen Creek. Like generations of teenagers from small towns, they all complained that there was nothing to do. The small commercial zones along the highway offered two Mexican restaurants, one department store, a nail salon, a dollar store, and a pizza parlor. Gas stations and the Walmart became sites where teens socialized. The charming downtown was even sleepier, with a small diner, an even smaller coffee shop, a couple of tractor and agricultural equipment and hardware stores, and a few office buildings. Despite nearly universal laments about boredom and small-town gossip, and frequent grievances about racism and discrimination on the part of black and Latino youth, most of the youth in Allen Creek liked the sense of small-town familiarity that came from knowing everyone in town. Allen Creek was home, and it was comfortable.

The small-town familiarity made me feel uniquely conspicuous when I first began my research. Over time, I learned to ignore the quizzical stares and gradually felt more comfortable approaching people to ask them about their experiences living in the small community. The more time I spent in Allen Creek, the more I began to feel like a member of the community, while simultaneously realizing that I was really an outsider in virtually every way. I am a white woman in my thirties. Although I am from a small town, I hail from suburban New Jersey, a far cry from this small Southern community. I once asked a man sitting next to me on the bleachers where the visiting soccer team was from. He told me, "They're from a town near Dunlan, you know, where the tractor pull is." I smiled when he said this. Not only did I not know where Dunlan was; I did not even know what a tractor pull was. I immediately looked it up when I got home. I knew I had considerable ground to cover if I wanted to become an accepted and trusted member of the community.

Luckily, I was not at a complete disadvantage, given that I speak Spanish and know a great deal about immigration both from my research and training and my personal life. I myself am the daughter of an immigrant and can relate on some level to the conflicting cultural pressures discussed by the youth in Allen Creek. My mother is from Norway and has a very different immigration narrative from the stories of the parents of the adolescents in my study. My mother moved to marry my father, and although her accent and even her culture differentiated her from her new neighbors, her Western European heritage allowed her, and my sister and me, to integrate into our surroundings quite easily.

Most of the immigrant families in Allen Creek had moved in search of better labor opportunities or to escape the dangers of urban violence either in their home countries or in urban areas of the United States. They were marked as clear outsiders when they moved to the small Southern community. Residents were uneasy with their new neighbors and all of the new Spanish-language products and store signs. They saw their town changing before their eyes. And though the town had overcome some of its initial growing pains, new struggles emerged between the established white population and the immigrant community as the schools became increasingly Latino.

Targeting the high school as my primary site of data collection, I began my research by observing and assisting in AVID college preparatory classes. Gradually, I expanded my engagement in the community. During the initial four-year study period from April 2007 to June 2011, I tutored high school students, volunteered at a community-based Latino Outreach Center, attended high school soccer games, played in pickup soccer games, taught salsa lessons to teenagers, attended county commissioners' meetings, mentored high school senior projects, and occasionally went out for meals with community members. I also conducted seventy-nine in-depth interviews with youth and key adult participants whom I met at the high school, at the Latino Outreach Center, or through individuals I got to know through my research. Sixty-three of these initial interviews were with youth: twenty unauthorized immigrants, three youths with temporary protected status (TPS),[6] sixteen citizen children of Latino immigrants, eleven black US-born citizens, and thirteen white US-born citizens (see Table I.1). Compared to their relative population in the town's high school, Latino youth, most of whom were Mexican and Guatemalan, were overrepresented in the interviewed sample. The student body comprised approximately 41 percent Latinos, 34 percent whites, and 25 percent blacks. Interviews offered insight into comparative perspectives of undocumented youth and their documented and citizen peers of various racial and ethnic backgrounds.

In 2011, I moved to New York and my contact with the youth became less frequent and largely Internet based. I returned to North Carolina twice in 2012 to revisit and reinterview a subsample of fifteen respondents. I returned once

Table I.1. In-Depth Interview Sample

	Female	Male	Total
Youth/young adult citizen (US-born) Latino children of immigrants	8	8	16
Youth/young adult noncitizen Latino immigrants	13	10	23
Youth/young adult black citizens	5	6	11
Youth/young adult white citizens	8	5	13
Adult community members involved with youth (teachers, parents, coaches, school administrators, nonprofit workers, county commissioners)	8	8	16
Total	42	37	79

before President Obama's announcement of DACA and once after. I continued to follow up with these respondents via phone interviews and conversations and through one additional visit to North Carolina in 2015. The fifteen respondents I selected for follow-up interviews had taken a wide variety of paths since high school. Though I would have ideally followed up with the entire original group of unauthorized youth, I was unable to connect with all of them when I returned in 2012. I reinterviewed thirteen of the original noncitizen sample (twelve unauthorized; one had TPS) and two citizen youths from the original sample.

When I first began my research, my initial aim was to discover how the small-town community influenced the incorporation process for youth from immigrant families. I did not anticipate all of the institutional and political shifts at both the state and federal levels. As I spent time with the youth in Allen Creek, however, I watched as they scrambled to make to new plans every time a policy shifted and the ground fell out from under them. I thus increasingly came to see their small-town experience as one that was in motion, as well as intrinsically linked to the larger state and federal contexts, which also shifted unpredictably.

The youth in the study aged into early adulthood during the Great Recession of 2008–11, a time period when working-class jobs offered increasingly less security and tuition costs grew (Grusky, Western, and Wimer 2011; Terriquez 2014). Moreover, and likely relatedly, they transitioned into early adulthood during a highly contentious time period in which politicians debated their right to reside, work, and go to school. Though the political vitriol reported in the popular press was largely directed at adult labor migrants in the region, the stories of the youth, more so than those of their parents, spoke to the demographic shift taking place in the Southeast. The study participants, raised in a small Southern community and educated in Southern schools, were the new North Carolinians and the new Southerners.

Outline of the Book

The remainder of this book details the experiences of unauthorized and liminally legal 1.5-generation Latino youth in North Carolina during the first two decades of the 2000s. Their stories are contextualized by the stories of their US-born Latino, black, and white peers, as well as the perspectives of their parents, teachers, coaches, and mentors. Throughout the book, I examine how constantly shifting policies at various levels prevented unauthorized immigrant youth from finding a full sense of membership in the country and state that they considered home. After developing the theoretical grounding of the book in Chapter 1, I examine in each subsequent chapter one tectonic interaction by focusing on a local-, institutional-, state-, or federal-level context and exploring how that context intersects with concentric contexts to frame the incorporation experiences of 1.5-generation unauthorized immigrants and, to a lesser extent, their second-generation peers.

In Chapter 1, I provide more background about the political and social climate at both the national level and in North Carolina during the time of the study. I build on key studies of immigrant incorporation in both new and established destinations (Alba and Nee 2003; Bean, Brown, and Bachmeier 2015; Gans 1992; Marrow 2011; Portes and Rumbaut 2001; Schmalzbauer 2014; Telles and Ortiz 2008) as I discuss how local, state, and federal policies and environments take on magnified or diminished influence in the lives of unauthorized immigrant youth depending on how these layered contexts move and respond to one another. By unpacking and illustrating in more detail my concept of tectonic incorporation, this chapter demonstrates how shifting multilayered contexts destabilize unauthorized immigrant youth as they attempt to navigate their pathways to adulthood. Moreover, I explain how disruptions in the multilayered context spill over to affect second-generation youth.

Chapter 2 focuses on the local context and the proposed local policies that emerged in response to immigration and associated population growth in Allen Creek. The chapter vividly depicts the research site of Allen Creek and describes how the community, its schools, and other local organizations framed the context of reception for Latino youth and their families. This chapter emphasizes how policy shifts at the local level, enabled by federal legislation, can breed fear among both immigrants and second-generation youth, even as community social supports remain strong.

In Chapter 3, I focus on the institutional context as I discuss how secondary school policies slowly adapted to the growing Latino student population and interacted with local- and state-level contexts. Utilizing ethnographic and interview data, the chapter illustrates how school clubs and supportive teachers helped buffer the undercurrents of racialized and class tensions that pervaded classroom, hallway, and community interactions. The chapter also examines how gender, time of arrival, and legal status affected students' attachments to school and ability to access supportive school programs.

Chapter 4 follows the youth out of high school and focuses on the exclusionary landscapes that unauthorized youth faced after high school graduation at the state and federal levels. The chapter also details a key shift at the federal level by highlighting DACA and emphasizing the ways in which the hostile state climate limited the impact of DACA. Even after DACA, many beneficiaries saw few opportunities for career advancement. Highly restrictive tuition policies and a weak state infrastructure of financial support programs largely excluded them from postsecondary education. Consequently, they struggled to acquire the necessary credentials to access upwardly mobile jobs.

Chapter 5 discusses how the federal programs of DACA and TPS positively affected young beneficiaries even when state and institutional policies curtailed the inclusionary impacts of these liminal statuses. The chapter focuses on youth who were well positioned to utilize DACA as a means toward advancement and security and juxtaposes their narratives of exclusion prior to DACA to their narratives of advancement and inclusion after the policy's adoption. The chapter also highlights the benefits of having TPS but points out that policy shifts in response to DACA complicated the lives of immigrants with TPS, as institutional gatekeepers struggled to differentiate between the two groups of immigrants. Though Chapter 5 illustrates how liminally legal statuses offered youth some advantages and an imperfect sense of membership even within a hostile state climate, the chapter emphasizes that youth would feel far more secure were these statuses made permanent and if they facilitated equal access to resources such as in-state tuition. When the Trump administration rescinded DACA in 2017, beneficiaries were poised to lose the jobs they had secured under the policy if Congress did not pass a legislative replacement before its expiration.

Chapter 6 discusses how some youth buffered the destabilizing impacts of constantly shifting policies by joining activist groups. Within these groups, they created spheres of membership and developed strong bonds with social contacts that they met through activist campaigns. Others, however, felt alienated from activism because of frustration with years of exclusion and disappointments at both the state and federal levels.

Finally, I revisit the main theme of tectonic incorporation as I discuss the North Carolina context in the 2000s and 2010s. The Conclusion reiterates how incongruent and inconsistent policies affected unauthorized immigrant youth and, by extension, their second-generation peers in North Carolina as they traversed journeys to early adulthood. Moreover, the chapter suggests ways in which tectonic incorporation may play out in states that are more welcoming to immigrants, particularly in the context of an increasingly hostile federal context. Consequently, I recommend policies to foster the advancement and incorporation of immigrant youth in the United States.

1 Shifting Contexts of Reception

As the 2016 presidential election neared, anti-immigrant fervor in the country mounted. Candidate Trump utilized unauthorized immigration as a key agenda item and whipped up support with enthusiastic "build that wall" chants at rallies throughout the country. As support for Trump grew, President Obama feared that his pro-immigration policies would unravel upon completion of his presidency. Though Obama faced harsh criticism from immigrants' rights activists for record numbers of deportations under his administration, he also initiated policies to grant more security to long-term immigrants during his second term. DACA and the associated Deferred Action for Parents of Americans and Lawful Permanent Residents (DAPA) both gave protection from deportation and work permits to long-term immigrants with established roots in the United States. Though DAPA was blocked by a lawsuit filed by twenty-six states, Obama remained vocal in his support for established immigrant communities in the United States. In a speech he gave prior to the 2016 presidential election, Obama urged Americans to recognize long-term undocumented immigrants and their children as national insiders who shared an American culture and outlook. He relied on research to support his position:

> Every study shows that whether it was the Irish or the Poles, or the Germans, or the Italians, or the Chinese, or the Japanese, or the Mexicans, or the Kenyans—whoever showed up, over time, by a second generation, third generation, those kids are Americans. They do look like us—because we don't look one way . . . we all share a creed and we all share a commitment to the values that founded this nation. That's who we are.[1]

As Obama described a nation of immigrants with a shared creed and commitment to national values, he called on Benedict Anderson's (1983) idea of an "imagined community," and he placed long-term immigrants and their children squarely inside this community.

Though President Obama stated that the research uniformly found that immigrants quickly become Americans over one or two generations, his classification of the research oversimplified a long academic dialogue surrounding immigrant incorporation and assimilation. In fact, recent research about immigrant incorporation has trended toward increasingly pluralistic models that stress differences among immigrant groups of distinct national origins and address incorporation processes across various social dimensions.

Incorporation and Membership

President Obama's characterization of assimilation research called on early models of assimilation based largely on European immigrant groups. Moreover, the studies he referenced emerged from time periods in which immigration status had less of an impact on incorporation than they do now. More recent research has labeled immigration status a master status, dictating the daily routines, mobility opportunities, and psychological outlooks of unauthorized immigrant youth, particularly at key transition points in their life courses (Gonzales 2016). Historically, assimilation theories have not accounted for immigration status. Instead, the theories tend to focus on adaptation patterns over generations, describing a gradual movement of immigrant groups into the mainstream middle class through both language acquisition and structural and cultural adaptation (Gordon 1964; Warner and Srole 1945). Though early theories of assimilation acknowledged diversity in assimilation processes based on ethnicity, culture, and structural access, the theories nonetheless largely followed a "straight-line" assimilation model in which immigrant groups gradually melted into the mainstream by adapting to the host society. More recent models of immigrant incorporation present a far more complicated picture than the straight-line route described by Obama and early theorists.

Accounting for the increased diversity in immigrant streams following the 1965 Hart-Celler Immigration Act, current discussions surrounding immigrant incorporation stress that different groups of immigrants may assimilate at different rates based on a variety of factors, including racial and ethnic discrimination, immigration laws, religious discrimination, coethnic community support, familial human capital, and available social capital (Alba and Foner 2015; Alba and Nee 2003; Bean, Brown, and Bachmeier 2015; Portes and Rumbaut 2001; Portes and Zhou 1993; Telles and Ortiz 2008). These model similation better align with Gans's concept of bumpy-line assimilation, which allows for "changing circumstances" and incorporation trajectories with "no predictable ends" (1992, 44). Acknowledging obstacles to integration, scholars have descriptively illustrated how various immigrant groups have followed varying pathways of incorporation. Despite emphasizing more complex contexts of reception and pathways to incorporation, these grand theories nonetheless continue to downplay the importance of immigration status.

The most pervasive theory on youth incorporation, segmented assimilation, outlines several pathways of assimilation for youth of different classes and social locations but focuses primarily on US-born second- and third-generation immigrants (Portes and Rumbaut 2001; Portes and Zhou 1993; Rumbaut 2005; Rumbaut and Portes 2001). According to segmented assimilation theory, interconnected factors, including discrimination, community context, and human capital, may facilitate either upward or downward mobility. Segmented assimilation theory recognizes upward mobility both via "straight-line" assimilation and through a reliance on ethnic social networks that foster "selective acculturation" or partial acculturation, whereby immigrant groups gradually obtain upward intergenerational mobility while retaining and benefiting from their heritage cultures (Portes and Rumbaut 2001, 63). Segmented assimilation theory also, however, describes a dangerous trend of downward assimilation into a "rainbow underclass" of urban minorities (ibid., 45). According to the theory, downward assimilation is most probable for lower-income second- and third-generation immigrants of color who face racism, discrimination, and chaotic, low-income urban neighborhood environments. The racial or ethnic discrimination described by Portes and Rumbaut, however, does not result from "spillover" assumptions about immigration status (Aranda, Menjívar, and Donato 2014). Instead, segmented assimilation theory stresses the dangers of urban youth culture.

Other scholars argue that segmented assimilation theory's emphasis on the downward trajectories of second- and third-generation youth of color oversimplifies the culture and experiences of low-income urban blacks and Latinos and underemphasizes the impacts of progressive policies and programs, such as affirmative action (Alba and Nee 2003, 7–8; Kasinitz 2008; R. Smith 2014). Emphasizing the far-reaching impacts of post–civil rights legislative advances, Richard Alba and Victor Nee (2003) highlight English-language acquisition, intergenerational gains in educational and occupational attainment, and interethnic and interracial marriage as evidence of upward mobility and of a diversifying mainstream population. Their perspective aligns with Obama's sentiment that Americans "don't look one way." The American mainstream, according to Alba and Nee's new assimilation theory, is ethnically, culturally, and economically diverse.

Recent data from a large-scale study of second-generation youth in New York City (Kasinitz et al. 2008) and from the nationally representative Current Population Survey (Tran and Valdez 2015) affirm Alba and Nee's argument that the second generation is making gains in educational and occupational attainment that take them, as a group, well beyond their parents. Although some Latino groups, including South Americans, most Central Americans, and Cubans, have advanced faster than Dominicans and Mexicans, all of the groups show evidence of intergenerational gains in terms of educational attainment and occupational status (Tran and Valdez 2015). Yet substantial evidence cautions against overly optimistic interpretations of intergenerational gains, as they may not predict long-term socioeconomic status mobility (Telles and Ortiz 2008; Terriquez 2014).

Building on Alba and Nee's focus on institutional and legislative advancement, Edward Telles and Vilma Ortiz (2008) point out that intergenerational gains reflect historical contexts that facilitate cohort advancements. But they also emphasize that these advances are smaller than what would be predicted by classical assimilation (Gordon 1964) or selective acculturation (Portes and Rumbaut 2001) models. Slower gains among Dominicans and Mexicans harken back to segmented assimilationist warnings of the crippling impacts of discrimination, isolation in poor urban neighborhoods, underresourced schools, and few work opportunities for individuals with low levels of education.

In an effort to explain the continued inequality, Telles and Ortiz point to the consistent replenishment of new Mexican immigrants to the Southwest as helping to sustain social distance between Mexican-origin populations and white populations in the region. Moreover, they argue that low-wage labor demands have helped facilitate stereotypes of Mexican immigrants as disposable, low-skill laborers. Adding further nuance to these arguments, Veronica Terriquez emphasizes that the low socioeconomic status of most Latino parents greatly disadvantages their children, who came of age during the Great Recession of 2008–12. Terriquez directly contrasts this population to Latinos who fared better in times of economic growth (Agius Vallejo 2012) and warns that the current population of Latino youth are primed to experience "working class stagnation" due to low levels of four-year college and few upwardly mobile job opportunities (Terriquez 2014, 383). Finally, Frank Bean, Susan Brown, and James Bachmeier stress that Mexican second-generation youth are doubly disadvantaged due to the high percentage that have "parents without papers." Children with undocumented parents are more likely to remain in economically insecure positions for long periods of time, thus placing strain on both parents and children and diminishing opportunities for intergenerational mobility. Bean and colleagues' "membership exclusion" theory places immigrant status as a central tenet of incorporation, but the theory nonetheless focuses on documented youth and emphasizes economic mobility without placing equal emphasis on the emotional consequences of exclusion (Bean et al. 2015, 17).

Incorporation and a Sense of Belonging

Though these theories of assimilation, incorporation, and integration have done much to advance our knowledge of the mobility patterns of various immigrant groups and their children and grandchildren, the major focus of these theories remains on markers of mobility and authorized immigrants. Most assimilation theories downplay the consequences of unauthorized status and exclusion on psychological and emotional well-being. Feelings of belonging and well-being, though harder to capture in large-scale quantitative studies, are equally important markers of incorporation as more tangible measures of mobility. As sociologist Andreas Wimmer writes, "boundaries of belonging" based on ethnicity and nationality confer "dignity, honor, identity, economic resources and political power" (2013, 5). Beginning with "dignity," Wimmer thus underlines the far-reaching impacts of successful incorporation that go beyond measures of mobility and move into psychological and emotional terrain. Similarly, Richard Alba and Nancy Foner argue that immigrants and their children lack access to full membership, as defined by "having the same educational and work opportunities as long-term native-born citizens ... and a sense of dignity and belonging that comes with acceptance and inclusion in a broad range of societal institutions" (2015, 1–2). Even as the mainstream adapts to growing populations of immigrants and their offspring, significant barriers to both mobility and dignity persist for immigrants and their descendants.

Immigration status, moreover, has taken on increased significance in recent years. As immigration law has become increasingly linked with criminal law, immigrants have become stigmatized as illegal border crossers capable of other illicit activities (Dreby 2015; Flores 2014; Golash-Boza 2015; Kanstroom 2007; Stumpf 2006). Heightened enforcement climates can have deleterious impacts on immigrants and their family members, as they face perpetual threats of deportation, family separation, and marginalization (Abrego and Lakhani 2015; De Genova 2002, 2010; Dreby 2015; Gonzales 2016; Gonzales and Chavez 2012;

Menjívar and Abrego 2012). Immigrants often experience chronic anxiety and associated health problems as they endure long-term uncertainty. For many unauthorized immigrant youth, the stigmas associated with their immigration status obstruct their feelings of membership and their opportunities for successful incorporation into the country that they know best. They are acutely aware of the negative stereotypes portrayed in the popular press and know that many within their communities of residence consider them intrusive outsiders.

Illustratively, as Trump began his campaign for president in 2016 classifying Mexican immigrants as "rapists" and "murders," he drew boundaries of belonging that placed Mexican immigrants decidedly outside inclusion, and furthermore undermined their dignity and honor. Throughout his campaign, Trump highlighted sharp boundaries between insider Americans and outsider immigrants who threatened the economic and physical safely of US-born Americans. His campaign strategy relied directly on Anderson's (1983) idea of an imagined community as he repeatedly recalled a nostalgic, though historically vague, era when America was "great" and presumably free of immigrant threats.

Of course, an imagined community of a cohesive national people residing neatly and exclusively within a bounded territory is unrealistic. Consequently, nation-states, and individual states within national borders, have adapted policies to address noncitizen residents. In response to the resultant incongruent political landscape, an "internal politics of belonging" (Brubaker 2010) emerges wherein long-term, noncitizen residents feel a sense of social membership in a nation where they face a vast machinery of exclusion. Chasms between formal and social membership may feel particularly wide for unauthorized immigrant youth who grow up and attend school alongside their US-born peers (Abrego 2008; Gonzales 2011, 2016; Silver 2012). Regardless of membership achieved in adolescence, however, research has repeatedly shown that youth tend to move into more exclusionary contexts as they age into adulthood (Abrego 2006; Cebulko 2014; Gleeson and Gonzales 2012; Gonzales 2011, 2016; Silver 2012). As undocumented youth graduate from high school and move on to the early stages of adulthood, they tend to confront constricting educational and occupational opportunities and more immediate threats of deportation, thus magnifying the salience of their immigration status in daily life.

In the longest study of undocumented youth to date, Roberto Gonzales (2016) finds that unauthorized young adults in Southern California face chronic uncertainty in adulthood and gradually adopt "illegal" identities. He carefully illustrates how young unauthorized immigrants navigate pathways toward illegality at different rates depending on when they leave educational institutions to pursue full-time work or family responsibilities. Following 150 unauthorized immigrants, he demonstrates that youth who do not attend college see their social and occupational worlds constrict around them at younger ages than youth who manage to delay their transitions to "illegality" by remaining in school through college and even graduate school. Devastatingly, however, Gonzales finds that youth who achieve high levels of education eventually join their "early exiting" peers as they too adopt psychological dispositions framed by their immigration status.

Immigration status alone, however, does not determine membership. Instead, immigration status intersects with various geographic and social locations, such as race, class, and gender, to frame immigrant experiences with discrimination and mobility (Brown 2013; Cebulko 2017; Enriquez 2017). For example, Latinos are far more likely to be profiled and stopped at traffic checkpoints than other groups in the South, thereby placing unauthorized Latino immigrants into the most vulnerable social spaces (American Civil Liberties Union and the Rights Working Group 2009; Coleman 2012; Shahshahani 2010; Weissman, Headen, and Parker 2009). Moreover, the impact of unauthorized immigration status varies widely by state and locality of residence. The influence of state, local, and institutional contexts should not be downplayed, as these more proximate contexts interact with federal policies to frame unauthorized immigrants' experiences of membership and exclusion at multiple levels and in multiple dimensions. And while unauthorized immigrants are of course most vulnerable to threats against their security, intersections between assumed immigration status and race, ethnicity, and locality affect second-generation immigrants as well. Because of these intersections, second-generation youth can face threats to their dignity as they too are maligned as potential criminals and national outsiders.

Layered Contexts and State Influence

Though theories about immigrant incorporation generally acknowledge the importance of context, most large-scale studies about youth and incorporation have focused on youth in traditional and largely urban, immigrant destinations (Gonzales 2016; Portes and Rumbaut 2001; Suárez-Orozco and Suárez-Orozco 2001; Terriquez 2014). Thus, even when research points to the dangers of substandard urban schooling, clearly a context-specific marker, the implications of these studies tend to be applied to second- and third-plus-generation immigrant populations nationally (Portes and Rumbaut 2001; Tellez and Ortiz 2008; Valenzuela 1999). And while research finds crippling impacts of undocumented status for youth in all areas of the country (Abrego 2006; Cebulko 2013, 2014; Gonzales 2011, 2016; Silver 2012), local contexts and institutional policies interact with federal actions to shape incorporation processes from state to state.

Research about immigrant youth incorporation in new, and particularly small-town and rural, destinations is scant. However, existing studies illustrate the complexity of these contexts, as immigrants in these areas develop deep attachments not only to their social contacts in these communities but also to the land itself (Marrow 2011; Schmalzbauer 2014; Striffler 2005). For example, in Leah Schmalzbauer's (2009, 2014) study of mostly Mexican immigrants in Montana, she describes how immigrants express heartfelt appreciation for their opportunities and the safety and beauty of their surroundings, despite frequent experiences with discrimination and perpetual fears of deportation. Similarly, in her 2011 study of immigrant incorporation in eastern North Carolina, Helen Marrow finds that many Latino newcomers to the rural South enjoyed the tranquility of their North Carolina neighborhoods even as they experienced racism and insecurity associated with their unauthorized immigration statuses. Moreover, despite grueling work conditions in food-processing plants, many of her study participants also felt relatively secure at work and made enough money to provide for their children.

Though later research has found working conditions in food-processing industries in the rural South to be far less secure, these studies also find that workers in the South carve out meaningful relationships with one another and, at times, with others in their communities, even in hostile workplace settings and political contexts that offer them very few protections (Ribas 2016; Striffler 2005; Stuesse 2016). These studies thus underline the importance of acknowledging how overlapping and often conflicting contexts of reception shape incorporation experiences and feelings of membership at different levels.

Even in the hostile climate of North Carolina in the first two decades of the 2000s, unauthorized 1.5-generation immigrant youth managed to find a sense of membership through their attachments to community organizations, schools, caring adults, and social networks (Silver 2012, 2015). These connections, moreover, propelled many toward upwardly mobile pathways despite an unwelcoming regional context (Silver 2012) and an economic structure that largely relegated their Latino immigrant parents to low-wage, insecure, and often dangerous jobs (Griffith 2008; Hernández-León and Zúñiga 2000; Kandel and Parrado 2005; Marrow 2009, 2011, 2017; Mohl 2003; Ribas 2016; Stuesse 2016). However, due to mounting legislation at the state level, their more localized feelings of belonging were tenuous and at times collapsed as policies shifted around them.

Because state and national legislative contexts are not static, more careful analysis of these overlapping contexts is needed. Particularly in new-destination areas where public policy and opinion continue to form and change in response to growing Latino populations, shifting policies can dramatically alter the context of reception for immigrants and their children. I next outline how these layered contexts shaped the experience of 1.5-generation youth in North Carolina during the first and second decades of the 2000s.

Tectonic Incorporation

Previous research has stressed the importance of examining incorporation across multiple dimensions (Bean, Brown, and Bachmeier 2015; Marrow 2011, 2017; Portes and Rumbaut 2001; Telles and Ortiz 2008), but research has thus far underemphasized how these different spheres move and interact with one another while in motion, thus becoming more or less influential in framing incorporation experiences and feelings of membership and exclusion. I use the term "tectonic incorporation" to illustrate how overlapping contexts shift unpredictably and respond to one another to frame the experience of incorporation for unauthorized 1.5-generation youth. For example, as federal policies become more inclusive, through actions like DACA, state contexts may be less influential in shaping feelings of membership and security for 1.5-generation youth. In contrast, the influence of state, local, and institutional actions may hold magnified influence over the daily lives of immigrants when federal protections are not in place. Focusing on institutional environments and state-level legislative actions in North Carolina, as well as the larger umbrella context of federal immigration policies, I illustrate how these constantly changing contexts destabilize unauthorized immigrant youth as they emerge from high school and attempt to carve their pathways into early adulthood.

Although tectonic incorporation most directly applies to unauthorized immigrant youth who face steep obstacles impeding their access to resources, the hostile political and social environment in North Carolina in the early 2000s affected citizen second-generation Latinos as well. Because Latino immigrants to North Carolina were a relatively recent population, most Latino citizens had unauthorized siblings, parents, cousins, and friends. Latino citizens, thereby, feared family separation and resultant heartache and economic insecurity as communities throughout the state partnered with ICE to enforce immigration law. Moreover, many Latino citizens in North Carolina faced assumptions of illegality and were profiled in traffic stops by police (American Civil Liberties Union and the Rights Working Group 2009; Silver 2017; Weissman, Headen, and Parker 2009) and were regarded as somehow distinct from their American peers by teachers and staff in schools (Silver 2015). Thus, as unauthorized immigrants in North Carolina were targeted by anti-immigration legislation at the state level, the impacts of hostility toward new immigrants in the state spilled over to affect Latino citizens as well.

Of course, concerns about racial profiling were not unique to North Carolina. As anti-immigration policies mounted in Arizona, for example, one study found that unauthorized, authorized, and US-born Latinos all discussed feeling increasingly surveilled and displayed high levels of psychological distress (Szkupinski Quiroga, Medina, and Glick 2014). DACA beneficiaries in more traditional immigrant destinations also continued to experience anxiety about racial profiling while driving (Aranda and Vaquera 2015) and feared the deportation of their friends and family (Aranda and Vaquera 2015; Gonzales and Terriquez 2013). Nevertheless, unauthorized Latino immigrants in all regions were most vulnerable to shifts in policies. In North Carolina, specifically, unauthorized immigrants were forced to adapt their behaviors and goals as sheriffs in cities and counties throughout the state entered into partnerships with ICE and educational institutions intermittently changed their policies on admitting or barring undocumented students.

The rapidly changing North Carolina context illustrates how institutional, local, state, and federal policies and actions interacted as tectonic plates, shaping the ways in which 1.5-generation Latino immigrants experienced belonging. When federal and state policies simultaneously shifted toward more exclusionary realms, unauthorized immigrants in North Carolina felt most vulnerable. When the federal context inched toward inclusion with the implementation of DACA, and the state context maintained its restrictive policies, the slightly more secure foundation continued to reveal fault lines as state policies prevented DACA beneficiaries from taking full advantage of the policy to build upwardly mobile futures. Finally, though institutions, such as secondary schools and nonprofit organizations, provided support and protection, they were limited in their ability to shield 1.5-generation unauthorized immigrants and, by extension, their families and friends from the unpredictable state and federal policy shifts that held more sway over their access to institutions and opportunities.

Magnified State Exclusion within a Shifting Federal Landscape

Despite bipartisan efforts in Congress to pass comprehensive immigration reform, federal action on immigration was repeatedly blocked in Congress in the early 2000s. Consequently, immigrants, including immigrant youth who had grown up in the United States, faced increasing insecurity because of the Illegal Immigration Reform and Immigrant Responsibility Act of 1996 (IIRIRA) and the multiple local and state ordinances and policies that emerged in the wake of the terrorist attacks of September 11, 2001 (Coleman 2009; Olivas 2007; Winders 2007). At the federal level, IIRIRA limited benefits available to immigrants and expanded categories of aggravated felonies, thus easing requirements for detention and deportation and drastically increasing the numbers of deportees (Golash-Boza 2015; Kanstroom 2007, 2012). IIRIRA also included section 287(g), which allowed local law enforcement agencies to enter into agreements with ICE, thereby strengthening the power of states and localities to enforce immigration law.

Restrictive policies targeting immigrant communities were particularly prevalent in Southern communities where immigrant flows were more recent and established populations were less diverse (Leerkes, Leach, and Bachmeier 2012). Research has demonstrated that 287(g) agreements resulted in more attention being placed on foreign origin during routine policing activities (Donato and Rodriguez 2014) and that Latinos are disproportionately apprehended under the policy (Armenta 2016, 2017). Hostile policies had measurable impacts on migration, as states with aggressive anti-immigrant legislation experienced notable decreases in Latino migration (Ellis, Wright, and Townley 2016) and decreased populations of unauthorized immigrants (Leerkes, Leach, and Bachmeier 2012). Prior to upticks in "internal border control" in 2005, however, immigration to these states had expanded dramatically (Leerkes, Leach, and Bachmeier 2012),

As immigration to North Carolina increased throughout the 1990s, anti-immigrant sentiment and legislation quickly followed. Despite its substantial distance from the border, North Carolina emerged as a national leader in immigration enforcement actions at the state level at the turn of the millennium. With eight active memorandums of agreement to participate in the 287(g) program at the time of this study, North Carolina ranked second in the country in its ability to train local law officers to enforce immigration law and begin deportation proceedings.[2] When North Carolina launched its participation in the 287(g) program in 2006 in Mecklenburg County, it did so with the goal of apprehending as many unauthorized immigrants as possible (Capps et al. 2011, 10). This model was subsequently implemented throughout the Southeast to encourage "self-deportation" by creating inhospitable environments. And while these policies emerged at the state level, enforcement efforts were enabled by a federal policy, which provided the framework for partnerships between participating states and ICE. In other words, state actions magnified the exclusionary provisions of IIRIRA.

During this heightened enforcement and hostility, the 2012 announcement of DACA came as a surprise to youth who had been campaigning for inclusion for more than a decade, as well as to legislators and interest groups who had been pushing for even more restrictions on unauthorized immigrants. DACA beneficiaries were granted legal presence through executive prosecutorial discretion procedures, but DACA did not provide lawful immigration status in the country or facilitate a pathway to citizenship. Consequently, state legislatures could continue to enact policies limiting the benefits given to irregular immigrants, including DACA beneficiaries, as long as these actions were consistent with established statutory laws within state boundaries (Arellano 2012). States like North Carolina that perceived DACA as an overreach of executive power pushed back against the policy on multiple levels.

For example, in January 2013, the North Carolina DMV temporarily revoked licenses previously issued to DACA recipients and ceased issuing new licenses. Ultimately, the DMV followed the state attorney general's recommendation to issue licenses to DACA beneficiaries, but only after substantial debate surrounding the design. Initially, the North Carolina DMV designed vertical licenses with a magenta stripe across the top and the words, "NO LAWFUL STATUS" and "LIMITED TERM" at the bottom and along one side in a red font. After much protest, the Department of Transportation modified the licenses to appear in horizontal format and removed the magenta stripe from the design. Even after the modifications, however, the licenses continued to bear the red label "LEGAL PRESENCE NO LAWFUL STATUS," clearly marking the license holders as outsiders within the state of North Carolina.

Although driver's licenses fell under state purview, the National Immigration Law Center (2013) deemed DACA recipients as fitting the general guidelines of state requirements for driver's license eligibility. Thus, the controversy surrounding the licenses came as a surprise to many DACA beneficiaries in North Carolina. Unauthorized youth in the state, however, were accustomed to political and social vitriol, as they were intimately familiar with debates surrounding their access to higher education.

No federal laws protect access to public institutions of higher education for unauthorized immigrants in the United States. In contrast, the 1982 *Plyler v. Doe* Supreme Court decision states that all children and youth, regardless of immigration status, deserve equal access to primary and secondary school

and equal protection under the law by virtue of their residence and person-hood.[3] However, because *Plyler v. Doe* was not decided on preemptive grounds but stressed personhood rights, it did not prohibit states from enacting state-specific policies addressing unauthorized immigrants' access to public institutions of higher education within their state borders (Motomura 2014; Olivas 2012). This lack of federal protection placed unauthorized immigrant youth in a precarious position as they approached high school graduation.

Undocumented youth generally have a much harder time accessing higher education than their citizen peers because of the high costs of tuition and the lack of federal funding support (Passel and Cohn 2009). Though some states have lowered obstacles to enrollment by offering unauthorized immigrant students access to in-state tuition and state financial aid, provided that they graduated from public state high schools or obtained a GED, other states have prohibited their enrollment in public institutions outright. Hence, unauthorized youth in more welcoming states have a much more accessible road to postsecondary education, while youth in states more hostile to immigrants have limited or no access to public institutions of higher education (Cebulko and Silver 2016; Olivas 2012; Rincón 2008).

In North Carolina, the debate about unauthorized immigrant students' access to college had been raging since the turn of the millennium, and it did not stop with the implementation of DACA. As increasing numbers of immigrant youth graduated from North Carolina high schools, they became a recurring feature in political debates. In the 2007–8 session of the North Carolina General Assembly, two bills were introduced to "prohibit illegal aliens" from attending North Carolina community colleges and public universities.[4] Similar bills seeking to bar college enrollment for undocumented students were introduced in the 2009–10, 2011–12, and 2013–14 sessions of the North Carolina General Assembly (2013). If one of these bills had passed, North Carolina would have become the third state after South Carolina and Alabama to officially enact a state policy prohibiting college admission to undocumented immigrants (National Conference of State Legislatures 2014; Russell 2011; Yablon-Zug and Holley-Walker 2009). In response to proposals to obstruct undocumented immigrants' access to higher education, some North Carolina Democrats introduced bills to prevent the solicitation of immigration status information from enrolled students and applicants. Ultimately, none of the bills proposed on either side of the aisle were enacted into law. The legislative stalemate left the door open for individual institutions to enact their own policies addressing unauthorized immigrant students. Politicians, however, remained deeply entrenched in the debates about educational access.

Lieutenant Governor Beverly Perdue, who was a member of the NCCCS board, publicly questioned the logic of admitting unauthorized immigrant students, stating in 2008, "I'm against allowing illegal immigrants who can never work legally in North Carolina to attend community colleges in North Carolina" (Redden 2008). In contrast, Governor Mike Easley issued a statement saying, "In the absence of federal action to the contrary, the Community College board should continue its current policy [of admitting undocumented students], which is consistent with other states" (Lee et al. 2009). Ultimately, the 2008 debates resulted in the NCCCS shutting its doors to undocumented students throughout the state.

Q. Shanté Martin, general counsel to the NCCCS, asserted that the 2008 ban on unauthorized immigrant students aligned with federal policies regarding unauthorized immigrants' access to state benefits.[5] However, Jim Pendergraph, executive director of the Office of State and Local Coordination for ICE, stated in a July 9, 2008, letter to the North Carolina attorney general that "admission to public post-secondary educational institutions is not one of the benefits regulated by the Illegal Immigration Reform and Immigrant Responsibility Act of 1996 and is not a public benefit under the Personal Responsibility and Work Opportunity Reconciliation Act of 1996 (PRWORA)."[6] The letter clearly stated that admission to institutions of higher education was not regarded as a benefit regulated by the federal government, as long as undocumented students did not receive financial aid. Yet, even after receiving this information, the NCCCS retained its ban on undocumented students, pending a thorough examination of the costs and benefits of undocumented students in state community colleges. The study's findings indicated that undocumented students placed no economic burden on the community college system if they paid out-of-state tuition and that such a policy would not invite legal challenges under federal law. In response to the study report, the NCCCS reversed the ban on undocumented students, allowing them to enroll for the 2009–10 academic year (Gonzalez 2009). The reversal marked the fifth change in the NCCCS policy on undocumented students since 2000.

The 2009 policy allowed undocumented students to enroll as full-time students in community colleges at out-of-state tuition rates, but it also stated that "students lawfully present in the United States shall have priority over any undocumented immigrant in any class or program of study when capacity limitations exist" (North Carolina Community College System 2009). Though more inclusive than the ban, the policy continued to relegate undocumented immigrant students to a second-tier position. Similarly, the University of North

Carolina (UNC) system's policy on undocumented students, established in 2004, explicitly stated, "When considering whether or not to admit an undocumented alien into a specific program of study, constituent institutions should take into account that federal law prohibits the states from granting professional licenses to undocumented aliens" (Redden 2008). The language of the policy thus allowed administrators to consider undocumented students' immigration status when making admission decisions to professional programs. Though undocumented students ultimately maintained access to four-year colleges and regained access to community colleges, the constant controversy and decidedly marginalized ranking in institutional policies made undocumented immigrant youth uneasy.

Undocumented adolescents in North Carolina knew that they would have had better access to higher education if they lived in a more welcoming state, and they directly compared their opportunities to their peers' postsecondary options in those states. Eleven states offered undocumented students in-state tuition in public colleges and universities in 2010. In the next five years, an additional seven states enacted legislation to provide in-state tuition to undocumented students who graduated from public high schools in those states. Yet Southern states maintained more restrictive policies. South Carolina and Alabama passed legislation banning undocumented students from state public institutions of higher education in 2008 and 2011, respectively. In Georgia, the Board of Regents for the University System in the state passed a policy in 2010 requiring all institutions that had not admitted academically qualified applicants in the previous two years to ban undocumented immigrants, effectively barring undocumented students from the state's most prestigious universities. Finally, though North Carolina never passed legislation barring enrollment of undocumented students, colleges throughout the state retained out-of-state tuition rates, even for DACA beneficiaries. In contrast, the governor of Massachusetts leveraged DACA as a means to offer previously undocumented youth access to in-state tuition (Cebulko and Silver 2016).

With almost thirty thousand DACA beneficiaries by 2016, North Carolina was home to the seventh-largest population of DACA beneficiaries in the country, trailing only the more traditional migrant-destination states of California, Texas, Illinois, New York, and Florida and the border state of Arizona (US Citizenship and Immigration Services 2016). Nonetheless, or perhaps in part because of the size of the DACA beneficiary population in North Carolina, DACA recipients in the state continued to be treated like second-class residents. They carried conspicuously different forms of identification, were offered lower-priority placement in community college classrooms, and had no access to in-state tuition. Their unauthorized peers were even more marginalized, as they had no access to driver's licenses, no work permits, and no protection from deportation. As hostile state policies increased, this population became increasingly uneasy.

Spaces of Incorporation within Exclusionary Landscapes

As the North Carolina political climate shifted toward increasingly exclusionary practices and policies, local institutions, such as secondary schools, churches, and community organizations, offered crucial support to help immigrants respond to changing and often conflicting policies at the state and federal levels. Due to the relatively short history of immigration to North Carolina, however, these institutions were not always well equipped to shelter youth from the hostile policies within the state. Moreover, research and public policies from other states could not always serve as guides for best practices, as the South offered unique challenges and resources to immigrant and second-generation youth and the institutions that served them.

Absent the pressures of urban poverty and pervasive neighborhood violence, adolescent children of lower-income Latino immigrants in North Carolina were arguably less likely to follow a path of "downward assimilation" (Portes and Rumbaut 2001), even in the face of a very hostile political context of reception (Clotfelter, Ladd, and Vigdor 2012; Perreira, Fuligni, and Potochnick 2010; Silver 2012). Nonetheless, the lack of resources and heightened immigration enforcement policies in the South threatened the successful integration of recently settled Latino populations.

Although youth in small-town Southern schools do not face the same challenges as their peers in dangerous urban schools, research about Latino students in Southern schools has suggested that incorporation processes may be more difficult than in more cosmopolitan urban areas due to school administrators' and teachers' lack of familiarity with Latino and immigrant populations (Bohon, Macpherson, and Atiles 2005; Griffith 2008; Kandel and Parrado 2006). Latino students in North Carolina schools report high levels of discrimination from other students and insufficient support in the form of tutoring, after-school programs, and Spanish-speaking staff and teachers (Behnke, Gonzales, and Cox 2010). Moreover, immigrant students in the region cannot rely on well-established networks of support or a long-standing infrastructure of resources to aid new immigrants or their second-generation peers. The size of the coethnic community in the region, however, is rapidly increasing. Though segmented assimilation theorists highlight coethnic communities as important resources for "selective acculturation," they qualify that such communities can either impede or facilitate upward mobility (Portes and Rumbaut 2001, 63). By this caveat, the coethnic community of new Latino immigrants in the South would be less able to leverage the necessary resources to foster upward mobility due to its large percentage of undocumented immigrants and low average levels of education (Kochhar, Suro, and Tafoya 2005).

Nonetheless, recent research has documented notable academic gains for Latino students in North Carolina schools, indicating that the state may be overcoming some of its initial strains in adjusting to the new population (Clotfelter, Ladd, and Vigdor 2012; Perreira, Fuligni, and Potochnick 2010). One study found that while Latino youth perceived more discrimination than their peers in Los Angeles, they also reported more positive school climates, more encouragement from adults who worked in the schools, and higher levels of ethnic identification (Potochnick, Perreira, and Fuligni 2012). Another study found that Latino youth who arrived in North Carolina by age nine closed achievement gaps with white students of the same socioeconomic status by sixth grade (Clotfelter, Ladd, and Vigdor 2012). Thus, even as teachers may be less familiar with Latino and immigrant youth in the South, preliminary evidence suggests that they are engaging in effective strategies to encourage their Latino students (Kandel and Parrado 2006; Potochnick, Perreira, and Fuligni 2012; Silver 2015).

One explanation for Latino immigrant achievement in Southern schools is that Latino immigrant students in the South benefit from being exposed to the English language and cultural practices of their US-born, non-Latino peers (Clotfelter, Ladd, and Vigdor 2012). With fewer ethnic enclaves, students in Southern schools may intermingle more with peers of different races, ethnicities, and classes than in highly segregated schools. More contact in classrooms may lead to better English literacy skills and increased feelings of understanding and membership.

While exposure to diverse communities and US-born English speakers may be beneficial, supportive coethnic communities within historically black and white neighborhoods can be equally important in promoting successful incorporation in schools. Research has repeatedly demonstrated that connections to ethnic and racial identities are associated with higher engagement in school (Chavous et al. 2003; Fuligni, Witkow, and Garcia 2005; Gibson et al. 2004; N. Lopez 2003; Oyserman, Harrison, and Bybee 2001; Silver 2015; Stanton-Salazar 2001; Suárez-Orozco, Qin, and Amthor 2008; Tatum 1997; Valenzuela 1999). Additionally, studies have consistently shown that teachers who acknowledge and understand the cultural backgrounds of their students will be far more likely to engage them in positive educational exchanges (N. Lopez 2003; Patel 2013; Stanton-Salazar 2001; Suárez-Orozco, Qin, and Amthor 2008; Valenzuela 1999). Conversely, if students feel isolated, alienated, or misunderstood in their schools, they may be more likely to form oppositional identities (Cortina 2008; Portes and Rumbaut 2001; Valenzuela 1999). Clearly, membership within a heritage community and recognition from teachers help immigrant and second-generation students establish a sense of belonging in schools that emphasize a white Anglo-Saxon history and perspective. Furthermore, in new immigrant destinations, coethnic communities, relationships with teachers, and involvement in heritage-based clubs and activities may serve as protection against isolation and help buffer community-level discrimination and hostile state policies.

Schools, of course, are not the only institutions active in creating spaces of inclusion and sanctuary against more hostile environments at the state level. Youth themselves, along with adult allies and nonprofit organizations, also create their own spheres of belonging and empowerment by establishing safe community spaces and advocating for immigrants' rights and inclusion. Nonprofit outreach organizations are crucial in connecting immigrant populations to resources and information, and they are also instrumental in promoting civic engagement and activism. Though previous research has found that Latinos are more likely to participate in activism when they live in cities with multiple well-established Latino outreach organizations (Martinez 2008), recent social backlashes and proposed anti-immigrant legislation have prompted immigrants in new destinations to become more politically engaged (Benjamin-Alvarado, DeSipio, and Montoya 2009; Deeb-Sossa and Bickham Mendez 2008; Okamoto and Ebert 2010).

In response to the proposed federal H.R. 4437, Border Protection, Antiterrorism, and Illegal Immigration Control Act of 2005, which included a measure that would have redefined illegal entry into the United States from a misdemeanor to a felony, coalitions of nonprofit organizations in states throughout the country helped unite immigrant and allied activists to mobilize in protest. Youth activists became increasingly visible as they took on leadership roles during the large-scale immigrants' rights marches of 2006 (Bada et al. 2010; Nicholls 2013). Finding membership and purpose through the social movement, unauthorized youth marched in immigrants' rights demonstrations, held mock college classes and graduations, occupied senators' offices, and went on hunger strikes as they campaigned vocally for their own inclusion.

While immigrant youth throughout the country united in a strong and effective immigrants' rights movement, youth in North Carolina and their allies in various local institutions and organizations faced very different challenges. Though some North Carolina youth responded to anti-immigrant rhetoric at the state and federal levels by deepening their commitments to their activist efforts, others retreated in frustration. For some, it was more meaningful to concentrate on helping their families rather than fight for access to expensive college classes (J. López 2007). Thus, even as activist organizations acted as supportive shelters from the growing anti-immigrant sentiment in the region, hostile policies threatened to undermine feelings of belonging and membership provided by activist organizations and community institutions.

Conclusion

Unauthorized immigrant youth in various states faced very different contexts of reception. Some, like those in North Carolina, faced hostile local policies and lacked access to in-state tuition as well as financial aid. Meanwhile, others in more inclusive states, like California, had access to in-state tuition, some public financial support for higher education, and, as of 2015, driver's licenses. In North Carolina, politicians, sheriffs, and school board members capitalized on the exclusionary provisions of the IIRIRA to introduce policies limiting access to resources and threatening the security of unauthorized immigrants in the state. As the state climate became increasingly hostile to undocumented immigrants, unauthorized immigrant youth struggled to find a sense of comfort or hope when confronted with state legislators that did little to protect them (Cebulko and Silver 2016). Nonetheless, supportive schools, organizations, and neighborhoods offered unauthorized youth support and a sense of membership. Yet, even as youth found spaces of belonging in supportive communities, shifts in policies at the state and federal levels threatened to destabilize the security and solidarity they felt as members of schools, youth-centered community groups, and activist organizations.

2 Local Policies and Small-Town Politics

> "I don't think that Hispanics should come here. I mean, I like my class-mates, but the other Hispanics are trashing the town. It used to be so pretty, and now they keep their cars in their front lawns, and some cars are just on cinder blocks, and there was one house that didn't even have a front lawn—they just had cement."
>
> Ms. Macy interrupted her and said, "Oh, like white rednecks don't park their cars in their front lawns or put them on cinderblocks?"
>
> Leslie responded by saying, "Yeah, but that's out in the country—like out in the boonies" (waving her hand to indicate the boonies far away).
>
> Ms. Macy laughed and looked at her quizzically. "Where do you think we are?," she asked her.

In this excerpt from field notes, April 10, 2010, sixteen-year-old Leslie, a white student, and her teacher, a white North Carolina native, respond to my request to interview Leslie about her experience growing up in Allen Creek. Although conversations surrounding immigration to Allen Creek were not always so negative, the reactionary tone taken by Leslie echoed the concerns of many within the community. Leslie recalled nostalgically that the town used to be nicer before the demographic shift. Her teacher, Ms. Macy, reminded Leslie that the behaviors she described were not unique to the Latino population and that Allen Creek was not so distant, either socially or geographically, from the "boonies" that Leslie referenced. Nonetheless, Leslie's concerns over changing demographics and aesthetics within her community reflected widespread complaints about recent immigrant flows into new-destination areas throughout the country (Brettell and Nibbs 2011; Flores 2014; Hernández-León and Zúñiga 2005). Rapidly shifting demographics and associated cultural shifts made many working- and middle-class white residents in Allen Creek uneasy as they saw their community changing around them.

Leslie used the broad term "Hispanics" to refer to Latino immigrants and newcomers in particular. She saw immigration to Allen Creek as an ongoing problem even though immigration to the town had largely plateaued by the time Leslie was ten years old in 2004. Indeed, many of her Latino classmates were born in North Carolina. Nonetheless, her comments revealed a persistent social distance between the Latino population and the more established populations of whites and blacks within the town. Most of the adult Latinos in Allen Creek were, in fact, immigrants to the United States, and Leslie was not alone in extending the immigrant label to their children.

Leslie's negative perceptions of Latino immigrants in North Carolina echoed the public rhetoric surrounding Latino immigrants in the South. Immigration to the region had stirred up fears about cultural incompatibilities, labor market competition, and rising crime rates, and longtime residents publicly vocalized their fears about demographic shifts in letters to the newspaper and on televised news clips (Sohoni and Bickham Mendez 2014; Stuesse 2016). In turn, political candidates responded to the public backlash by campaigning on platforms highlighting their tough stances on immigration. Although North Carolina was a swing state, candidates on both sides of the aisle were decidedly anti-immigrant in the 2008 political debates. In one of her televised campaign advertisements, North Carolina senator Elizabeth Dole (Republican) approved a message criticizing competitor Kay Hagan (Democrat) for voting to "give illegal aliens driver's licenses." The ad flashed a photograph of about a dozen presumed "illegal aliens" scaling the wall at the US-Mexico border as a voice-over intoned, "So here they came, costing us a billion dollars each year; billions in lost wages."

The advertisement's claims were both far-fetched and inaccurate. Driver's licenses likely had little to do with immigration across the US-Mexico border, which was located more than one thousand miles from the southwesternmost point of North Carolina. And Kay Hagan had in fact voted to ban driver's licenses for persons lacking Social Security numbers in 2006. Hagan's response ad highlighted her vote to ban driver's licenses for "illegal immigrants" and trumpeted her endorsements from fifty-three sheriffs. The ad claimed that Hagan "cracked down on a[n immigration] crisis Washington created." Kay Hagan won the election, and in 2010, she voted against the DREAM Act.

The claims made in senatorial campaigns were tamer than proclamations made by the sheriffs that the candidates were courting. Because Latino immigration was a key issue in political debates throughout the state, the popular press was soliciting interviews with public officials in counties that had large immigrant populations. Sheriffs from largely conservative counties had been quoted in the press making bold claims about the criminality and moral dispositions of Latino immigrants, and their comments quickly gained the attention of watchdog organizations like the American Civil Liberties Union (ACLU).

One article in Raleigh's *News and Observer* quoted Sheriff Terry Johnson of Alamance County saying, "[Mexicans'] values are a lot different—their morals—than what we have here. In Mexico, there's nothing wrong with having sex with a 12-, 13- year-old girl. . . . They do a lot of drinking down in Mexico" (Collins 2007, A1). A different article quoted Sheriff Steve Bizzell of Johnston County calling Mexicans "trashy" and musing that "all they do is work and make love, I think" (Collins 2008b, A1). He nostalgically recalled the days when Mexican farmworkers were sequestered on farms. Though he acknowledged that isolation in work camps was "bad for [immigrants] as human beings," he asserted that native North Carolinians did not have the same issues with immigrants when they were segregated onto farms instead of integrated into the community. These comments were picked up by additional local news outlets and subsequently quoted in an ACLU report examining racial profiling in the region (Frederickson et al. 2009). After receiving harsh criticism for his comments, Sheriff Bizzell issued a written apology. The controversy, however, did not hurt his career. He remained in office and won elections again in 2010 and 2014. Sheriff Johnson of Alamance County remained in office as well. A federal lawsuit accusing Johnson of racial discrimination was dismissed by a judge in August 2015, citing a lack of sufficient evidence to prove that the police department was targeting Latino drivers in traffic stops and searches.

Though public policies addressing immigrants in the region specifically targeted unauthorized immigrants, the comments made by the sheriffs, similar to Leslie's comment about "Hispanics," addressed "Mexicans," not unauthorized immigrants. Thus, the public narrative emerging from these statements simplistically categorized all of the Latino newcomers to the region as "Mexicans" and simultaneously racialized and demonized them as morally corrupt. Previous research has shown that similar language racializing Latino populations in Arizona paints Hispanic populations as undeserving of social benefits and can result in more hostile policies addressing immigrant populations (Brown 2013). In turn, more hostile policies addressing immigrants tend to have negative impacts on Latino communities in general, who report feeling surveilled and distressed in areas with active immigration enforcement policies (Szkupinski Quiroga, Medina, and Glick 2014). In North Carolina, the derisive language leveled against Mexicans set the stage for hostile legislative measures addressing unauthorized immigrants in the state. The rhetoric also placed documented Latinos and Latino citizens into marginalized social spaces along with unauthorized immigrants.

Public officials in Allen County did not court the same amount of controversy as their peers in other counties, but Allen Creek had also grappled with its own adjustment to immigration. Although public outcries had quieted by the time I began my research, members of the community and surrounding towns had staged an anti-immigrant rally attended by members of the Ku Klux Klan earlier in the decade. Like other small towns experiencing influxes of immigrants, a large percentage of residents were uncomfortable watching their communities change so dramatically. "Diversity transitions" (Alba and Foner 2015, 14–15) in small towns were particularly conspicuous, and other studies have documented similarly panicked reactions to initial waves of immigration in new-destination towns (Cuadros 2006; Lacy and Odem 2009; Marrow 2011; Sohoni and Bickham Mendez 2014; Torres, Popke, and Hapke 2006). In the tense adjustment period, it was unsurprising that Leslie attached such negative characteristics to her Latino neighbors.

Although Leslie liked her Hispanic classmates, her comment that "other Hispanics" were "trashing the town" was reminiscent of the comment made by Sheriff Bizzell that the Mexicans in the state were "trashy." Of course, Leslie was only a teenager when she made these offhand remarks about immigrants in Allen Creek, and her comments were not reflective of a well-developed philosophy about race or ethnicity. In fact, Leslie's experience with race and ethnicity was more complex than her comment might suggest. She had a diverse group of friends and often struggled to justify her friendships and romantic relationships to her parents. Leslie's parents referred to her Latino peers as her "friends that worked at the chicken plant." The derogatory joke clearly referenced social divisions around race and ethnicity and alluded to the labor opportunities that had initially attracted Latino immigrants to the region.

Allen Creek specifically drew immigrants because of its proximity to several chicken-processing plants, textile mills, and plastics-manufacturing plants. Poultry-processing plants, in particular, were greatly in need of an increased labor supply in the 1990s, and immigrants were quick to respond to labor demands (Kandel and Parrado 2004, 2005; Parrado and Kandel 2008; Striffler 2005; Stuesse 2016). The expansion of work opportunities in the poultry industry was directly linked to increasing consumer interest. As health concerns associated with eating red meat began to emerge in the popular press, the poultry industry was primed for growth. To maximize profit and best respond to consumer demand, the poultry industry integrated vertically, linking growing, feeding, processing, and production in proximate facilities. Food-processing companies in sparsely populated towns, such as Allen Creek, were unable to fill the demand for laborers with local populations and actively sought immigrant laborers. Moreover, meat-processing work is physically demanding and often results in crippling injuries from taxing and repetitive labor (López-Sanders 2009; Ribas 2016; Striffler 2005; Stuesse 2016). High turnover rates thus required a larger supply of available workers.

Companies based in the South advertised jobs on billboards in Mexico, and some provided incentives for employee referrals for friends and families (Mohl 2003). As the word spread through social networks, immigrants began to travel to North Carolina from other states and countries to fill expanding labor opportunities (Hagan, Hernández-León, and Demonsant 2015; Hagan, Lowe, and Quingla 2011). When Latinos began to arrive in larger numbers in the South, their entrance into the labor market complicated race relations, which had been marked by a binary racial division and a history of racial oppression through slavery, Jim Crow, and persistent structural racism and inequality. Because of class differences rooted in long-standing racial inequalities, whites in rural Southern regions were more likely than blacks to be employers or in managerial positions from which they could offer work to Latino newcomers to the region (Marrow 2011). Like research in more traditional migrant receiving areas (Waldinger 2003), research in the South has documented white employers' preferences for Latino immigrants (Ciscel, Smith, and Mendoza 2003; López-Sanders 2009). Because of irregular immigration status and a lack of cultural capital, immigrants are generally perceived to be more compliant and less likely to complain about harsh working conditions (Ciscel, Smith, and Mendoza 2003; López-Sanders 2009; Ribas 2016; Waldinger 2003). Perceptions about immigrant workers in Allen Creek spilled over onto Latinos in general.

Poultry was fundamental to the local economy, but because of its association with Latino immigrants, "working in the chicken plant" was a derogatory phrase signifying failure, lack of motivation, and a lack of options. Even Latino youth viewed "working in the chicken plant" as a dead-end future. Many had witnessed their parents and relatives struggle under harsh and exploitative labor conditions, and they wanted something different for themselves. They internalized pejorative remarks about poultry-plant work and would openly distance themselves from associations with the chicken plant when discussing their ambitions for the future. They had picked up on the segregated labor market in their community, and they understood the shame attached to particular jobs.

Though immigrant youth did not comment on residential segregation as much as they discussed labor market stratification, they were nonetheless aware of neighborhood segregation within their community. Although Allen Creek was small, discrete neighborhoods separated residents by race and class. Most obvious to passersby, three trailer parks were home to a majority of Latino residents. Close to the highway, these communities offered affordable housing options, particularly for newly arrived immigrants. Despite coming from humble origins, many of the Latino youth that migrated to Allen Creek were unfamiliar with trailers, and some youth recalled their shock upon seeing trailers for the first time. Zaíra, an immigrant from Guatemala, remembered seeing trailers at age nine when she first arrived and thinking that they were "cages for dead people." She was horrified to learn that one of these cages was her new home. Others were not shocked by the trailers themselves but complained about their neighbors, who occasionally drank too much and disturbed the neighborhood by yelling or fighting.

On the other end of the spectrum, and farther from the highway and commercial sections of town, the country club neighborhood was populated almost exclusively by white, wealthier families who lived in big houses with yards. The neighborhood was named for the small country club and golf course in town, and youth were aware of the status attached to this neighborhood. Teenagers of all races and ethnicities spoke of "living by the country club" as a euphemism for being rich, and the phrase often demarcated a social (if not literal) distance between families who lived there and families who lived anywhere else in Allen Creek.

The intersection of the main highway and another main avenue marked a third identifiable neighborhood in the community that was home to many of the African American families in town. Spray-painted graffiti and gang tags infrequently marked an adjacent underpass, visibly distinguishing this area of town. Although there were occasional threats of fights between black and Latino gangs in the community, most youth were quick to classify both black and Latino adolescent gang members as "wannabes," and violence in the town was rare. Teenagers admitted that there was a fair amount of drug use but also stated that most drug trades and drug use involved marijuana. Teens who had lived in urban areas in other states, moreover, commented that drugs were far more visible in those cities than in Allen Creek. In Allen Creek, criminal activity beyond drug use and driving under the influence rarely went beyond petty thievery. When I asked if there were gangs in town, one Guatemalan American girl responded, "There are people who think they're in gangs." Her comments reflected the sentiments of most of her peers. Some parents and teachers spoke about other community members being scared of emerging Latino gangs, but no one that I spoke with directly voiced this concern.

Other neighborhoods were less segregated. While most people within these neighborhoods discussed pleasant relationships with their neighbors, others discussed tensions and discrimination. One Latina woman spoke in heated frustration about her neighbors calling the police every time her family had a backyard barbecue. She attributed what she identified as harassment to anti-Latino discrimination by her white neighbors and the predominantly white police force in the community. Though she was well integrated into the community as a nurse and frequent parent-volunteer at the high school, she occasionally considered moving because of what she felt to be oppressive discrimination. People of color in the community could easily call to mind experiences with discrimination in Allen Creek, usually with police or store or restaurant owners. Nonetheless, most identified race relations as peaceful, though distant.

The community gradually became more accommodating to immigrants as residents and school officials organized centers and programs to help integrate new immigrants and their children into the community. In the mid-1990s, community members started a Latino Outreach Center to assist immigrants with job hunts, legal issues, and food and housing concerns. The local schools implemented English as a Second Language (ESL) programs, and more recently the high school created one club to help Latino students access and apply for college and another that allows high school students to assist in after-school programs at the elementary school with Spanish-speaking children.

Despite these proactive measures to incorporate Latino immigrants into the community, some long-term white residents obstructed other efforts to integrate Latino children of immigrants and black children into the largely segregated primary schools. As the Latino population of the county and town increased by more than 400 percent between 1990 and 2010, county commissioners discussed how to best respond to the influx of residents. One proposed response was to rezone the school districts to ensure that no school district was saddled with disproportionate responsibilities to address the needs of new immigrant students. Like parents in other new immigrant destinations (Hernández-León and Zúñiga 2005), white parents in Allen Creek resisted integration out of fear that their children's education would suffer. The debate that ensued in response to the proposed rezoning reaffirmed the residential and social boundaries present among the three major demographic groups in the county. Alvaro García, the vice principal of Allen Creek High School, explained that white parents spoke out to oppose the proposed redistricting: "I mean, you're talking about a school that didn't get integrated until like the '70s, and so, you know, you have parents and grandparents that still remember that. . . .

We just went through this rezoning thing where they were trying to rezone the school districts, and it did not fly because the parents said that it was 'tradition' instead of 'I don't want my kids going to school with colored kids, whether they're brown or black.'"

Mr. García perceived the opposition to rezoning as a strategy to maintain borders between the established white population and both the black and Latino populations in Allen Creek. And like other Latinos in the region, he linked the social position of Latinos to the social position of African Americans (Jones 2012; Marrow 2017). Both were mapped into different neighborhoods and elementary schools from those of their white peers.

White parents' concern with "tradition," at least according to Vice Principal García's interpretation, illustrated what sociologist Eduardo Bonilla-Silva has described as an increasing trend of coded language replacing overt racism. Their opposition to rezoning was rooted in legacies of racial inequality, but parents spoke out in a manner that obscured "direct racial discourse but effectively safeguard[ed] racial privilege" (Bonilla-Silva and Forman 2000, 52). Their "color-blind" (Bonilla-Silva 2003; Gallagher 2003) rhetorical strategies echoed other political movements in the region that emphasized words like "tradition" and "heritage" to garner support for policies excluding unauthorized immigrants from participating in state and local institutions (Gill 2010; Lacy and Odem 2009, 150). For example, in Alamance County, one city displayed banners with the slogan, "Preserving Our Heritage, Promoting Our Future"; in a less coded action, legislators in Beaufort County made English the official county language (Gill 2010). Because of their immigration enforcement policies, both counties had gained reputations among immigrants for being places to avoid. Anti-immigrant fervor arose in reaction to fears about the rapidly shifting demographics of the region as well as in response to widespread beliefs that incoming populations of Latinos would lead to increased crime (Gill 2010; Haddix 2008; Sohoni and Bickham Mendez 2014). Fears about changing populations played out in political debates in small towns throughout the state.

In the case of Allen Creek's rezoning debate, white parents won the battle, and the "tradition" of largely segregated schooling remained intact, at least at the elementary and middle school levels. In the town's sole public high school, however, black, white, and Latino students all took classes, participated in school activities, and played on the same sports teams. Nevertheless, adolescent cliques reflected the social distance among students of different races and ethnicities. Alonso, an undocumented immigrant from Mexico, described the social scene among teens in Allen Creek: "It's very cliquey by race. Hispanics are with Hispanics, Americans are with Americans, and the African Americans are with African Americans. The groups are really separated. The ideas that the Americans have about us is that we're not going to talk to them, and they're not used to having us around. They didn't grow up with us, so their parents don't like us. I have some friends who aren't Hispanic, but mostly I hang out with just Latinos." In his description of segregation across racial and ethnic groups, Alonso equated race with nationality as he referred to his white peers as "Americans." Previous research has found that adult labor migrants in Mississippi made similar linguistic differentiations between (white) "Americanos" and black "morenos" (Stuesse 2016, 111), symbolically excluding both Latinos and African Americans from full national membership. Speaking from personal experience as an undocumented immigrant, Alonso described feeling distant from his white peers. He experienced racism from their parents and felt that his white classmates were unfamiliar with Latinos. By emphasizing the perspective of whites in his response, Alonso situated white Americans as the dominant members of the community, in control of constructing social boundaries.

Both Leslie's comments about Hispanics "trashing the town" and Alonso's description of racial segregation acknowledged hierarchal ethnic and national boundaries that organized the social groups within Allen Creek. Their perspectives also reflected a regional dynamic where Latinos were conspicuous newcomers in an area long populated almost exclusively by blacks and whites. Uneasiness about the Latino population tended to magnify when Latino populations asserted their cultural and linguistic differences in public places.

For example, each year at homecoming, the community held a parade that traveled down Main Street. High school students would decorate cars, wave flags, and raise banners, and community members would line the normally sleepy street to watch the day's events. Though the event was typically one of community unity and pride, some community members felt that the school's Latino students were trampling on the long-held tradition by speaking or singing in Spanish in the parade.

The high school's Action Inspiration Motivation (AIM) club, an offshoot of the North Carolina Migrant Education Program, comprised almost exclusively Latino students who helped with translation services in the elementary schools and engaged in other community service work.[1] The club's director, Ben Ryan, explained that his students' actions during the parade made some residents uneasy: "[My students] were in the homecoming parade last year, shouting some things in Spanish, and they got some nasty looks from some people in the town. The soccer team too—they were singing 'Olé, olé, olé, olé, Los Tigres.' They were calling themselves 'Los Tigres' [The Tigers], so they got some nasty looks. I think some of the old-time residents in Allen Creek might frown upon that kind of pride." According to Mr. Ryan, some of Allen Creek's older residents felt that students chanting the school's mascot in Spanish and singing Spanish songs in a community parade were signaling their unwillingness to adapt to the norms and customs of Allen Creek. These community members saw the traditions that youth brought with them, or took from their parents, as changing their community for the worse.

The small-town atmosphere did not allow Latino immigrants or their children to easily blend into their surroundings. Some youth would implement strategies to combat assumptions of illegality and low achievement that they felt were placed on them because of the color of their skin. For example, Luz, a US-born citizen with Salvadoran parents, intentionally wore college T-shirts when she went with her parents to flea markets or to Walmart. She explained that she was tired of people assuming that she was stupid because of the color of her skin. She also bought her parents T-shirts that said the name of her university followed by the word "mom" or "dad." She wanted people to know that her parents had children in college. She claimed that she never felt pigeonholed because of her ethnicity in her North Carolina college town, but in her home town and surrounding rural areas, she took symbolic action to upend assumptions and stereotypes. Like Luz, other youth complained about feeling surveilled and judged because of their skin color and use of Spanish, but they also found comfort in their small-town surroundings. As legislation targeting immigrants in the state began to spread from town to town, however, the safety of home felt increasingly less secure.

Federal Immigration Enforcement on a Small-Town Stage

Allen County did not have a reputation for being particularly hostile to immigrants, but increased police surveillance in other North Carolina counties incited apprehension in immigrant communities throughout the state. In 2006, the state banned driver's licenses for individuals without Social Security numbers, making unauthorized immigrants more easily identifiable and far more vulnerable. Latinos in Allen Creek noted a heightened police presence and were often followed by police or stopped at traffic checkpoints set up in predominantly Latino neighborhoods. Even the Latino high school vice principal spoke with frustration about the close police monitoring.

When I asked Vice Principal García to compare Allen Creek to other places where he had lived, he replied, "One thing that has been a revelation for me here in this town is that this is the first time in my life that I have thought of myself as Hispanic." I asked how he classified himself before, and he responded, "As a person. Here I'm treated differently. . . . My wife and I have been pulled over here more times in three years than I have been pulled over my whole life in Orlando. Once my wife got pulled over and she had just moved here, so she had a Florida license. So instead of giving her a warning or something, he gave her a one hundred fifty–dollar ticket for not having a North Carolina license. That kind of stuff."

Mr. García should have been recognizable to the police as the vice principal of the town's only high school, yet he was stopped often and frequently felt out of place. He could map out a geography of places that he felt unwanted in the town. Unfortunately, all of the roads in Allen Creek would appear on that map. As he explained, "I get pulled over all the time. . . . And there's a couple of restaurants that I feel very uncomfortable in. The bowling alley sometimes too. I get a lot of stares. Sometimes when you go into certain stores, you get a little look." Despite his prestigious position in the school, Mr. García confronted significant discrimination in Allen Creek. Earlier in our conversation, he told me that he liked his job and the town because it was safe and had very little gang activity. Yet his personal experiences with the police were far more negative in Allen Creek than in Orlando or Chicago, where he had lived previously.

Tensions between Latino residents and the police became even more charged as the counties surrounding Allen County implemented the 287(g) program, which deputized local law enforcement to enforce immigration law. Allen County was not involved in the program, but as the state's political climate became increasingly hostile, many undocumented immigrants began to fear driving both within and beyond county lines. Then, in late 2008, chatter began to appear on community message boards about bringing 287(g) to Allen County. To calm concern among residents, the mostly Democratic County Board of Commissioners proposed a resolution to prevent local law enforcement agencies from entering into agreements with ICE. County residents came out en masse to debate the issue at the subsequent town hall meeting in February 2009.

The small courtroom was filled to standing-room-only capacity even before the meeting began, and there was scarcely room to park on the normally sleepy streets surrounding the courthouse. About two hundred people crowded into the room, and the county commissioners sat in the front of the room facing the constituents. After commencing the meeting with a prayer and the Pledge of Allegiance, the presider announced that the meeting had been extended from the normal meeting time of sixty minutes to ninety minutes to allow time for all speakers. Local residents lined up behind the microphone at the front of the room and took turns addressing the commissioners and their neighbors. Some spoke against the resolution and in support of the 287(g) program, which they considered necessary to uphold federal law and protect local communities from crime. Others spoke in support of the resolution, which they believed would help keep immigrant families together and maintain peaceful relations between the police and community members. They did not want a culture of fear to permeate immigrant neighborhoods in Allen Creek. Attempting to bridge the two sides, one middle-aged white woman approached the microphone. She asked her fellow community members, "Are we raiding homes? Are we breaking up families?" Her questions were asked rhetorically, meant to quiet concerns and remind her neighbors that Allen Creek was a peaceful community without high-profile deportation raids or contentious relationships between immigrant communities and local police. A chorus of voices shouted, "Yes!" in response.

As she spoke, several Latino teenagers whispered to each other and shifted uncomfortably in their seats. Less timid and better integrated than their parents, close to twenty Latino youths from Allen Creek had attended the meeting. Victor, the high school soccer coach who also ran a scholarship fund for Latino students in the region, took the microphone next. Victor was Latino, and he sympathized deeply with the youth in the room. He remembered feeling isolated in school when he was their age and saw that he could mentor and champion them.

Pointing to the teens, he addressed the audience: "When thinking about this resolution, we have to ask ourselves, are these our kids?" He then looked directly at the bench where a number of recent graduates of Allen Creek High School were sitting. He pointed to one and said, "Itzel, can you stand up? Itzel is going to Carolina Tech [pseudonym] and studying to become an FBI agent." He pointed to another and continued, "Eduardo, stand up. Eduardo is also going to Carolina Tech to become a mechanical engineer." Angling toward the back corner of the courtroom, he pointed to a high school senior. "Vicente is a finalist for the Morehead scholarship at the University of North Carolina." He continued, "Isabel is studying to become a nurse at North Carolina State. Lidia is also studying to become a nurse at North Carolina State. Luz is on a full scholarship at UNC. José graduated from Allen County Community College [pseudonym] and is now working in a hospital."

He paused and looked around at the young adults standing all around the courtroom before speaking again. "I'll ask you again. Are these our kids? We educated them in our schools, and we saw them grow up in our town, so now we have to decide if they're our kids. You can't change what's happening, so you should embrace it. Real leadership cuts against the grain. Thank you."

Victor knew that several of the youth he spoke about were US citizens, but he saw the 287(g) policy as an attack on the Latino community in general. Itzel was an eighteen-year-old US-born child of Mexican immigrants. Certainly, the previous speaker's assumption that local police did not raid homes or tear apart families did not ring true to her ears. Although Itzel was a citizen by birth, she knew that the resolution debated in the town hall meeting was not an abstract policy affecting anonymous strangers. She knew the faces of the people who might be deported through 287(g). They were her family members, her friends, and her neighbors. She already knew the heartbreak of having her own family torn apart because ICE officers had raided her home and arrested her father and brother.

Itzel's family had lived in Allen Creek since she was three years old. She was born in California, but her undocumented parents felt that North Carolina was a safer place to raise their children, where they could also capitalize on family connections. They had especially high hopes for Itzel, their one US-born child. As the only citizen in her family, Itzel had opportunities her siblings lacked. Having attended school in the United States since kindergarten, she spoke better English than her siblings, and she was far more engaged in school than they had been. Itzel's citizenship status also protected her the day the police raided her home.

Itzel recounted the morning that she last saw her father and brother. She and her father were driving to school when they were surrounded by police. She described what happened next:

> Once we got to that first stop sign, police cars started pulling out of everywhere. So, there were two cars in front, and three in the back, just surrounded us. And so they took my dad out of the car, and I was just in the passenger seat. I had no idea what was going on. So they took us back to our house and went in our house and took other people that lived with us. So there was three gone that day: my dad, my brother, and the brother of my brother-in-law. They didn't tell us nothing. They didn't show us a warrant or anything. They just went inside our house and woke everybody up. . . . The door was open, so they just went in. So they took everyone to the police station, I guess, and I never saw them after that. A lot of people don't know this, but that's what happened.

Itzel did not know the exact details of the events leading up to the raid, but she knew that her father had been engaged in a monetary dispute with a lawyer. According to Itzel, the lawyer had reported her father to ICE. Though she told me the story in October 2009, only six months after the police surrounded their family car and escorted them back into their home, she struggled to recall the details of that morning. She knew that the police took everyone they found in the home who could not produce documentation proving their legal residence, but the trauma of the day was too much for her to relive. The one detail that she could not forget was that she was not allowed to say good-bye to her father or brother.

I asked Itzel why they allowed her mother, who also lacked the proper immigration authorization, to remain behind. She responded, "I have no idea. I think she hid and the agents weren't able to locate her. And I wasn't saying anything or telling who was there. I don't even remember what they were saying. I sort of blocked that whole scene out of my mind." Shortly after her father was deported to Mexico, Itzel's mother decided to return as well. Itzel had just turned eighteen, and she struggled with the decision of whether to stay in the United States or move with her parents to Mexico. She ultimately decided to remain in North Carolina. After having worked so hard to give their children opportunities to succeed, Itzel's parents were forced to miss her high school graduation. But they supported her decision to remain in the United States in the hopes that she would continue her education and be the first in the family to go to college and build a professional career.

The deportation of her father and subsequent departure of her mother were a harsh introduction into adult life for Itzel. She became depressed and withdrawn. She attended her graduation but did not move forward with her plans to attend college. Instead, she moved in with her sister and got a job to help pay for household bills. She did not want to be a burden to her sister, so for months Itzel moved quietly between her work at a fast-food restaurant and her sister's home. She stopped playing soccer on her club team and isolated herself. Itzel essentially put her life on hold as she recovered from the trauma that had ruptured her childhood world.

Slowly, and with help of Victor, her soccer coach, Itzel began to refocus. After taking the semester off, Itzel applied to college and enrolled for the spring semester. Victor convinced her to help him coach the high school girls' soccer team that spring. After six months of painful adjustments, Itzel felt confident in her decision to remain in the United States, and she regained her sense of belonging in her community.

She missed her parents deeply, but she did not describe her story as tragic. Instead, she juxtaposed her experience to those of others less fortunate, proclaiming herself one of the "lucky ones." Itzel was born in the United States and she was well aware of the opportunities this afforded her. Despite the distress she suffered during and after the raid, she maintained that she was more fortunate than many of her unauthorized peers. She spoke empathetically about their struggles to attend school and find work. She also pointed out that she had the choice to stay in the United States or move with her parents to Mexico. For her brother and father, this was not a choice.

As one of the lucky ones, Itzel was able to enroll in college, get financial aid, and remain connected to her passion of soccer and to the teachers who encouraged her throughout high school. She had two important elements operating in her favor: she was a citizen, and she had many social supports within her close-knit community. Her mentors helped her navigate through a very difficult time in her life, and her legal status gave her the ability to pause her education to recover from the stress of witnessing her brother and father's deportations without losing the option to return to school.

Itzel also considered herself one of the lucky ones because, though extremely traumatic, her encounter with police raids was less harrowing than what many others had experienced. She explained, "I've heard about a lot worse situations than mine with the police. In most counties, they have 287(g), so then police will just stop any cars and then older people will get arrested and the kids will be left there all night. So I've heard a lot worse situations than mine. At least mine was peaceful." As Itzel astutely noted, sloppy implementation of the 287(g) policy had endangered immigrants and their families. Itzel's description of "the kids . . . left there all night" referenced a highly publicized case of three children abandoned on a North Carolina highway after their mother was pulled over and subsequently arrested for immigration violations late at night in July 2008. The police left the children with another adult who was in the car, but, fearing his own deportation, he fled. The case had been written about in popular press publications and an ACLU report examining the repercussions of 287(g) (Collins 2008a; Fredrickson et al. 2009). Incidents like this one sowed fear among Latino immigrants in the state. It was this fear that brought many out to the town hall meeting to voice their support for a resolution to ban 287(g) from Allen County.

Itzel knew that the resolution would not bring back her family or undo the anguish that she felt watching her loved ones handcuffed and removed from her home, but she sat in the courtroom in support of her friends and her principles. She knew some of her peers might experience what she had gone through, and others might be deported themselves. She was relieved when the resolution passed, though she knew from personal experience that it would not protect all families with mixed-immigration status from being torn apart. Nonetheless, the resolution helped keep events like the one she endured from becoming routine. Moreover, it signaled that the county commissioners recognized the human rights and dignity of their immigrant neighbors and perhaps even regarded them as true members of the community. For the moment, the commissioners' decision seemed to signal that the immigrant youth in the room were indeed "[their] kids" instead of the children of immigrant outsiders.

Yet this victory for immigrants' rights was short-lived; newly elected conservative-leaning county commissioners overturned the resolution just two years later in 2011, a decision that signaled a local political shift that matched the more hostile context of reception in the rest of the state. Immigration to Allen Creek had declined in the intervening period, but popular sentiment held that immigration was a problem of public safety. When concerned voters elected local representatives who represented their views, policies changed accordingly. Despite overturning the resolution, the county did not enter into a memorandum of agreement (MOA) with ICE. The reversal of the resolution without an MOA was an uneasy compromise to appease voters on both sides of the issue.

Conclusion

Though Itzel was a US-born citizen, her story indirectly illustrates tectonic incorporation and directly demonstrates its spillover effects. As anti-immigrant hostility spread in North Carolina, unauthorized immigrants were increasingly targeted for deportation. In turn, deportation was made easier by the federal policy of 287(g), which allowed local police to enforce immigration law. Though Itzel's father was not deported as a result of 287(g), she knew that the policy could result in even more families torn apart. Itzel's citizenship status could not protect her from experiencing the heartbreak of forcible family separation. Yet, even as the state embraced augmented immigration enforcement tactics, Itzel had strong community support that helped her recover after the trauma of family deportation shattered her life as she knew it. Moreover, she felt confident to voice her convictions and stand up in resistance against local policy shifts when the county debated 287(g).

Though local anti-immigrant policies specifically targeted unauthorized immigrants, they were not the only affected parties. Just as in other localities with immigration ordinances and augmented enforcement policies (Brown 2013; Szkupinski Quiroga, Medina, and Glick 2014), Latinos in North Carolina felt acutely surveilled, regardless of their immigration status. When comparing his experience in the more traditional immigrant destinations of Florida and

Illinois, the vice principal noted that he was pulled over far more frequently in Allen Creek than in any other place he had lived. Itzel was scarred by witnessing her unauthorized immigrant parents become so disempowered and subsequently experienced profound losses as her brother and father were deported and her mother moved shortly after. The trauma of her encounter with ICE brought to light the complexity of the terrain in which she and peers entered adulthood. While neither Vice Principal García nor Itzel feared deportation for themselves, they were both intimately connected to people far more vulnerable than themselves. Documented immigrants, undocumented immigrants, and their citizen children were part of the same families and ethnic communities, and the "legal violence" (Menjívar and Abrego 2012) enacted on unauthorized immigrants spilled over to affect entire communities.

Unauthorized immigrant youth faced political exclusion as a result of immigration enforcement and anti-immigrant sentiment in their home state and community. And both unauthorized and second-generation immigrants saw their friends deported, families torn apart, and their opportunities blocked as the result of increasingly hostile state and federal policies targeting unauthorized immigrants. Yet unauthorized immigrant youth felt the support of their friends and their mentors and relied on this support to help buffer the stress of exclusionary policies and the constant anxiety of "deportability" (De Genova 2002). Having benefited from small-town community support herself, Itzel, along with her coach and other community members, also provided this support to her unauthorized immigrant friends as she sat in that courtroom alongside them.

Although Itzel's experience shook her to her core, she knew that her ability to rebuild her life after the devastating separation from her parents was largely enabled by her citizenship status. Her unauthorized peers would have faced even higher barriers in her position, as she sympathetically pointed out. Unauthorized immigrant youth were acutely aware that their daily routines were increasingly monitored and feared that they would become even more so if 287(g) were brought to Allen Country. The constantly shifting landscape made them feel unsteady as they attempted to build their futures. Nonetheless, they took comfort from their connections to local institutions and social groups and from relationships with their peers, teachers, and other influential adults in the community and at school. Through these interactions, they found spaces of belonging in contexts of exclusion. Yet, as policies at the local, state, and federal levels continued to shift around them, they knew that any feelings of security they had were tenuous at best.

3 Pathways to Membership

On September 16, 2010, five students lined up in the hallway and boisterously began to sing, "And I'm proud *not* to be an American, where at least I know I'm *not* free." The students, who were all of Mexican descent, were singing an adapted version of "God Bless the U.S.A." by Tennessee-based artist Lee Greenwood in a jovial celebration of Mexican Independence Day. As they filed into their classrooms, they continued the chorus. Ms. Macy smiled and raised her eyebrows at Mani, a US-born child of Mexican immigrants, as he walked into AVID class singing. He smiled back, "No, we're just singing that for Mexican Independence Day!" Both Macy and the other students laughed as Mani and his classmates continued to joke around on their way to their seats. Although they were joking, their adapted lyrics conveyed a sentiment of profound national exclusion. Yet their choice of this classic country music song to parody also displayed a national and even regional knowledge. And their ability to sing it in school showed that they were comfortable enough to joke about their lack of belonging in the national community. Other students thought the song was funny, and they were not admonished by their teachers or administrators for their actions.

The incident poignantly illustrated how Latino youth in Allen Creek High School, regardless of immigration status, walked a tightrope between incorporation and exclusion. Their decision to sing this song on Mexican Independence Day illustrated a bicultural capital reflecting attachments to both their country of origin and their country of residence. Within their coethnic community, they bonded over feelings of marginalization and created spaces of inclusion among friends. In turn, their US-born black and white peers appreciated their humor and saw them as fellow students, though not necessarily fellow Americans.

Latino students knew that they were regarded as distinct from the other students in their school because of their, or their parents', immigrant backgrounds. They did not step into school as blank slates but instead brought their experiences from the community with them. They were aware of discrimination in their town, and they were not immune to prejudices at school either. Yet the school, like the community, had also adapted to help incorporate Latino students by creating structural support systems through clubs, sports teams, and inclusive curricular materials. Though their ethnicity and immigrant history marked Latino students as newcomers and partial outsiders, they found ways to celebrate their ethnic identities through friendships, ethnic clubs, targeted academic coursework, and athletic participation on majority Latino teams. They thus found footholds of stability on otherwise unstable terrain by embracing their culture and forming a coethnic community within their school.

Ironically, the perception of Latinos as new, or foreign, provided a pathway toward incorporation that was not available to black students in the school. School administrators promoted ethnicity-based extracurricular programs for Latinos, but they were less comfortable with the idea of clubs that celebrated African American heritage or offered black students a safe space in which to discuss racial discrimination. Noting a recent history of school segregation under Jim Crow–era politics, both teachers and students were hesitant to embrace separate programs for black students. Yet they supported clubs for Latino students, whom they did not view through the lens of a racially oppressive history. Because black students were viewed as national insiders, they had fewer formal groups where they could discuss their experiences of prejudice or celebrate their own cultural heritage. Thus, even as Latino students were marked as foreign, they benefited from resources that facilitated integration and opportunity within the school.

Previous research about immigrant and US-born Latino students has stressed that children do best when they are able to draw on and navigate both their heritage cultures and the surrounding US culture (Bejarano 2005; Portes and Rumbaut 2001; Stanton-Salazar 2001). However, schools are often structured to isolate US-born students and more recent immigrant students, thereby limiting the exchange of cultural capital between the two groups (Valenzuela 1999). As federal policies, such as No Child Left Behind and Race to the Top, have tended to stress test scores and English acquisition over language maintenance, school policies that focus on improving test scores instead of facilitating environments of inclusion and intellectual curiosity tend to isolate and exclude immigrant students and too frequently result in declining achievement for immigrant youth (Morales, Trujillo, and Kissel 2016; Patel 2013; Suárez-Orozco, Suárez-Orozco, and Todorova 2008; Valenzuela 2005).

For unauthorized youth stresses about life after graduation begin to increase in their junior and senior years of high school (Gonzales 2016; Silver 2012), and they are more likely to lose interest in school and show declining achievement than their documented peers (Suárez-Orozco, Suárez-Orozco, and Todorova 2008). Without a clear path to upward mobility and security in adulthood, unauthorized immigrant youth begin to doubt the value of school. Unless school policies can foster a culture of engagement regardless of status, the federal and state policies that limit mobility for undocumented youth tend to encroach on educational experiences. Just as exclusionary local and state policies can magnify the impact of exclusionary federal policies, institutional policies can similarly exacerbate or buffer governmental policies.

Though second-generation students do not face the same challenges as their unauthorized immigrant peers, they nonetheless continue to face exclusion in school. Studies about immigrant and second- and third-generation youth in schools have stressed how harmful stereotypes limit opportunities and feelings of membership for youth of color. Ample research demonstrates that 1.5-, second-, and third-generation immigrants of Latino and Caribbean descent have been criminalized by teachers and staff in urban school settings (N. Lopez 2003; Rios 2011; R. Smith 2002; Telles and Ortiz 2008; Valenzuela 1999). Young men of color, in particular, frequently face suspicions of gang involvement and expectations of academic failure (N. Lopez 2003; Rios 2011; R. Smith 2002, 2006). Unauthorized youth of color who are limited by both immigration status and criminalization struggle on two fronts to find security and membership. However, when administrators and teachers act deliberately to combat hostile stereotypes and restrictive state and federal policies, students benefit. Moreover, deliberate actions of engagement would ideally promote a schoolwide culture of learning and inclusion.

Allen Creek High School

When I asked students to describe their high school, all but five of the sixty-two youths I interviewed began by proudly discussing the diversity of the student body. Of the remaining five students, three described the school as segregated, one spoke about its small size, and one described the school as run-down and dirty. Administrators and teachers celebrated the school's diversity in official school events like graduation, and the students had clearly caught on. Patricia, an immigrant from Honduras, speculated about how students learned to embrace the school's diversity: "I think it's because of how small [the school] is. You get to know the people, and you get to fall in love and go deep with the people here. . . . Somehow you become a family." The small school facilitated opportunities for youth to interact with their peers of different backgrounds.

Students who had moved from other schools echoed Patricia's sentiments and noted that Allen Creek High School was different. After moving from Orlando, the Latino vice principal told me that his son was surprised by the racial harmony at Allen Creek High: "[My son] got here from Orlando, and he did not understand why these people got along so well. The school that he was at, if you looked at someone, he wanted to fight. He did not understand why people were so friendly. It freaked him out. . . . As school went on, he got white best friends, black friends, Spanish friends. They generally like each other." Youth involved in extracurricular activities were especially likely to make friendships that crossed racial and ethnic boundaries, but even youth who were less involved noted that the school was known in the area for its diverse student population. Indeed, simply because of the small school size, it would have been impossible for students to go through four years of high school without having multiple interactions with peers of different races, nationalities, ethnicities, and social class backgrounds.

Allen Creek High School enrolled about eight hundred students, and approximately one-half of them participated in the federal free/reduced-cost lunch program. The school served a large low-income population, and many students or their parents were unauthorized immigrants. Like other schools in low-income neighborhoods, Allen Creek High School struggled on some measures of school performance. In 2010, the school's four-year graduation rate was about 75 percent, and dropout rates were highest among Latinos. Graduation rates were improving, however; between 2005 and 2010, the four-year graduation rate increased by eight percentage points, and the five-year graduation rate increased by ten percentage points.

Educational disparities were also reflected in academic achievement. In the 2008–9 school year, white students ranked highest on both end-of-grade and end-of-course exams, followed by Hispanic students and then black students. This pattern remained in the 2009–10 school year for the end-of-grade tests, but African American students scored one percentage point higher than Hispanic students on the end-of-course tests. On average, however, Latino and black students continued to lag well behind white students, reflecting a pattern evident in secondary schools throughout the country, in spite of similar levels of ambition across major demographic groups (Kao and Thompson 2003; Kao, Vaquera, and Goyette 2013). As the population of Latino students was projected to rise dramatically over the next decade, the school board became increasingly concerned about this academic gap.

To improve retention and engagement among Latino students, Allen Creek High School partnered with a nearby university to implement a Latino Achievement Club (LAC). The club offered SAT preparation, college application support, and an early, noncredit college course focusing on issues related to immigration and Latinos in the United States. During the time of the study, LAC offered approximately sixty-five high school students (between twenty and twenty-five per grade) three years of close mentorship from college undergraduates and guidance from college professors involved with the program. The program promoted a climate of academic achievement and specifically linked this achievement to Latino identity.

Administrators also implemented other programs to lower dropout rates, including a support group for teenage mothers and expectant mothers (implemented in 2010), a support group for students experiencing emotional problems and troubled home lives (implemented in 2010), and an AVID program for students in need of additional academic support (implemented in 2006). Finally, the school board made high-profile adjustments to its staff. In 2006, the school hired a Latino vice principal and a Latina parental outreach coordinator to facilitate communication with Spanish-speaking parents and students. The vice principal explained that his ethnicity was a primary factor in his recruitment: "There's never been a Hispanic administrator in Allen County, so I got the honor of being the first one. I think that they saw that the trend was that this school was going to be more and more Hispanic based on the elementary and middle schools that feed us, some of which are almost ninety percent Hispanic at this point. I think that they were looking for someone who would be effective with that population."

Though the school's Latino population was projected to rise annually, the demographic breakdown of students split fairly evenly along racial and ethnic lines during the time of the study. Between 2007 and 2011, roughly 41 percent of the students were Latino, 34 percent were white, and 25 percent were black. Though Allen Creek High School was a minority-majority school, the staff did not mirror this racial and ethnic composition. Of the fifty-seven teachers, seven were African American and only one was Latino.

Though interethnic and interracial relationships within the school were generally harmonious, school structures nonetheless distanced groups from one another. Students who were active in extracurricular activities or in advanced placement classes were often most able to bridge the racial and ethnic divide between cliques. Luz, for example, enrolled in all advanced placement (AP) classes and was involved in several student clubs. She complained that she sometimes got chastised for acting snobby due to her association with white students. She explained,

> People consider me a very Americanized Hispano, which I don't like. I don't consider myself a very Americanized Hispano. I mean, I hold on to my culture and my language, but just because I took AP classes, I had a lot of friends who were gringos. And sometimes I would sit with my friends, and my Hispanic friends would say things about how I thought I was American. But I just didn't see why I couldn't talk to them.

Academic tracking led to segregation among students and, of course, as illustrated in other studies, offered students separate and unequal schooling experiences (Ochoa 2013; Tyson 2011). Though most classes enrolled a racial and ethnic mix of students, white students were overrepresented in both AP classes and agriculture classes. While Latino and black students were not absent from advanced classes, they also recognized that they stood out. As one student, Vicente, noted, he initiated a relationship with his white girlfriend after spending time with her in class. He explained, "That's how you can tell I'm a little more assimilated. It's just the courses I take. I mean, if I was . . . taking basic courses, I'd probably be a little more with the Latinos. But I want to be successful in life, so I want to take these courses." Though most students of color in AP classes did not discuss acute feelings of isolation in these settings, several Latinos, like Vicente, mentioned being friends with "Americans" as a result of their enrollment in advanced classes, and some, like Luz, discussed feeling judged for these friendships.

Similarly, white students with Latina friends also faced occasional judgment from their white peers. For example, Erika, a US-born citizen of Guatemalan parents, recounted an incident when a white classmate asked Erika's white boyfriend, Andy, why he was dating a "Mexican girl." Andy brushed off the comment, but the sting of the remark stayed with Erika. The classmate was a good friend of her boyfriend, so Erika was shocked by the question. She explained, "I'm Guatemalan. So that hit me hard, and I was like, maybe I shouldn't be in this relationship." Because of stereotypes surrounding the Latino population in town, Erika felt misunderstood in spite of her citizenship status. She was not alone. Regardless of being born in the United States, many Latino youths who were US citizens had to navigate around the expectations of illegality (and Mexican nationality).

Remarks like the comment directed at Erika's white boyfriend reflected the social distance among white, black, and Latino students, even as the commonplace nature of interracial and interethnic couples suggested simultaneous integration. Carlos, a US-born child of Mexican immigrants, explained how he developed interracial and interethnic friendships while simultaneously articulating how his relationships with his Latino peers were different from his other friendships:

> We're all together, like difference races. I mean, like yeah, we have groups of people that stay with groups of people, but if we go to big events with the school, like an assembly, you'll see kids with everybody, like not just blacks with blacks or Hispanics with Hispanics—just like random. . . . I have a good variety of friends. [My elementary school] is primarily white. . . . So that's where my friends came from, most of them. . . . It's not like I was just gonna leave the friends that I grew up with to go with some kids that were just my color and that was the only reason that I was gonna be their friends . . . but now through soccer, most of my friends are Hispanic.

Carlos connected with his Latino friends in high school through soccer but also through shared life experiences. He continued, "Most of my closer friends are Hispanic I guess, and I think we kind of motivated each other to do well in school, you know, to not live the life our parents are living so we won't have to do what they did." Like Carlos, most students had friendships with students outside their race or ethnicity but nonetheless bonded with students who shared similar life experiences. Due to cultural distinctions and structural inequalities associated with race, ethnicity, and immigration history, these shared similarities tended to break along ethnic and racial lines.

Other students also discussed racial and ethnic cliques, and they could all identify geographic spaces occupied by particular ethnic and racial groups within their school. Gisella, an eighteen-year-old Mexican American student, provided a social cartography of the lunchroom: "We always used to make fun, like, as soon as you walked into the cafeteria, the furthest table was the footballers or the black table. The two middle ones were the more high social class kind of thing, and the Hispanics always hung at the round tables. So as soon as you walked in, you could tell how you divided yourself. Yeah, you could definitely tell." While most students saw segregation in the cafeteria as the most conspicuous, the hallways also had defined territories for jocks, white agriculture kids, black footballers, newcomer Latinos, and more acculturated 1.5- and second-generation Latinos. In this way, Allen Creek was typical of other American high schools with racial cliques in their cafeterias and hallways (Bettie 2003; Ochoa 2013; Tatum 1997).

Small-School Support

Mornings at Allen Creek High School would look familiar to anyone who has ever seen US high schools portrayed in movies or on TV. Diverse groups of students congregate in the entryway and in front of the main doors every day to socialize before the school bell rang. As I entered the school in the morning to sign in at the front office, and as I left in the afternoon, I dodged students flirting and running in the halls, navigated around cliques congregated in large clusters, and occasionally averted my eyes from the multiple conspicuous couples with their arms and legs entangled and draped intimately around each other.

Though most students socialized with each other in the hallways, there were always a few who spilled over into classrooms and offices, chatting with teachers and guidance counselors. Vanesa Tevez, the bilingual parent-outreach coordinator, had a warm and inviting personality, and students were drawn to her. She felt that her presence in the school provided Latino students an outlet that they lacked prior to her arrival:

> The Hispanic kids always come to talk to me about their problems. There's so much drama, so much "he said, she said." And sometimes I see that they have problems with some of their teachers, and the teachers will really go the extra mile to help out the white kids, but they won't always do that with the Hispanic kids, so I'm glad that I'm there at least so that I can be that support for them. And I can hear what's going on in the school because then at least I can stand up for them. I won't be quiet anymore. I speak up when something happens, and I don't think it's right. At least they have me.

She was very involved in students' lives and took her role as an advocate seriously. Though she spoke highly of the majority of the faculty members, she felt that a few teachers and staffers treated Latino and white students differently, and she saw herself as a support to help buffer some of the institutional inequalities at the school. When describing unequal student experiences, she focused exclusively on the white/Latino divide, identifying white students as the dominant group within the school. When I asked her about support systems for black students, she commented that they had a lot of support through football, failing to note that this support would be available only to black male students who played football. Tevez saw herself as an ally for the Latino youth within the school, and she did not apologize for this position. As one of only three Latino staff in the school, and the only one that was not in control of either grades or disciplinary issues, she felt that she offered Latino students a sanctuary that was absent in the school before she was hired.

Like Ms. Tevez, many students agreed that particular teachers or coaches could be discriminatory toward Latino students. Sofia, a US citizen born to Bolivian and Peruvian immigrant parents, noted that the recently arrived students faced more discrimination at school. She explained, "We have the ESL program at our school, and I feel like the teachers don't think that those kids are as smart, so the teachers treat them like they're dumb or they don't have that potential." Though Sofia perceived most of the discrimination against Latinos as being directed toward more recent arrivals, other Latino students discussed more widespread discrimination at school. Eduardo, an unauthorized Mexican immigrant and honors student at Allen Creek High School, noted that teachers treated him and many of his friends differently: "[Discrimination is] still there, but it's starting to become more integrated. Especially because they're starting to look at people individually, not as a whole group. 'Cause like at school when they see me, like the teachers and coaches, they know that we're good kids. Then they see the kids with the saggy pants and stuff, and they're more strict toward them. . . . So I mean they see that not all Hispanics are the same."

In noting his own favorable treatment, Eduardo alluded to general discrimination against Latinos within the community and in the school. In spite of a general lack of gang violence in the town and school, some teachers and staff at the school viewed Latino boys as potential problems. In 2009, for example, a temporary replacement school resource officer (SRO) arrested several Latino boys suspected of gang involvement. The boys were lined up and handcuffed on school grounds and arrested for minor offenses before the school's administration was consulted. The arrest of the boys mirrored descriptions of Latino and black boys in urban areas being regarded with suspicion by their teachers and treated like criminals by school security, police, and passersby (N. Lopez 2002, 2003; Rios 2011; R. Smith 2006; Telles and Ortiz 2008; Valenzuela 1999; Waters 1996). Unlike in the urban high schools depicted in previous research, however, the arrest in Allen Creek High School was an isolated incident that invoked a harsh response from a multitude of teachers, parents, and coaches.

After staff, parents, and concerned community members spoke out against the incident, the SRO was replaced with a permanent officer who had undergone more extensive training for the position. No similar incidents occurred subsequently, at least during the time of this study. Nonetheless, students remained aware of stereotypes facing Latino boys. Negative stereotypes about Latinos seemed to affect male students more than female students. Indeed, several teachers and students identified a group of newly arrived Latino boys who sometimes fought with a black clique in the school. The conflict between these two small groups stood apart from the normally tranquil relations within the school. Moreover, among immigrants who arrived at later ages, male students seemed to face more academic struggles than their female peers.

Ben Ryan, who taught Limited English Proficiency (LEP) classes, noted that a few girls who had been in the LEP program dropped out due to pregnancy or to care for their younger siblings, but he generally found that his female students moved through the program more quickly than their male counterparts. He described this discrepancy between boys and girls:

> More LEP students on our list are boys, and I think it's because mothers, if
> Dad isn't around, have more control over their daughters than their sons. I
> have an eighteen-year-old sophomore who's been here for seven years who's
> still LEP, and I think Mom isn't able to push him in school the way Dad might
> have been. Another kid has been in this country seven or eight years, and he's
> been LEP the whole time. He does the bare minimum. His older sister gradu-
> ated with honors and went on to college. Their father was deported a few years
> ago, and Manuel was the oldest boy, so he feels like he's on his own.

Mr. Ryan pointed to gender as a clear indicator of academic success and complained that boys and young men were quick to lose interest in school, particularly if their fathers were absent due to deportation or other factors. His emphasis on gender echoes previous research into gendered disparities in urban schools. For example, Robert Smith (2006) argues that adolescent second-generation men can adopt a hypermasculine identity as a means of asserting dominance over a societal structure that has in many ways disenfranchised and excluded men of color from achieving societal respect through upward career mobility. In Allen Creek, recent immigrants who lacked immigration authorization and struggled with English had few opportunities for upward mobility through work. Moreover, as both Eduardo and Sofia noted, they were devalued in school because teachers tended to treat new immigrants and the "kids with the saggy pants" differently than students who appeared more motivated. Teachers were more encouraging of female students, whom they perceived to be more engaged and respectful.

Ryan attributed girls' motivation to mothers keeping tighter control over their daughters than sons. Similar scholarly analyses of "lockdown" or "shut-in" girls described in research about Latino youth from immigrant families have likewise pointed to academic benefits of strict parenting for girls (R. Smith 2002, 2006; Suárez-Orozco and Suárez-Orozco 2001). Although research acknowledges familial tension that arises as a result of strict rules, studies have more often found positive outcomes of protective parenting (Feliciano 2012; Feliciano and Rumbaut 2005; R. Smith 2002, 2006; Suárez-Orozco and Suárez-Orozco 2001). Indeed, daughters who are inside the home helping with household chores may be less likely to get into trouble and have more time to focus on their schoolwork. Nonetheless, many girls in Allen Creek noted that their strict parents were holding them back academically. Absent the pressures of urban gangs and violence, gendered expectations and resultant familial rules and restrictions operated very differently in the small community of Allen Creek.

Female students complained about their parents restricting their after-school activities, even when they were school sanctioned. Cristina, an eighteen-year-old second-generation Mexican American, discussed the fights that she had with her mother about playing soccer. She explained, "My mom has the mind-set of, you're a girl, you're staying home, and you're cooking, cleaning, and doing what you're supposed to be doing. And if I did something wrong, she would always threaten me, 'You're not going to play anymore!' So she would really find anything to tell me I couldn't play anymore, but I kept playing. And I would cry because I would get so mad." Of course, US American parents can also have different expectations and rules for their sons and daughters, but only the Latina children of immigrants talked about regular after-school activities causing familial tension, even when these activities would help prepare students for work or college.

Some students fought with their parents, not only about participating in extracurricular activities but also about remaining enrolled in school when they were old enough to contribute in meaningful ways to household expenses or labor. Knowing that his students faced substantial parental pressures to work or help out at home, Ryan struggled to convince some of his LEP students that staying in school was worthwhile. He found this battle particularly hard for his unauthorized immigrant students as they struggled to envision potential pathways toward college or upwardly mobile work because of their unauthorized immigration status. At times he even struggled to convince himself that their time was better spent in school than in activities that would more immediately help their family members:

Some of the kids who are undocumented ask me, "Why should I come to school if I can't go to college?" And I just tell them that this place is better than the alternative, and they're getting something here that no one can take away from them. . . . We have too many students, and too many that don't do what's required of them, and so they get way behind and just drop out, maybe to work, maybe to take care of family members, or because they're pregnant or to go back to their home countries. And that's fine, but some of them just aren't willing to do the work. They see [their senior] project or a class project as not necessary. "Why should I put in all this time to learn all this stuff about US history when I'm undocumented and I won't be able to go to college anyway?"

Mr. Ryan found it difficult to come up with compelling reasons for his students to choose school over family needs or other pressing life circumstances. In highlighting the US history course, he also noted that some LEP students felt excluded not only from the national community but also from the school curriculum. Knowing that he could not promise them a pathway to legal residence or college after high school, Ryan struggled to motivate his LEP students, particularly boys, who felt especially pressured to work. Many felt very little incentive to succeed in school if they could not parlay their success in school into rewards later in life. As the only full-time faculty member teaching newcomers, he struggled to address the needs of this particularly vulnerable group of students and wished that he had a stronger support system.

Presenting a more optimistic view, Vice Principal García explained how he used his own cultural capital to connect with Latino students, including Latino males whom other teachers may have overlooked as disinterested students or gang members. He frequently spoke to the Latino boys about his brothers being involved in gangs in Florida. He did not consider gangs to be a serious issue in Allen Creek, but he used his personal experiences to bond with teenagers whom he thought might become involved in risky behaviors.

I asked Vice Principal García whether he approached all students in the same manner or whether he varied his approach based on gender or race or ethnicity. He responded, "Different. . . . With the Hispanics, I have that common thing. And they see me and they know that I'm successful, so they know that they can do it too. . . . I joke with kids and I say I'm your daddy, or you're my school daughter or school son, so I've been able to connect with them. . . . Once they realize someone cares about them, they start cooperating."

García believed that his role as the assistant principal aligned naturally with the role of a Latino father figure. Relying on cultural connections, and at times cultural stereotypes, he explained:

Hispanic fathers are strict, but they're also very loving. So when you deal with these Spanish girls, you have to be strict with them, but you also have to show them that you care about them. . . . A Hispanic father, the ones that are older generations, it's very difficult to show emotion. The way that you do it is by providing for your family. . . . So, here at the school, you just have to show that I do care about you. It might be something as simple as having snacks on my desk. There's always food on my desk. There was more food here this morning, but a couple of pregnant girls came through and ate all the crackers. So that's just an example. Show them that you'll provide for them, that you care about them.

García stressed his cultural similarities to Latino students, and he used his connection to the students to motivate them. He told me that he connected with all students, but he spoke at length about how he reached out to Latino students. Moreover, his use of familial language to describe his relationships was reserved for Latino students.

Mr. García was not the only interviewee to describe student-teacher relationships in familial terms. The use of familial language crossed racial and ethnic lines, but white and Latino students tended to use familial language more readily than their black peers when discussing relationships with the predominantly white faculty. Because many of the Latino parents in Allen Creek were lower-income immigrants without formal educations beyond primary or early secondary school, Latino students relied heavily on teachers and coaches for assistance with schoolwork, college applications, and even personal problems. Faculty and staff felt an obligation to help guide and nurture students whose parents lacked the cultural capital to navigate the educational process. These relationships extended beyond classrooms and sports fields to include visits to college and teachers' homes. Because Latino immigrant parents often worked irregular hours or feared driving without a license, teachers found themselves driving Latino students to school-related events more frequently than white or black students. Moreover, because many of these parents did not celebrate US Thanksgiving, teachers sometimes invited the Latino students to join their families for the holiday meal. I also heard from interviewees that in at least three cases, teachers opened their homes to Latino students whose parents had been deported or who left home because of familial conflicts.

Teachers and college advisers were not always able to articulate how these close relationships developed. For example, Ms. Connor, the college adviser, commented that she worked with roughly equal numbers of black, white, and

Latino students. Yet she found herself developing especially close relationships with Latino students:

> I have to say the biggest highlight of my job thus far is working with a particular student who, when I met him at open house and said, "I'm here to talk about college," he said, "Oh I'm not going to college." Didn't even want to talk to me, and I [said], "Well, before you leave, you have to give me three reasons why." And he was like, "Okay." So he kept walking by, and I [asked], "Do you have those reasons? Do you have those reasons?" and finally he [answered], "I'm undocumented, I'm broke, and I'm going to work in the chicken plant. Those are my three reasons." And I [said], "Okay, see you on Monday." So I've gone to his soccer games and I've seen him since, and I've been reaching out to him, and the Tuesday before Thanksgiving break he came and poked his head sheepishly around the corner and said, "Can I talk to you about college?" And I [responded], "YES!" All of this talking and maybe berating since August has finally come to fruition!

Teachers and mentors in the school often went out of their way to reach out to Latino students because they were aware of the obstacles these students faced. Ms. Connor maintained a steady connection to this student precisely because she knew that his parents could not advise him about his options for college. Through her persistence, the student eventually felt comfortable enough to ask her about his options for college.

Even when teachers offered opportunities to all students, Latino and white students were often more likely than black students to participate. When Ms. Connor organized a college-visit with twenty students, she was surprised to see that the white and Latino students self-segregated on the bus and the tour. She made no mention of the black students in her description. When I asked her if the trip included only white and Latino students, she responded, "Yeah, actually. I don't know how that happened, except I had a sign-up sheet and had made a bunch of announcements and it was first come, first served. And I think they just came—like, they got their groups of friends and signed up and then when there were twenty signatures, it was done. It was full."

Though most of the teachers supported and genuinely cared about all of their students, they also did not necessarily feel the same obligation to reach out to black students in the same way that they reached out the Latino students. One possible explanation for this discrepancy was the teacher training, which focused on addressing different national and linguistic backgrounds. Though the teachers met several times throughout the academic year to discuss racial and ethnic achievement gaps in testing scores, the school addressed strategies to improve learning outcomes for children of immigrants more directly than it addressed strategies to better support African American students. None of the interviewed teachers could recall any teacher training specifically addressing strategies to improve engagement for black students.

One white teacher, Laura Macy, was frustrated with the meetings about test scores. She explained that she recognized all of her students as individuals and worked to address their individual learning styles. She felt that the meetings implied that teachers were "almost racist" in their teaching styles without offering any effective strategies to bolster the academic achievement of black and Latino students. She then recalled one formal training session that she found beneficial but insufficient: "We have had some positive training in the school in regards to teaching ESL students that has addressed cultural sensitivity with Latino students in terms of seeing their cultural difference as a resource as opposed to a negative, but probably not enough [training]. I've still heard about teachers saying things to their students like, 'What does it matter? You're going to be working in the chicken plant like your father anyway?' But I heard that from a student, so take that with a grain of salt."

Ms. Macy's comments suggest that issues between teachers and Latino students persisted in spite of the training, but other teachers spoke more directly about the strategies that they used to better engage Latino students as a result of the training. One African American teacher recalled a training session in which teachers were encouraged to ask students about their cultural traditions, particularly when discussing holidays or historical events in class. Thus, teachers asked Latino students how particular holidays were celebrated in their countries of origin and put up posters of Latino authors in English classrooms. Because of their shared national origins, the teachers did not see the need to implement these types of inclusive practices in relation to black students. Instead, they tended to view black and white students through a color-blind lens and spoke of teaching individual students instead of students of particular races.

Perhaps as a result of training, and perhaps because of different comfort levels, close mentorships tended to form more easily between the majority-white teaching staff and Latino and white students. With Latino students, teachers purposefully reached out in ways that went beyond their job descriptions. With white students, relationships formed naturally as many teachers shared a church or had long-standing family friendships with their students' families. One white student, Evan, commented that the agriculture teacher would sometimes come over on weekends to help his family repair their tractor. Michelle, another white student whose parents had attended Allen Creek High School with some of her teachers, commented, "Well, one of the teachers, we went to church together, and then I had her AP class and I just felt like I could go to her for anything. And I felt that way with all of my teachers. I kind of viewed them as an extension of my family." Because churches and community spaces in Allen Creek were often segregated by race, the majority-white teachers did not develop relationships with black students in the community as readily as they did with the white students. In contrast, the cultural difference between white teachers and Latino students prompted teachers to form intentional relationships with their Latino students.

Ethnic Identity Formation through Extracurricular Engagement

The school climate of Allen Creek High School, though certainly not immune to issues of racial and ethnic discord or distance, offered Latino youth opportunities to find spaces of inclusion and belonging. Friendship ties and formal clubs and organizations facilitated opportunities for Latino students to simultaneously embrace their ethnic identities and enhance their attachment to the community. Students frequently noted positive school-based interactions, which made them aware, sometimes for the first time, of their ethnicities. For example, Jack, a US-born son of a Colombian immigrant mother and white US American father, described how going to Allen Creek High School opened his eyes to his heritage. Jack did not feel connected to his Latino heritage in primary school. Though his mother was a Colombian woman who had worked in the local chicken plant, Jack had never considered himself Hispanic prior to enrolling in high school. His father was a white army officer, and Jack had moved from state to state for much of his childhood. He told me that attending Allen Creek High allowed him to connect to his ethnic heritage in a way that he never had before:

> Coming to Allen Creek High was a big transition for me because I had been to schools that had been over ninety-five percent black or over ninety-five percent white, so coming to a school that had a large Hispanic population was different. In the white school I was in, I was just white. . . . Then going to a black school and being someone of mixed race, that was a benefit because I wasn't white. It was in southern Georgia, and it was a very dangerous school. Twenty-seven hundred students, ninety percent black, and that year they had just mixed up [the school] zones, so they mixed gangs. . . . Actually, that's the

first experience in my life that I had heard that I wasn't white. Some kids came up to me in the hall and said, "You're not full white, are you?" . . . And I said, "No, I'm Colombian." And he could tell that just from looking at me, and that made my life a lot easier.

Jack's ethnic identity became even more pronounced after he enrolled in Allen Creek High School. He explained that his identity began to change after he started playing soccer with his mostly Latino teammates:

> Getting to Allen Creek High, it affected me through the soccer team, mostly because the soccer team was so Hispanic and they were so proud of it that I couldn't hide from it. . . . They'd be like, "You know, you're Colombian. Don't act any other way." And I never thought I was, but they wanted to make sure. So my experience at Allen Creek High definitely highlighted the fact that I am biracial. . . . It made me realize that I had to make a point of not hiding it. And in turn, they made going to the family outings and the pig roasts and the non-stop dance dance revolutions, they made that a lot more enjoyable, because I saw that they were a tradition. And the way that they spoke Spanish even, it made me take a little more pride in the uniqueness of the Colombian culture.

Jack learned to celebrate his Latino heritage as something that made him feel connected to a larger ethnic community. Unlike his school in Georgia, where he considered his identity in terms of the benefits of being regarded as "not full white," in Allen Creek, Jack's Colombian heritage did not offer him protection from gangs, nor was it symbolic of an oppositional identity against whites or mainstream institutions. In contrast to previous research that has shown isolation and oppositional ethnic identities emerging in response to discrimination and exclusionary school policies (Ochoa 2013; Portes and Rumbaut 2001; Valenzuela 1999), Jack's social interactions with his teammates taught him to be proud of his history and ethnicity even as he remained connected to his school and community.

The students on the soccer team came from various national backgrounds, but they united as a team of Latinos. In this small school, ethnic factions did not emerge among Latinos, who were largely viewed as a uniform group by their black and white peers and teachers. Jack learned the words to Spanish-language songs on the team bus, and he began to examine his ethnic heritage as a part of his history and identity. There were a few white students on the team, and they too had fun picking up Spanish words and learning Spanish songs. They also felt protective when other teams, or their fans, made racist comments, calling their Latino classmates "wetbacks." On the team, ethnic and cultural pride was a unifying force. Similar cultural bonding occurred on the girls' soccer team where Guatemalan and Honduran players would jokingly refer to themselves as "honorary Mexicans," and a few of the girls would display a Mexican hand salute during the US national anthem.

Youth, teachers, and community members had to fight against a resistant administration and community to create structures of support in school. Prior to administrative shifts, "meso level" (Ochoa 2013, 13–15) structures of exclusion were normative, and hostility to programs of support was openly articulated. In spite of clear benefits of the soccer teams, students who graduated in the late 1990s and early 2000s recalled outright discrimination as they battled to create a school soccer team. One white Allen Creek graduate, Eamon, recounted a conversation he had with the principal when he was a senior in high school in 2000. In response to Eamon's plea to create a soccer team, the principal told him that he would not support the team because "soccer [was] a Mexican sport." Even after the school implemented the soccer program in 2003, the Latino soccer coach said that the school continued to privilege the football team and that occasional ethnic discrimination was directed at the majority-Latino soccer team by the school's groundskeeper or other coaches. The coach was extremely frustrated when, in 2010, the school added a new "Allen Creek Football" sign to the scoreboard, which was shared by both soccer and football. He saw this as an intentional slight against his teams, which largely comprised Latino students.

In addition to soccer teams, formal school organizations and clubs provided supportive environments for Latino students to find, and create, a sense of belonging. Heritage-based clubs allowed students to celebrate their cultural backgrounds among peers, discuss political issues facing Latinos, and utilize their bicultural and bilingual skills. Moreover, like school clubs depicted in previous studies (Gibson et al. 2004; Ochoa 2013), these clubs helped students resist negative stereotypes and form critical and politically engaged mind-sets. By offering tools of empowerment, supportive school clubs encouraged unauthorized youth, to fight back against meso-level structures of exclusion both within the school and the state. The LAC, in particular, provided Latino students with a supportive community of academically and civically engaged coethnic peers.

The club offered a nurturing environment where students discussed issues related to their ethnicity and migration history in an academic setting and received support with the college application process. Moreover, LAC partnered with college professors to offer students college-level coursework focused on issues related to Latinos and immigration. Finally, LAC connected students to private scholarship funds (available to undocumented immigrant students as well as citizens) for higher education. As Vicente, a US-born son of Salvadoran immigrants, explained:

> [LAC is a] program that allows Latinos to take college courses early to allow you to go to college. So they give us readings for us to analyze. And I think it initiates a spark for us to want to go a little further. And it opens more doors; like they show you how to apply to college and things that Latinos really don't know how to do. They give you all mentors from the university . . . and I would send [my essays] to [my mentor] on Monday, and probably two or three hours later he'd have it back to me. They show you around, introduce you to professors, and they try to, like, spark it up and keep you interested.

Vicente was already deeply invested in school when he joined LAC, but LAC helped him envision a path to college by giving him the tools to apply and feel confident that he could succeed in that setting.

Like Vicente, other students saw LAC as a crucial tool in propelling them toward higher education and furthermore pointed out how the club helped the Latino community. In 2011, the LAC students elected Mani, an eighteen-year-old Mexican American, and one of the students who sang the parody of "God Bless the U.S.A," to give a speech at the club's graduation ceremony. He told the audience, "We are an inspiration to the millions of Latinos that don't have a chance to get higher education. Being Latino does not equate to being a day laborer, working in a chicken plant, or in landscaping. Being Latino means having the initiative to go further. We are the Latino Achievement Club, and we are a success." Taking pride in his ethnic heritage while noting the racialized socioeconomic inequalities of his surrounding community, Mani celebrated LAC and the opportunities it provided. Mani's words echoed findings of previous research that has shown that educational experiences help shape ethnic identities (Feliciano 2009). Clearly, students in LAC linked their heritage cultures to their academic achievement and took pride in both.

During the graduation ceremony, students repeatedly referred to LAC as a "familia." Offering a wholehearted endorsement of the program, one parent stated, "If it weren't for LAC, I think I would have lost my daughter because of all the high school drama, but LAC gave her a place to belong." LAC supported its members to grow during high school, both academically and personally. LAC also worked with families to help them understand the benefits of the club. Echoing the comments of other young female students, Luz, a US-born child of Salvadoran parents, explained that she struggled to convince her parents that she was staying after school for legitimate reasons:

> I think my mom was always supportive because she thought that it was school related, but my father wasn't. Well, I shouldn't say that. My mom had to be convinced. I think that LAC helped instill that in her and explain that to her. My mom would have to explain to my dad that I was staying after school for academic reasons and not to be with my boyfriend, and it wasn't easy because none of my siblings had ever stayed. I should say that my dad wasn't just worried for no reason. He was really hard on us, and both of my sisters semi ran away with their boyfriends, but then they came back home.

Luz's comment again speaks to the distinct experiences that students had depending on gender. Her experiences struggling against gendered expectations echoed the experiences of adolescent girls described in previous research who commented that living under strict household rules felt "oppressive" (Suárez-Orozco and Suárez-Orozco 2001, 80) or as if they were living under "lock down" conditions (R. Smith 2006, 171). Luz knew that the dangers of Allen Creek were a far cry from the gangs, drugs, and violence of south-central Los Angeles, where she had lived prior to moving to North Carolina. In a small town like Allen Creek, staying at home meant that girls had fewer opportunities to develop leadership skills or engage in extracurricular activities that would augment their human capital. LAC leadership worked with key community members to reach out to parents in Spanish and explain the benefits of the program so that parents would allow eager students to participate, regardless of gender.

For many, LAC was a source of motivation and a reason to engage in school. It gave students hope that they could reach for college in spite of the substantial obstacles in their way. Mariano, an unauthorized immigrant from Guatemala, explained that he struggled to stay motivated in school until LAC invited him to apply:

> During my freshman year, I was really kind of lost because I wasn't sure that I was going to go to college because of that uncertainty [with my immigration status]. But then when I was a sophomore, I got invited to LAC. And we have great mentors, and they told us that if we did good in school that they would help us do well in college. That's when I really became motivated to do better in school, and that's when I realized that I might be able to go to college. Because my parents have always been truthful with me, and they told me, "We do want to send you to college, but we don't have the money to do it, so just

so you know for the future, we won't have the money to help you pay for college. So you'll have to help yourself on that end." So thanks to LAC, they really motivated me to do better in school, just knowing that there's an opportunity for me.

Offering undocumented students hope that they could access college, in spite of the out-of-state tuition and capricious community college admittance policies in the state, helped create a culture of achievement among the Latino students in the school.

LAC was an amazing resource for the students who were accepted into the program, but enrollment was limited to about twenty-five students per grade. For Latino students who were not in the program, the school had other programs that allowed them to use their bicultural and bilingual skills. The AIM club also celebrated Latino students' heritage and contributions to the community. The ESL teacher at Allen Creek High School started a chapter of the AIM club in 2002 with the mission of helping students advance academically and build self-esteem. The AIM club was open to all students, but one of the primary activities of the club was to volunteer as tutors and translators at an elementary school in Allen Creek. Only Spanish-speaking students were able to participate in this activity, and as a result the club remained almost exclusively made up of Latino students. By translating for parent-teacher conferences, AIM club members gained valuable professional experience and made social connections that helped them in the job market. One AIM club member was offered a job assisting with Spanish classes at the elementary school. When I asked him how he got the offer, he replied, "Well, the principal really likes me because I went there and my little sister went there too, so sometimes I would go and drop her off or pick her up. And then I volunteer there with the AIM club, translating for parent-teacher conferences, and I'm really good at that, so she likes me a lot."

Though Ovidio chose to go to college instead of accepting the position, he was gratified to receive praise and encouragement from a well-respected person in the community. And through his volunteer work, he learned about working in a school. He planned on pursuing a career in secondary science education and believed that his experience with the AIM club had influenced this professional goal. By connecting students with community members and institutions, the AIM club acted as a mechanism to integrate students into the community. Moreover, both AIM and LAC encouraged students to engage their bicultural capital in ways that deepened their connections to their school and community. Previous research has shown that youth benefit from drawing on bicultural capital and tight-knit coethnic community resources (Feliciano 2001; Portes and Rumbaut 2001). The resources at Allen Creek High School demonstrate that even in the absence of a coethnic community with a well-developed academic support network, school-based support structures can be extremely effective in encouraging academic engagement and ethnic identities of achievement.

Older 1.5- and second-generation immigrants in Allen Creek did not have access to clubs like these when they were in high school, and they noted how different the school environment was. Support structures for Latino students gradually increased as teachers and administrators adapted to the new and growing student population. Several students who attended the school before LAC started, and before the student population was majority Latino, recalled feeling lost and isolated. Julio, a US-born citizen of Mexican parents, who graduated from Allen Creek High School in 2005, struggled in school without an extensive network of support. He explained, "Your parents start talking to you about dropping out—you know, really close to graduation day, a semester left, half a semester. And it's like, why are you going to bother to graduate? Why don't you go out and work? Why not start right now? And it is really frustrating because I'm pretty sure some of my friends thought the same way I did, like, 'Why am I wasting my time? If I can start working now and start saving money, why am I wasting my time?'" Julio stayed in school through graduation, but many of his friends left early. He told me that his younger siblings had access to many more support clubs than he did when he was in high school, and he sometimes wondered whether his experience would have been different had those resources been available to him.

Though the clubs were generally accepted by the school community, other programs caused some tension. For example, when the school screened *Papers*, a documentary about undocumented students, in 2011, some students and teachers complained that they discussed issues facing only Hispanics, to the neglect of other student issues. Even some Latino students were unhappy about the screening. As one student said, "I already live this every day. Why do I want to watch it?"

College preparation programs designed to involve Latino parents were also met with some resistance by administrators. Ms. Connor, a guidance counselor, described the pushback she received when she brought a college access program targeting Latinos to campus:

> Things were kind of a little testy last year [in 2010] when a program called
> JUNTOS came, and they were doing information sessions about barriers to

college. And all throughout the spring semester they talked about a different aspect of the college application program, and oftentimes meetings were conducted in Spanish. And I know that our principal, who is black, was very open with me about not targeting just one population. If you have organized nights, they have to be open to all students. There was some tension around that. And luckily at Allen Creek High School we have these amazing headsets that people can wear, and then a translator can translate and they'll hear it in their headsets—the same presentation.

Fortunately for the guidance counselor, Allen Creek High School had acquired translation technology that not only translated English to Spanish but also translated Spanish to English. However, the program nonetheless incited tension between the guidance counselor and the principal, as the program focused on outreach to Latino parents. The principal noted that efforts directed at the Latino population were not necessarily matched by efforts to engage the black population, and she wanted to ensure that programs addressing college readiness were available to all students.

During my research, I often asked students and teachers whether there were clubs for African American students, such as a Black Student Union. Some commented that Upward Bound, a federally funded educational program designed to help lower-income students attend college, was primarily utilized by African American students. Others said that the AVID program included African American students. Finally, several teachers and students mentioned sports, particularly football, as the main source of support for black students at Allen Creek High School. Though most were surprised by my questions, some black students noted the disparity, and one student, Ashlyn, explained how she made sense of it:

> I've thought about that like, how come they do have the Latino Achievement Club because they help them, and they can [get] full rides to college, and I always wondered how come they don't do that for black people because we're minorities too, you know? . . . We do need help. . . . I think that they should do it for more than one race, [but] Latinos are having it harder than black people right now or any other culture because if they're undocumented, they're trying to say that they can't get into college.

Ashlyn was aware that Latino students were getting support that was not available to her, and though she was frustrated by the disparity in resources, she ultimately decided that the club served the needs of undocumented students who had fewer resources than she. The LAC, however, included citizen, documented, and undocumented Latino students. Nonetheless, by emphasizing her classmates' struggles with immigration status rather than ethnicity, Ashlyn justified the need for the club.

Unlike Ashlyn, most people did not see a particular need for clubs that specifically targeted African American students or celebrated African American identity. This opinion was expressed not only by whites and Latinos but also by African Americans. For example, Braden, a black senior commented, "I kind of feel like . . . I don't want to say I'm completely against having clubs for certain groups of people, but I just feel like, instead of separating people by the color of their skin or their race, I just think that if someone wants to be in a certain club that they should be able to be. I mean, you can all relate and have equal opportunity."

Similarly, an African American teacher commented, "I think that [the] AIM club is good because it gives the Latinos a chance to get their feet wet and learn that they can participate in the community first within their own space and then with everybody, so I think that's good, but I think that clubs should be open to all students. I don't like the separation." Having grown up in the segregated South and in Allen Creek specifically, Ms. Bartlet was uncomfortable with the idea of separation by race. She did not see the Latino clubs as separating the students by race but instead distinguished the Latino students as newcomers. Although many of the Latino students had been born or raised within the community, Ms. Bartlet's perception of them as new was a sentiment shared by many.

Finding Membership from the Outside

Latino students in Allen Creek High School developed their ethnic identities in the broad context of a hostile state climate where Latinos were perceived by many as "illegal" and threatening. Yet these identities also emerged in the local context of a small-town public high school forced to respond to a changing student population. Teachers' and administrators' proactive, if somewhat slow, responses to the new population of Latino students facilitated pan-ethnic group formation geared toward positive incorporation and upward mobility. As a result of school programs targeting Latinos, Latino students were freer to assert their ethnic identities through formalized school structures than were black students, and they consequently found spaces of belonging within the school. By explicitly linking Latino ethnicity to student organizations, these structures served to expand the cultural scripts attached to Latinos within the school. Though the stereotypes of Latinos as underachieving chicken-plant workers or potential criminals persisted in Allen Creek, heritage-based clubs offered a counternarrative of Latinos as hardworking immigrants and engaged and upwardly mobile students.

As anti-immigrant legislation in the state increased, the need for programs targeting unauthorized students became more apparent. Teachers were aware of threats to their unauthorized Latino students and saw the school clubs and programs as crucial to their success. Identity-based academic and social clubs were beneficial to Latino students who used their bicultural and bilingual skills at school-sanctioned functions and meetings. These clubs also provided Latino students with space to discuss their status as immigrants and children of immigrants. Teachers and administrators generally accepted the presence of these clubs because they needed translation services to communicate with immigrant parents of elementary school students and because they viewed the Latino students as newcomers.

Nonetheless, issues arose when programs targeting Latino students threatened to alienate other students. The black principal, in particular, wanted to ensure that resources for Latino students were not denied to other students. In directing programs toward Latinos exclusively, the school did not facilitate student coalitions between black and Latino students, nor did it provide spaces for black students to embrace their heritage as it did for Latinos. In contrast, it was precisely because teachers viewed the Latino students as different, foreign, or new that they encouraged clubs for Latino students. In embracing their heritage identities and utilizing their bilingual and bicultural skills, both unauthorized 1.5-generation and second-generation immigrants became better integrated in their school and in the community of Allen Creek.

Conclusion

Though race relations were not completely harmonious, Allen Creek High School had overcome many of the initial difficulties associated with incorporating a new Latino population. The Latino students who graduated in the early 2000s benefited from the ESL program, but they did not have access to any additional resources. Gradually, school policies shifted to more deliberately incorporate immigrant and second-generation students, even as the state climate shifted in the opposite direction. The school added Spanish-language materials, parental outreach programs in Spanish, clubs for Latino students, Latino administrators and staff, soccer teams, and Spanish classes for native speakers. These clubs, programs, and resources helped Latino students find a place of belonging in the school and community regardless of immigration status. Furthermore, by hiring a Latino vice principal, the school district demonstrated its recognition of the growing Latino population in the town and high school. Though there was still only one Latino teacher during the study period, the school's proactive responses to this demographic change resulted in progressively better graduation rates, rising academic achievement levels among Latino students, and growing Latino representation in school organizations.

In contrast to the efforts of teachers and administrators to incorporate immigrant and second-generation Latino youth, state policies toward undocumented immigrants in the region were increasingly hostile and restrictive. The educational strategies at Allen Creek High School went against the political tide at a time when North Carolina legislators and NCCCS board members were proposing measures to ban undocumented immigrants from higher education. Simultaneously, Alabama state legislators passed a law to collect immigration information for students in primary and secondary school (Alabama HB 56), and Arizona state legislators banned the Mexican American studies program in Tucson public schools (Delgado 2013). The successes of clubs such as AIM and LAC offered important reminders of how heritage- and identity-based clubs, teaching strategies, and course content can provide spaces of incorporation and foster cultures of achievement among students who often feel marginalized and silenced by state policies and school curricula.

These strategies, however, were not always seamlessly implemented and did not erase all discrimination in the school. The Latino students at Allen Creek High School remained aware of their outsider status and occasionally lamented discrimination in formal complaints that the football team was treated better than the soccer team or through jokes and adapted songs they sang in the hallways. Yet Latinos received resources and guidance through culturally sensitive programming. For many Latino students, high school thus provided a nurturing and supportive environment that they recalled fondly after graduation. Though second-generation students could continue to build on the skills and confidence they gained in high school, in part as a result of the community and critical thinking they developed though heritage-based clubs, their unauthorized 1.5-generation peers faced a far harsher transition out of high school. Once undocumented youth graduated, the supportive structures that helped foster a sense of inclusion fell away, leaving them with far less protection against the destabilizing forces of anti-immigrant lobbying and legislation.

4 Graduation, Isolation, and Backlash after DACA

For many unauthorized immigrant students, high school graduation marked a firm transition from membership into exclusion. With the announcement of DACA, eligible youth hoped that the policy would help them retain some sense of belonging and continue the forward momentum they had initiated in high school. When President Obama announced DACA, he appealed to the sympathies of the American public: "These are young people who study in our schools, they play in our neighborhoods, they're friends with our kids, they pledge allegiance to our flag. They are Americans in their heart, in their minds, in every single way but one: on paper" (White House Office of the Press Secretary 2012).

With these words, President Obama proclaimed that undocumented immigrant youth were already members of the nation, and he emphasized their loyalty to America as the justification behind DACA. He continued,

> They were brought to this country by their parents—sometimes even as infants—and often have no idea that they're undocumented until they apply for a job or a driver's license, or a college scholarship. . . . It makes no sense to expel talented young people, who, for all intents and purposes, are Americans—they've been raised as Americans; understand themselves to be part of this country—to expel these young people who want to staff our labs, or start new businesses, or defend our country simply because of the actions of their parents—or because of the inaction of politicians. It is the right thing to do . . . for the American people . . . because these young people are going to make extraordinary contributions, and are already making contributions to our society. (White House Office of the Press Secretary 2012)

Echoing the arguments of immigrant youth activists (W. Perez 2009; Vargas 2012), the president considered undocumented young persons as deserving of authorization because of their feelings of national identity and their connections to American institutions and communities. Moreover, he stressed their innocence in migration decisions and their drive to contribute to the nation.

Even after DACA, however, the unauthorized youth in Allen Creek continued to face significant barriers to higher education and the labor market because of financial restrictions on postsecondary education in North Carolina. Consequently, most unauthorized immigrant youth with dreams of college found themselves frustrated and stuck in spite of the implementation of DACA. For many, the realization that they could not access higher education forced them to reimagine the lives they had envisioned in high school.

In Allen Creek High School, the dominant message impressed on students was to aim for college. The hallways were papered with fliers reminding students of application deadlines to area schools, and admitted students were celebrated on classroom bulletin boards announcing their college destinations. College was promoted as the primary end goal of high school, and teachers often discussed the expectations of college professors as a tactic to implore students to pay better attention to coursework. "In college, your teachers won't remind you about due dates" was a common refrain among teachers in Allen Creek High School, who dutifully reminded their students of upcoming deadlines and allotted class time for work and discussion of assignments. Teachers were aware of the demanding work schedules of many of their students and tried to do everything to prepare them for college during the school day. Though only about 75 percent of the student body graduated in four years (slightly lower than the state average of 80 percent), nearly 70 percent of eligible students took the SAT (equal to the state average). In spite of the overwhelming marketing of college in Allen Creek High School, administrators and teachers knew that not all students would attend. Nonetheless, they continued to stress the importance of college in the hope that students would improve their classroom performance and aim for higher education.

Undocumented youth experienced the same institutional culture that stressed college and academic achievement as their documented and citizen peers. As a result, many felt devastated when they confronted the almost insurmountable barriers to college. During school, educators and administrators seldom discussed postsecondary pathways aside from college, but at the high school graduation ceremony, speakers explicitly addressed the various journeys that the graduates would take after high school. Allen Creek High School teachers and administrators took great care to celebrate graduation as an accomplishment in and of itself, and they urged students and parents to do the same.

In 2009, just as in years before and after, Vice Principal García welcomed the graduating seniors and their families to the graduation ceremony first in English and then in Spanish. He urged the students to enjoy this moment, as it was the only high school graduation they would have. He added that for some, it would be their last graduation altogether, reminding students that not all would continue on to higher education. He spoke of the value of hard work and manual labor, urging the students to take pride in whatever path they embarked on next. By speaking in English and Spanish, he ensured that all of the parents could understand the ceremony. Moreover, by referring to higher education, the labor market, and the armed forces, his speech paid homage to the diversity of the student body.

When College Is Not an Option

Vice Principal García's words acknowledged the plight of 1.5-generation unauthorized youth, for whom college was increasingly out of reach. Many undocumented graduates went straight from high school to work, and for some, their distinct experiences from their college-going peers gradually broke up friendships. Gustavo, an undocumented immigrant who had come from Mexico when he was thirteen, told me, "It's really hard knowing that after [high school] you can't do nothing. . . . Just thinking that after that all you have to do is work. I felt so attached to high school, and I just didn't want it to end." Gustavo missed high school and struggled to adjust to his new routine after graduation. He worked as a welder and spent weeks or months out of town and away from his friends and girlfriend who remained in Allen Creek. He saw his friends who had gone away to college even less frequently, and it was hard for them to relate to one another because their lives had taken such different turns. He recalled high school nostalgically: "Everybody was so close, and you knew everybody, but now when you're grown and you want to see your old friend, you don't really get to. It's hard now because, I mean, it's a small town and we grew up together. Like we shared everything—soccer, going out to eat. Like we were real close and stuff, and now like going to college, like [my friend] Carlos . . . I miss him." Gustavo never excelled in high school, and he frequently faced disciplinary actions until he found an outlet through art during his senior year. He did not have the grades to qualify for private scholarships or the immigration status to access financial aid.

Gustavo explained that his issues in high school haunted him in early adulthood:

I was never prepared to go to college because my life was just problems, problems, problems until now. I had it rough. . . . And right now, I want to go to college, but it's extremely hard for me because my grades throughout high school weren't the best. I was always going out, skipping school, not showing up or coming late. . . . I wish I could go, but everything is getting harder and harder. I have to work, and I would love to stay here in Allen Creek. I can't really get a good job because of all of the papers, and it's like, you want to be here so bad, but you know that you can't.

Gustavo felt stuck both because of his trouble in high school and because of his immigration status. Though he lamented his adolescent behavior and took some responsibility for his current situation, many of his undocumented peers who received good grades in high school found themselves in similar positions.

Carmen, a nineteen-year-old 1.5-generation Mexican immigrant, graduated from high school in 2007, the year before NCCCS implemented its ban on undocumented immigrants. She wanted to become a nurse, and she had the grades to pursue her college dreams, but she saw no point in paying for school if she could not work after she graduated. She explained, "I could have continued taking classes, but they wouldn't give me the [nurse's aide] certificate. Then I thought about going to community college to become a dental hygienist, but they told me that I would need to take an exam at the end of that as well and that I would need a Social Security number to do that. And if I didn't have that, then I could give them an ID, but since I didn't have that either, I just couldn't study anymore." Carmen had very concrete ideas about what she hoped to do after college, yet, without work authorization, she saw no way to reach her goals. After the implementation of DACA, she felt she had been out of school too long to return. She worked for a dentist making plaster molds, but she had few options for career growth even with a work permit.

Like Carmen and Gustavo, others struggled to advance without a college degree. Their daily routines at work provided stability, but many felt as though their lives were in a holding pattern. They awaited policy changes that would help them find a space of belonging and purpose. Yet their hopes that a DREAM Act would pass dwindled as they saw the political pendulum swing toward a more restrictive climate for unauthorized immigrants. When the president announced DACA, most unauthorized immigrant youth were shocked. Many hoped that the policy would finally open up doors to higher education and upwardly mobile jobs, but the lack of access to in-state tuition and financial aid made college a seemingly unreachable goal for many DACA beneficiaries in North Carolina. The policy also made potential beneficiaries nervous.

DACA and Its Aftermath

The memorandum of prosecutorial discretion from the Department of Homeland Security announcing DACA states: "Our nation's immigration laws are not designed . . . to remove productive young people to countries where they may not have lived or even speak the language. Indeed, many of these young people have already contributed to our country in significant ways" (Napolitano 2012). Emphasizing the fact that many within the 1.5 generation are more at home in the United States than in their countries of origin, the language of the memorandum positioned young immigrants as deserving of national residence and at least partial membership. By 2016, DACA had granted authorized presence to 844,931 individuals in the country and 29,846 individuals in North Carolina (US Citizenship and Immigration Services 2016).

Two years after his June 2012 announcement of DACA, President Obama announced an expansion of the policy to exclude the age limit for eligibility, thus allowing an additional 330,000 immigrants older than thirty to apply for DACA (Krogstad and Gonzalez-Barrera 2014). Additionally, the expansion lengthened the work authorization from two to three years. In the same November 20, 2014, announcement, the president introduced DAPA to offer more protections to the parents of US-born citizen children and lawful permanent residents who had resided in the country since 2010.

DACA and DAPA were, in some ways, a response to Obama's critics on the left who had been campaigning against the administration's deportation policies that had removed record numbers of unauthorized immigrants from the country. Yet, as immigration scholars Marjorie Zatz and Nancy Rodriguez (2015) point out, the policies of prosecutorial discretion were far less secure than legislative actions. Both the initial DACA policy and its 2014 expansion sparked controversy. And while the 2012 iteration of DACA was implemented despite vocal opposition from conservative legislators, its 2014 expansion faced more consequential resistance when Texas and twenty-five other states—including North Carolina—filed a lawsuit to halt DAPA and the expansion of DACA.

The lawsuit evidenced wide divisions in state and federal ideologies surrounding immigrant residents, even for the least controversial immigrant groups such as children who were brought into the country through no choice of their own. At the time of this writing, a court-ordered temporary injunction was in place that kept the November 2014 policies from taking effect. Though the injunction was temporary, oral arguments to the Supreme Court resulted in a 4–4 split vote, issued on June 23, 2016.[1] With the triumph of Donald Trump in the November 2016 presidential election, the future of the expanded policies looked bleak. On June 15, 2017, the Trump administration officially rescinded DAPA and the expanded version of DACA. The memo put out from the Department of Homeland Security stated that the 2012 iteration of DACA would remain in effect but did little to reassure recipients of their long-term security (US Department of Homeland Security 2017). Moreover, after the memo was released, the Texas attorney general, Ken Paxton, along with other attorneys general from nine additional states, not including North Carolina, sent a letter threatening additional legal action if the Trump administration did not move to phase out DACA. The letter was effective. On September 5, 2017, Attorney General Jeff Sessions announced that the Trump administration was rescinding DACA.

With the termination of DACA, hundreds of thousands of young immigrants were poised to lose work permits and protection from deportation unless Congress were to pass legislation extending protections prior to the expiration of the policy in March 2018. DACA had granted temporary legal presence to approximately 63 percent of the 1.3 million immediately eligible individuals as of March 2016 (Hipsman, Gómez-Aguiñaga, and Capps 2016). The remaining 37 percent either did not apply or did not complete their applications for various reasons, including application fees, incomplete educational credentials, and concern that temporary authorization was not worth future risk of deportation if the policy were to be revoked (Batalova, Hooker, and Capps 2014). Interestingly, higher percentages of youth in hostile states, like North Carolina and Arizona, applied for DACA than their eligible peers in more welcoming states like New York and California (Singer, Svajlenka, and Wilson 2015). The incentives of applying for DACA in less welcoming states, it seems, outweighed the potential risks, particularly given the dangers of driving without licenses in these states.

Applying for DACA

Following their initial reactions of disbelief in response to the announcement of DACA, most eligible youth in the study spoke to teachers or trusted advisers in churches or nonprofit organizations who encouraged them to apply. Youth who were not enrolled in college and who lacked strong connections to community organizations were more skeptical of the policy. Sada, an unauthorized immigrant from Mexico, did not trust the policy and waited until after President Obama's reelection to apply. She explained, "I was excited but scared at the same time. They had no clue that I was here illegally, and it was at the time that they were arresting a lot of people and deporting a lot of people, and I was scared. I actually filed after [the 2012] presidential elections. I didn't want to do it before because I didn't know if it was just a setup." Sada was nervous about giving her name to the federal government and worried that the policy was a ploy to gather data on the undocumented immigrants in the country. Her fears were echoed by other applicants. Karla, a Guatemalan-born immigrant noted, "I was so nervous to get my fingerprints taken because I didn't know what to expect. But in the end, it was no big deal."

Even potential beneficiaries who knew that the program was authentic worried that their actions prior to DACA might jeopardize their security. Valentina, a Guatemalan immigrant who worked with false documentation after high school, worried that she would be deported if she applied for DACA: "I was scared that I would get punished or deported and never be able to get my papers, because I had been working with false papers for so many years. But then I talked to Mariela [the founder of the Latino Outreach Center] and met with a lawyer that she knew, and then I felt more comfortable applying. My sister had applied at her church, because they brought in a lawyer who helped them with the application, and she got approved, so after that I felt better about applying."

Revealing oneself to the government was anxiety provoking, but activists, church leaders, school officials, pro bono lawyers, and nonprofit workers were instrumental in easing DACA applicants' worries. Yet the application process was much easier for some youth than others. For youth enrolled in school, gathering the necessary documentation for DACA was straightforward. But for youth like Sada, who had worked to remain undetected since high school, it was difficult to gather proof of eligibility. Ironically, it was an interaction with the police that gave Sada her proof of residence:

> There was a hiccup with getting [DACA] because I had no proof of me being here back in 2009. I proved that I graduated in '08, and that I started [taking a course in] school in 2010, but I had nothing in 2009. I had nothing under my name, no bills, nothing, absolutely nothing. So I didn't know what I was going to do, but then my mom remembered that I got stopped in 2009, and they gave me two tickets. So I went to court and asked them for my records. And it was back in September 2009 that I got stopped, and it proved that I was here then and at all the court dates. So finally, I had to wait six months, but I finally got it.

As previous research shows, women and immigrants with fewer social and institutional attachments have a harder time proving eligibility for authorization programs because fewer records exist of their presence (Hagan 1994, 1998). By trying to minimize her chances of deportation, Sada had inadvertently jeopardized her chances of receiving DACA.

Sada lived in her parents' house after high school, and none of the bills were in her name. She had records of her presence from her work at a grocery store, but she had used a false Social Security card to obtain the job. Working with false documentation made her fearful of deportation and ultimately led her to quit her job after what she felt was a too close run-in with ICE. She recalled, "At my job, there was another Hispanic guy working with a fake Social, and immigration was there, and I walked in and I just wanted to leave. I called my mom to come get me, but she said that the person that gave me the Social was fine with it, and it was a real Social. But that was the first and last time that I worked with a different Social Security number." Because the chronic stress was too much for her, Sada quit her job and began babysitting so she could get paid under the table. Because her job was informal, Sada felt that she was no longer working in violation of the law, but the work also made it harder to prove her continued residence in the United States.

Even with DACA, beneficiaries continued to worry about their security. Sada explained her uneasiness: "My understanding is that DACA isn't a law, so it could change. What if this president isn't happy with us having an opportunity and wants to take something away from us? You do get kind of scared. What if this next person wants us out? If they do want us out, then they have us on file, and we're ready to go." As Trump gained momentum in the primaries, Sada's anxiety grew. She knew that she took a leap of faith when she identified herself to the federal government, and she remained uneasy about the future.

Stagnation after DACA

Most DACA beneficiaries felt some trepidation about exposing themselves to the government, but ultimately most decided that the protection from deportation was worth the risk. Especially in states like North Carolina where a lack of public transportation and programs like 287(g) made the risk of deportation a constant source of anxiety, DACA provided much-needed peace of mind. Even with the added security and work authorization, however, many beneficiaries struggled to advance socioeconomically.

Sada hoped to attend college but could not afford out-of-state tuition. She asked a lawyer if her DACA status made her eligible for in-state tuition, but of course, in North Carolina, it did not. Still, she hesitated to ignore rumors of loopholes that gave her some hope. She explained that an acquaintance, who was also a DACA beneficiary, told Sada that she "argued with the [college] and the school gave her in-state tuition." She continued "My friend told me [she] did a bunch of stuff and she caused a fuss and got in-state tuition from the school, but I haven't really done the research to find that out." After hearing this story, Sada decided that there must be a way to attend college. She did not, however, learn any additional details about her friend's tuition policy. The one official loophole that existed for DACA beneficiaries in the state was a business sponsorship exception that allowed North Carolina employers to pay the community college tuition of their DACA employees at in-state rates (North Carolina Community College System 2013). Without a business willing to sponsor and pay for Sada, she, and most other DACA beneficiaries, would still be required to pay out-of-state tuition.

Sada had started community college a year after high school but dropped out because of the high costs of tuition. She had been taking one class each semester and paying one thousand dollars per class. She grew frustrated when she compared her own educational trajectory to her citizen friends' and sister's: "When you're in high school, you don't really think about this stuff, being undocumented, but after graduation is when it hit me hard because the college wanted all this money and my friends who are US citizens, they were all happy needing to pay five hundred dollars, six hundred dollars, and I would be like, how am I going to pay five thousand dollars for one semester?" Instead of attempting to apply to college after receiving her DACA status, Sada continued to work. She retained the hope that, like her friend, she might one day be able to convince the college that she was entitled to in-state tuition. By delaying her college application, she avoided having to confront prohibitively high tuition costs and abandoning her dreams. College remained something that she could abstractly hope for in the future.

Sada's US-born sister, Cristina, expressed guilt that her undocumented sister, only a year older than she, faced so many constraints. She and her sister were very close, but they had never discussed these feelings. The silence surrounding their different opportunities weighed heavily on Cristina. She cried as she explained, "I just kind of feel bad that I am going to college and she can't. You know, it hurts my feelings. I get real sensitive about it. Sorry [for crying]. I know that she can't go, but one day if I can help her, I will." Cristina was very emotional when discussing her older sister, and she found it nonsensical that she and her sister had such different opportunities. Their difference in citizenship status drove a wedge between the two sisters, who, despite remaining close, could not bring themselves to discuss their unequal opportunities.

DACA did not level the playing field between the two sisters. Cristina graduated from college and found work as a paralegal. She lived with her husband and two children in a house roughly twenty minutes from her childhood home. The girls' younger brother also left home when he joined the army. Despite being the oldest, Sada continued to live at home with her parents and her youngest brother, who was still in high school. Knowing that her immigration status delayed her transition to independence, she joked, "Hopefully, I'm married and out of the house before [my little brother] leaves to go to school." She was happy for her siblings' success but also knew that her own ambitions were constrained by policies obstructing her access to educational institutions and, as a result, professional opportunities.

Like Sada, Alonso, another unauthorized immigrant from Mexico, hoped DACA would facilitate a pathway to college. Alonso struggled to fit in at Allen Creek High School. He felt more at home in the town's Latino Outreach Center youth group, where he participated in community projects with other Latino youth. At school, he felt other students judged him for his clothing and for being an immigrant. He arrived in the United States at age thirteen, and he recalled Mexican school uniforms as an equalizing force that protected students from judgment for being poor. He did not have good grades in high school and often arrived at class unprepared. Alonso's high school teachers complained to me that he did very little schoolwork, but Alonso nonetheless had dreams of going to college. Without private scholarships, however, out-of-state college tuition was prohibitive.

Moreover, Alonso could not justify paying for school tuition when there were household bills to pay. Alonso's mother worked in a textile factory, and his older brother worked in a lumber mill. Alonso's mother had moved the children out of their family home when their father became abusive. After they lost the additional support of his father's income, Alonso began working part-time at the Kentucky Fried Chicken (KFC) in Allen Creek during his junior year of high school.

Alonso did not want to stay at KFC indefinitely, but he was not yet ready to leave his mother. After high school, he took on a full-time position, but he never viewed it as permanent. He had cousins who worked in factories in Chicago, and he thought about moving there if he could not find a better-paying job locally. His greatest hope, however, was for the federal DREAM Act to pass so that he would be able to go to college.

Three years after high school graduation, however, Alonso was no closer to enrolling in college. But he felt comfortable in his life and was proud of his growth in his job. After working full-time at KFC for two and a half years, Alonso was promoted to management, and he enjoyed the added responsibility. He felt like a role model to the younger workers. In many ways, Alonso had "learned to be illegal" (R. Gonzales 2011), accepting, or at least ignoring, his immigration status. He chose to focus on his accomplishments at work and his relationships with his friends and coworkers to find a sense of peace and purpose. In this way, much like many of the young unauthorized immigrants in Roberto Gonzales's (2016) large-scale study of unauthorized youth in California, he resisted the label of "illegal outsider" and instead embraced his space of belonging within his immediate social network. Though he tried his best to concentrate on the positive aspects of his life, Alonso knew that he lacked security and that his opportunities for advancement were limited.

Alonso was ecstatic when he heard about DACA. He recalled the day of the announcement: "Lorena [the former youth group leader at the Latino Outreach Center] called me and . . . told me all about Obama. And I was like, wow, that's awesome. I can do what I always wanted to do, which is go back to college. I got excited." Sadly, Alonso's excitement about DACA stemmed largely from misinformation. Alonso initially believed that DACA would allow him to pay in-state tuition and access federal financial aid. Even after he completed the application process, Alonso maintained his beliefs, recalling,

> When they sent me the approval letter and my card, my heart dropped. I was so excited. . . . It was just a big step. It was so cool. Now we can apply for college and have benefits. I don't have to worry about people doing background checks or getting fired from my job. It's just less stress. Now I'm just waiting for my license. That will be a big, big change without worrying about getting stopped without a license. I'm going back to school this year. I'm going to apply in August to go to community college. I want to study something with nursing. I want to work with special kids. I'll keep my job while I go and take classes. I didn't have enough money to take classes before, but now I can apply for FAFSA [Free Application for Federal Student Aid].

Upon hearing the news that DACA would not offer him the federal financial aid benefits or in-state tuition available to his citizen peers, Alonso struggled to accept that he still would not be able to attend school. The policy ultimately had little effect on his educational and career trajectory. Three years after receiving DACA status, Alonso had made no major career shifts, and he had not enrolled in school.

Slipping Backward after DACA

Even youth who had managed to transition to college did not necessarily view DACA as the boost that they needed to advance toward meaningful and fulfilling careers. Indeed, DACA did nothing to help offset the high cost of out-of-state tuition. Thus, the policy did very little to help youth remain in college when facing financial strain. For example, Dalia, an unauthorized immigrant from Mexico, and Karla, an unauthorized immigrant from Guatemala, were thrilled when they received full scholarships to private four-year colleges with the help of LAC, but they were both heartbroken when the money they received for their first year of school was not available for their second year. Because their scholarships were funded with soft money, they were not guaranteed the same amount of scholarship money each year. During their senior year of high school, the director of the scholarship fund had received a large one-time donation, but he was unable to raise the same amount of money the following year. Consequently, Dalia and Karla fell through the cracks. In parallel experiences, both girls had to leave college after only one year despite receiving DACA protection.

The semester she left college, Dalia explained her disillusionment:

> Initially, I had thought that I'd be there [at the private college] all four years because the way I was told, well, I knew that LAC wouldn't be able to give me the same amount of money every year, but in my mind I had thought, well, they're not just going to put me in school and then the next three years not keep me in school because that wouldn't make sense at all. But I knew the amount wouldn't necessarily be the same. So when things started changing, I was like, okay, so now I know that I won't be able to stay in three more years without some help. So I was looking everywhere to find more money. And they gave us a list of scholarships that undocumented students were eligible for, but most of those scholarships were California based, and a lot of them were for seniors in high school, so it was really hard. Not a lot of people are trying to give money or scholarships for undocumented students. So it was really hard to figure out, well, I can't find this money, so what am I going to do? I tried to get in contact with so many people, but nothing came through. Now I'm at home for the semester. I was trying to get into at least a community college for the semester but I can't afford that now. . . . I miss school.

For Dalia and Karla, the cost of private college was unaffordable on only a partial scholarship, as was the out-of-state tuition North Carolina public colleges charged to DACA recipients. Dalia was frustrated by the limited opportunities in her home state, and she was well aware that students in similar positions in California had more opportunities for in-state tuition and scholarships than she had.

Dalia's path through primary and secondary school had put her on a clear trajectory toward college, and she was dismayed at the turn her life had taken. Dalia's parents brought her to the United States when she was only six months old. She grew up thinking that she had been born in the United States until she brought home a camp application in middle school that required a Social Security number. Crushed at having to disappoint their daughter, her parents reluctantly told her that she did not have one. This was Dalia's first memory that signaled to her that she was different from her middle school peers, who were mostly US born and white. Despite being born in Mexico and not having legal documentation to be in the United States, Dalia grew up feeling unattached both culturally and linguistically to her Mexican heritage. NASCAR and country music were far more ubiquitous in her home than soccer or *banda* music, and while she loved Mexican food, she ate hamburgers and hotdogs just as frequently. Only when she began high school did she begin to embrace her ethnic identity and interact more regularly with other Latinos.

Dalia's experience with the Latino community in her high school provided an opportunity for her to explore her heritage. Because the majority of her friends from her primarily white elementary and middle schools went away to private high schools, Dalia was forced to make new friends when entering high school. She explained how her high school also introduced her to her Mexican heritage:

> In middle school, where I went, we weren't really diverse. Like, me and my cousin were the only Hispanic kids in our class, and there were maybe four or three black people in our class, so it was mostly white. So usually I would just hang out with white people. So when I got here, it was kind of weird because most of them went off to boarding schools and private high schools. . . . And I guess here there's more Hispanics. And in middle school I really didn't, like, explore my culture as much. Here, having so many Hispanic friends [now], I can explore my culture more, and I feel like I can use more Spanish. . . . I was just accustomed to speaking English. So here now, with all my Hispanic friends, I'm getting more into speaking Spanish, and we have Spanish jokes now, and to me that explored more like, "Oh, this is more how I should be speaking sometimes. Why don't I take up more Spanish classes to learn?" That's actually what encouraged me to take more Spanish classes and actually

learn how to speak better and enunciate better and write better and read better. That really influenced me.

Dalia discovered her ethnic heritage through her interactions with coethnic peers in Allen Creek High School. Through friendship ties with other Latino students in her school, she began to feel pride in her heritage, linking it to academic pursuits as well as social interactions.

In college, however, the connection between her background and her education was strained due to her immigration status. Dalia found herself lying about her citizenship during college orientation. She reluctantly chose to identify as a citizen, because she felt it was the closest option to her experience. She recalled, "We actually had this thing at orientation, and I remember, someone asked an ice-breaker question, and it was like, something like, if you count yourself as a US citizen or if you're a foreign exchange student—something like that—and I just kind of stayed back, but then I figured, I'd been here all of my life, so I may as well count myself as a citizen. It's just awkward situations like that that you don't know where to put yourself."

Orientation was not the only time Dalia faced an "awkward situation" at a school event. She also remembered an experience she had in class: "In another class [the professor] asked about driver's licenses just because everybody drives, and so everybody puts their hands up in the air to say that they have a driver's license, and I just couldn't. That was an awkward situation too. It was just an example, I can't remember what it was, but it was supposed to be that everyone would raise their hands and I couldn't."

Like Dalia, most unauthorized immigrant students in North Carolina colleges were similarly isolated from social networks of unauthorized student peers because so few of them could afford tuition at out-of-state rates. Moreover, most professors had very little experience with undocumented students. Unlike their peers in large California schools, they had no access to undocumented or "AB 540" student organizations, named for the California bill that offered undocumented youth in-state tuition (Abrego 2008). Moreover, most of their peers and advisers had little knowledge of immigration issues. Dalia claimed citizenship at orientation, but circumstances like the class question about driver's licenses and, even more poignantly, her struggles to obtain scholarship funding for the second year of college reminded her that she was excluded from national membership. Though DACA finally provided Dalia with legal presence in the only country that she had ever known as her home, it did not facilitate her continued enrollment in college.

Because tuition policies did not change following the announcement of DACA, the new status provided a path not to education but only to work. Karla, who also dropped out of school after receiving DACA, explained her reaction: "What would have been even better is if we had in-state tuition. It's extremely hard for me to get funding for my second year because LAC only gave us seven thousand dollars for the whole year. So we went from getting twenty-three thousand dollars from LAC to only seven thousand dollars. At least now I know that if I can't get the money, then I can work and maybe go back to school later, or go to community college."

In spite of their anger that DACA would not help them remain enrolled in college, Karla and Dalia were grateful that they would at least be able to work. They planned to save money to eventually return to school and finish their college educations. Dalia was resolved to earn a nursing degree from a community college and hoped to eventually complete a four-year degree. Nonetheless, the transition out of a four-year institution felt like a big step backward. She said, "I feel like I'm being pushed back more and that I haven't really accomplished anything. . . . I feel behind. . . . It's very frustrating. Very, very frustrating." Even with DACA status, Dalia felt like an outsider in North Carolina as she struggled to move forward with her educational and occupational goals.

Her backslide out of college was not the first time Dalia had described feeling left behind. Before DACA, Dalia had expressed a feeling of arrested development when comparing herself to her citizen brother: "I sometimes feel like my brother is so much older than me. I mean, he's seventeen and I'm twenty, but he's the one that can drive, and he can go wherever he wants, and I just have to stay home because I don't have a license. And he'll get to go to college. I just get so frustrated because he's so much younger than I am, and yet I feel like I'm younger because I can't do anything."

Dalia's early childhood experiences were very similar to those of her citizen brother. Yet upon entrance into adulthood, Dalia watched as her younger brother advanced in ways that she was unable to. DACA allowed Dalia to take the first steps toward catching up with her brother when she began working and, eventually, taking community college classes. Even after the enactment of DACA, however, Dalia continued to struggle with her inability to drive. She waited while the state attorney general and DMV debated whether DACA-status individuals would be eligible for licenses. She explained her reaction to DACA and the driver's license debate:

I'm excited [about DACA]. It's exciting because I feel like it's a step closer for me to actually be a citizen here. The only thing is, like, it's still a little confusing to me because I don't think that we can get financial aid, and now they've changed it up so that we can't get licenses in North Carolina. So now it's kind of like, well, that doesn't make sense if we get a work permit to work but we can't get licenses to drive to work, so it's really like, it just doesn't make sense at all. I mean, how does that make any sense? My dad showed me online, and we saw this interview that said that they suspended licenses for DACA recipients, and I was just like, that doesn't make any sense at all. It just seems like people are just trying to figure out a way for us to not get stuff that we need.

Dalia saw North Carolina politicians as trying to limit access to resources and maintain exclusion for undocumented immigrants. Despite her ability to work legally and contribute to her family, state policies continued to stunt her ability to develop to her full potential. She viewed the state backlash as nonsensical in the face of DACA, and she very clearly articulated how frustrated the conflicting contexts made her feel.

Even after Dalia received her license, she remained anxious about driving with a license that bore the words "NO LAWFUL STATUS." She noted, however, that her brother was pulled over more frequently by police than she was because he "looked Mexican," while her skin tone was light. And she did not take for granted her newfound independence. With a license, a stable work schedule, and a new academic focus in early childhood development, Dalia hoped she had at least reinitiated her forward momentum instead of taking steps backward.

Unlike Dalia, who had enrolled in part-time community college two years after receiving DACA, Karla had not yet found a route back to college three years after the implementation of DACA. Dalia's parents helped her pay tuition at community college, but Karla lacked similar family support. Karla's mother had returned to Guatemala with her new husband when Karla was twelve, and Karla remained in North Carolina with her aunt, who was on a tight income. In spite of the hardships that Karla faced as an undocumented immigrant living in the United States, she was happy that she had made the decision to stay. At the age of eighteen, shortly after she had been admitted to college, she told me,

If I had to move back to Guatemala, it would be hard because I would have to leave everything that I knew behind. And I would have to leave my family because they're already residents. And I would have to leave my friends. I've been with them all my life, and my teachers and people I've known all my life. I'd miss the lifestyle. It would be really different over there. And I don't know who I would go to, because I wouldn't go back to my mom, or my dad, or my aunts or uncles down there. I don't really keep in contact with them.

Karla was heartbroken when she was forced to leave college, and she was further deflated when she realized that DACA would not facilitate a path back to school. In spite of her disappointment with the scope of DACA, however, the policy gave her hope that she would gain more secure standing in the United States. Describing her reaction to the announcement of DACA, she told me, "I was excited, because I was hoping that maybe from there, it will open opportunities to become a resident or something, so I was really excited and hopeful."

Although DACA did not allow Karla to realize her educational ambitions or put her on a pathway to legal permanent residency as she had hoped, the policy opened up work opportunities that were previously out of reach. Before DACA, Karla had never worked in the formal labor market. After DACA, she found a job as a project manager's assistant in a construction company. She dealt with big-name clients, and she felt far less stressed with a steady income. Karla enjoyed her job, but her options for growth were limited without a college degree. Thus, although DACA offered her legitimacy and security, the lack of in-state tuition continued to limit Karla's potential development.

The Stigma of Having "No Lawful Status"

Obstructions to education, and as a result, the highly skilled labor market, were not the only barriers to full inclusion for DACA beneficiaries in North Carolina. Even though beneficiaries were thrilled to finally have access to driver's licenses, they quickly realized that these licenses were not equal to those of their citizen peers and siblings. Sada explained,

> The license, it kind of does bother you, because they stamp you, they put a stamp on you, saying, "This person is undocumented." I didn't see the need to do all of that. Because we know we're here undocumented, but if we have the privilege to drive, why put that on the license? We already know that. Why not just make it like every other license? When someone asks you for your license, you see the stares and it's like, "What's wrong?—I'm just like every other person. Pay no mind to the red letters."

Sada's frustrations with her license stemmed from experiences she had while using it in routine interactions. She recounted one incident with a store clerk that highlighted the impact of her differentiated license:

> I went into a furniture place to get my niece a new bed set for her room, and

they always ask for an ID with the credit card. And this guy asked me for another form of ID. He wanted to make a big issue out of it. I was like, that ID is just as valid as any other ID. If you don't want to take it, that's fine. I'll go to another furniture place. My mom told me to calm down, and I'm like, "No, I'm not going to calm down! I'm doing this right! We don't need to put up with that stuff." So I just went to another store. . . . But most of the time it's fine, and you just let the stares roll off your back.

Sada's experience at the furniture store, and the stares that she got in other interactions, signaled to her that not everyone viewed her license as a legitimate form of identification. Even after DACA, she knew that many continued to view her as an outsider. She became extremely frustrated when people discriminated against her because of the color of her skin or because her license was stamped with red letters.

DACA recipients were acutely aware that the licenses explicitly marked them as alien residents without a legitimate claim to membership in the state of North Carolina. Alonso commented that the differentiated license would open him up to harassment by police. When the DMV was considering issuing licenses with a magenta stripe, Alonso reacted by saying, "I don't like the fact that they're going to put a pink stripe on the license so that they know that we're not from here, that we're not legal. We already know that, so I don't like that. So whenever a police person stops you, they'll already know that you're illegal. It just makes me mad and disappointed. What does that have to do with a license for driving? They don't have to put all of your business out there. And plus, we didn't choose to come over here; they [our parents] just brought us."

Alonso saw the distinct license as a form of punishment for an act that was not his choice. In his mind, the license symbolized Alonso's second-class position in the social structure of his state, shaming and outing him as an "illegal" immigrant, and making him vulnerable to police harassment. Alonso was happy when the magenta stripe was omitted from the design, but he still lamented that the license made his status public knowledge.

Both Sada and Alonso noted that they already knew they were undocumented, and they perceived the red lettering as a deliberate mark of their exclusion. DACA beneficiaries felt that the differentiated license made them more vulnerable to harassment or embarrassment, as they needed to show their licenses to bouncers, store clerks, bartenders, and restaurant workers who asked for identification. Nonetheless, they were happy to finally be able to legally drive. Sada recognized that having a driver's license, marked or not, improved her daily life. She explained,

> My life has been a lot easier. I don't need to be looking behind my back checking do I have a cop there, do I have cop there? Because you never know what kind of cop you're going to get. In the beginning, I forgot. It was hard to get used to. I used to see a cop behind me and get so nervous, and then people would ask me, "Don't you have your license?" And I'd be like, "Oh yeah!" You're so used to looking behind your shoulder. But it's so much easier now, and I don't have to take people's time for them to drive me places.

Sada felt like a burden for a long time after high school when she was forced to rely on her citizen siblings and friends to drive her places. Without a driver's license or work permit, it was difficult for her to help her parents. With DACA, she felt far more comfortable driving, working, running errands for her parents, and signing her name to public documents. Though she remained blocked from college because of financial constraints, she did not take for granted the decreased anxiety she felt after receiving DACA.

Like Sada, many unauthorized youth in this study were unable to achieve upward mobility in the first few years after DACA was implemented, but the policy nevertheless improved its beneficiaries' feelings of security and membership. Karla discussed the notable difference that having a license had made in her life. First, she could drive herself to work. Second, she felt far more comfortable moving through her daily routines, and, in spite of the visible markings on the license, she felt that some of the stigma of illegality had been lifted. She explained that having a license removed a chronic source of stress from her life: "It's so exciting. . . . I don't feel guilty or scared that they're going to stop me and give me an extra ticket, or worse. It was scary, but I didn't have to drive that often. . . . You know, I didn't have any documentation. At least to me, it's incriminating [not to have documentation]. Just to know that I can have the right kind of ID is such a relief." Even though DACA recipients continued to have no lawful status, the temporary authorization provided by DACA did much to remove the stigma of criminality that many had experienced during routine activities before implementation of the policy. Nonetheless, the pushback at the state level continued to stigmatize DACA beneficiaries in North Carolina and limit their opportunities for upward mobility.

Where Plyler v. Doe Left Off

After high school, fissures between authorized and unauthorized immigrant youth became far more apparent as their access to resources and benefits diverged dramatically. Regardless of immigration status, youth residing in the United States have the right to attend primary and secondary school as a result of the 1982 *Plyler v. Doe* Supreme Court ruling. Unauthorized immigrant youth in different states, however, have vastly different access to higher education.

The *Plyler v. Doe* decision protected undocumented youth from exclusion in primary and secondary schools throughout the nation, but the decision did nothing to prevent states from creating state policies excluding undocumented immigrants from access to resources or benefits controlled at the state level. Writing for the majority in the *Plyler v. Doe* case, Justice Brennan argued, "It is difficult to understand precisely what the state hopes to achieve by promoting the creation and perpetuation of a subclass of illiterates within our boundaries, surely adding to the problems and costs of unemployment, welfare, and crime."[2] Brennan argued that a state policy to charge tuition to immigrant children was against the interests of the state because educating immigrant youth was both just and socially beneficial. Yet even as it struck down this policy, the *Plyer v. Doe* decision acknowledged states' rights to protect their own interests. The explanation behind the decision focused on the equal protection of children and not on preemption surrounding the federal enforcement of immigration law.

The majority decision differentiated immigrant children from their parents, specifically stating that state laws could exclude "those whose very presence within the United States is a result of their own unlawful conduct."[3] The decision thus rested on the protection of innocent children rather than the argument that individual states or school board policies should not preempt federal law (Motomura 2014; Olivas 2012). Because the decision was grounded in the principles of equal protection and not preemption, the case had little influence on subsequent state policies affecting immigrants. It did not prevent individual states from passing legislation regarding immigrants' access to higher education in general or in-state tuition in particular. Moreover, states remained in control of issuing driver's licenses. In other words, the case did not prevent state legislatures from enacting state laws addressing immigrants, even though immigration has typically fallen under the purview of federal law.

Under the current patchwork system of variable state policies, twenty states offer in-state tuition to undocumented immigrants who graduated from public secondary schools within those states, and an additional six states offer some access to in-state tuition for DACA beneficiaries. In contrast, colleges and universities in North Carolina continue to charge out-of-state tuition rates, and other states such as South Carolina, Alabama, and Georgia have banned undocumented students outright from public institutions of higher education. This uneven legislative field gives youth in more hospitable states partial access to membership through policies that facilitate college entrance while marginalizing their peers in more hostile states through policies that obstruct college access. Even after the implementation of DACA, states continued to utilize their power to maintain mechanisms of exclusion or enact idiosyncratic policies regarding the incorporation of 1.5-generation immigrants. As youth in North Carolina quickly learned, DACA did not seamlessly open pathways to membership or remove restrictions to public colleges and universities in the state.

Conclusion

DACA granted work authorization and reprieve from the threat of deportation to its beneficiaries, yet youth in North Carolina remained blocked from in-state tuition and equal driver's licenses. They felt that the federal government was granting them a legitimized space within the country while the state was blocking avenues toward inclusion. Revisiting the tectonic plate metaphor, the implementation of DACA and the subsequent state-level backlash in North Carolina revealed fault lines that emerged as federal and state policies slid past each other in opposite directions. The friction created by the moving political shifts at the state and federal levels caused youth to stumble as though they were climbing mountains atop crumbling rocks.

In North Carolina, differentiated driver's licenses magnified the outsider status of DACA recipients, even as they felt relieved at their ability to drive legally. Likewise, they struggled to obtain the necessary credentials for upwardly mobile jobs, even as they celebrated their newly acquired work permits. Youth felt themselves sliding backward, grasping to maintain the progress they had made but unable to combat institutional policies limiting their mobility. Some youth who had made the difficult leap from high school to college experienced backslides in their trajectories, as DACA did not have the legislative power to override exclusionary policies. For most DACA beneficiaries, policies blocking their access to in-state tuition and financial aid kept their dreams for college just out of reach. Youth who rebelled or struggled in high school, like generations of adolescents before them, were doubly hampered in their ability to move forward in life. Their more high-achieving peers, however, also struggled to advance.

DACA beneficiaries celebrated their new "legal presence," but they wished the policy offered more. Dalia and Karla's reduced private scholarships were insufficient to cover the cost of their tuition, and both young women were forced to drop out of college as a result. Alonso assumed incorrectly that DACA would provide access to in-state tuition in North Carolina. Sada had heard rumors that her friend had successfully argued for access to in-state tuition. Rumors and assumptions aside, DACA beneficiaries, with few exceptions, were not eligible for in-state tuition in the state of North Carolina. Without this access to in-state tuition or public financial aid, most were unable to find any immediate pathways toward more upwardly mobile jobs or educational opportunities. Nonetheless, DACA provided its beneficiaries with more security to work, drive, and travel within the United States. State-level resistance to the policy, however, blocked opportunities that were available to DACA recipients in other states and continued to mark DACA beneficiaries as outsiders in North Carolina.

5 Toward Upward Mobility and Incorporation

DACA was far from perfect, but like other temporary authorization programs such as TPS, it allowed beneficiaries access to resources and opportunities they previously lacked. Just as the name suggests, temporary protected status is a temporary designation given to individuals from countries that have sustained armed conflict, environmental disasters, or other extraordinary circumstances that prevent them from returning safely to their home countries. As occurs with DACA, individuals with TPS are given temporary protection from deportation and must renew their status periodically. The application and renewal processes are arduous, and studies have illustrated that living with "liminal legality" for lengthy periods of time can have both material and psychological repercussions (Cebulko 2013, 2014; Menjívar 2006; Menjívar and Abrego 2012). Yet these legally gray areas also offer some advantages to individuals and open up resources not available to unauthorized immigrants.

Even in states that pushed back against perceived federal overreach, federal policies like DACA and TPS nonetheless gave immigrant youth better access to higher education and jobs than they would have had without protected status. The temporary nature of these policies and the confusion surrounding entitlements afforded with these statuses, however, complicated the lives of individuals with liminally legal status. As state policies moved to limit resources available to unauthorized immigrants, institutional gatekeepers struggled to figure out how to classify liminally legal youth. Because of the ambiguity and impermanence of both DACA and TPS, beneficiaries' journeys toward upward mobility tended to be slow and interrupted.

Trading School for Security and Independence

For many undocumented youth, the transition out of high school was a movement from inclusion to frustration. As they neared high school graduation, many struggled to successfully bridge the transition to adulthood when avenues to college and work were so heavily obstructed for unauthorized immigrants. Though some considered returning to their countries of origin, the vast majority chose to remain in North Carolina in spite of the harsh political climate.

Eduardo migrated to North Carolina at age seven. When I asked him at age seventeen if he would ever consider returning to Mexico, he replied,

> I would like to stay [in North Carolina] because that's where I grew up. . . .
> Even though we're Mexican and Hispanic . . . we have nothing to do in our
> country 'cause this country is the country that's given us everything: food,
> shelter, education, everything. You don't have anything there [Mexico]. It's like
> [he spreads his arms out to the side, one after the other], here's your life; here's
> where you [were] born. You got nothing to do with Mexico. . . . You have ev-
> erything to stay, but you can't stay here because you're not legally here. You're
> no one here. You're just transparent. They don't see you.

Eduardo's immigration status left him trapped between two nations, without a sense of full membership in either. He felt attached to his home state of North Carolina because of his childhood memories and his connections to his friends and community. Nonetheless, he identified himself as a "transparent" outsider due to his nationality, ethnicity, and immigration status. Eduardo's feeling of being nationless was particularly acute due to his unauthorized status, yet previous research has illustrated that second-generation youth can also feel stuck between national identities without full access to membership in either the United States or their ancestral countries (Kibria 2002; Levitt and Waters 2002; Wolf 2002). And while race and ethnicity certainly influence feelings of membership, Eduardo specifically referenced his immigration status. Though he previously commented that he would occasionally get looks around town due to his ethnicity, he also felt included and supported in his small community. He had developed close relationships with his teachers, and he wanted to continue to build on his academic successes. More than any other factors, Eduardo felt that his immigration status held him back and precluded him from attaining a sense of belonging in the United States.

Eduardo arrived in the United States with his brother and sister in 1998. Their aunt drove them to the border, where their uncle, who lived in the United States, picked them up in his truck. The children pretended to sleep as they passed through the border checkpoint, and the border agent made no attempt to wake them. Their uncle drove them from Texas to North Carolina, where they reunited with their parents. Their father had already been living in North Carolina for two years, and their mother had migrated six months before the children.

He recalled the move as easy. The houses looked different, but the farm-lands were similar to the land he left in Mexico. He learned English quickly in elementary school and was tracked into honors classes in high school. Eduardo's passions were soccer and school, and he excelled at both. Eduardo saw his parents struggle to find secure work, but his achievements in school made him feel like he was in a different category. He tried to fulfill his end of the "immi-grant bargain" (R. Smith 2006), working hard in school to repay his parents for their sacrifices. He took AP classes and joined the school's LAC. Because of his immigration status, Eduardo knew that enrolling in a four-year college would require creative financing and considerable assistance. Nonetheless, he hoped that his dedication in school would pay off in the form of private scholarships for student-athletes.

On their end, Eduardo's parents did all they could to shelter him from the strains of his immigration status. They wanted him to concentrate on his stud-ies and strive for college. Despite their hard work, however, it became harder and harder to protect Eduardo from the limitations of his own undocumented status.

In 2006, his family's challenges with their unauthorized status grew more intense. The North Carolina state legislature instituted a provision requiring all driver's license holders to have valid Social Security numbers. Simultaneously, police checkpoints began to pop up in areas with dense immigrant popula-tions. Eduardo's father grew uncomfortable driving the long commute to his construction job for fear that he might be stopped and deported. Not wanting to leave his children with a "suddenly single" parent as a result of deportation (Dreby 2015, 31), he quit his job. Eduardo's mother tried to make ends meet by picking up as much work cleaning houses as she could. The family cut back on expenses, and Eduardo offered to work, but his parents encouraged him to focus on his education. They stressed that college would lead to better jobs and a brighter future, and Eduardo embraced their dreams as his own.

Eduardo's athletic abilities and academic achievements, along with his fam-ily's income level, would have made him a perfect candidate for scholarships if not for his immigration status. Fortunately, however, he had strong advocates helping him search for alternative pathways to finance his college education.

His soccer skills enabled him to connect with a soccer coach at one of the state's community colleges. Between private scholarship money secured by the soccer program at the community college and additional funds acquired by the LAC, Eduardo found enough money to fund his tuition. Eduardo went to visit the community college, and he began to envision his future there. He hoped that the more affordable tuition at the two-year college would ease the challenge of funding the remainder of his education at a four-year college.

Eduardo's carefully crafted plans, however, suddenly collapsed months later in 2008 when the NCCCS board passed a resolution barring undocumented students from attending community colleges throughout the state. Both Eduardo and his parents felt crushed by the ban. Steadfast in their commitment to help their son become the first in the family to attend college, his parents decided to send Eduardo to Mexico for his education. Distressed at the idea of returning to Mexico, Eduardo scrambled to find ways to remain in North Carolina near his friends and family. Luckily, his strong network of social support allowed him to come up with an alternative. Eduardo's soccer coach also ran a scholarship fund associated with the LAC and consequently had connections at various area colleges. He capitalized on his connections with a four-year technical college close to Eduardo's hometown, and he set up a meeting with an admissions officer even though the application deadline had passed. Eduardo was admitted, and he was able to hold on to the scholarship funds from the LAC.

Although Eduardo found a way to remain in North Carolina, he was traumatized by the community college ban on unauthorized immigrant students. It was the first time in Eduardo's life that his immigration status caused him to lose something that he had already earned. And while he did, in fact, attend college, the inequity of the NCCCS resolution became the catalyst for his emotional transition to living as an undocumented individual. He began to lose any sense of national membership and internalize an undocumented identity. He also stopped vocalizing life plans for fear that his status might cause them to fall apart. He lost the optimism he once had and resigned to focus on his day-to-day life instead of looking toward the future.

Shortly after Eduardo made the decision to attend the technical college, I asked him what he imagined he would be doing after college. He responded, "We can't even be certain about what's gonna happen in the next month! . . . Like me going to [community college], like that [policy] came up and we just had to deal with it. Look for alternatives." Eduardo was grateful that he could stay in North Carolina near his family and friends, but his immigration status continued to haunt him throughout college.

Despite feeling somewhat isolated in college, where he had few Latino peers, Eduardo's first three years went remarkably well. His dream of graduating from college, however, was temporarily derailed in his fourth year. Since his first year of college, Eduardo had relied on the help of the school's multicultural student adviser to navigate class registration and secure a tuition plan each semester. But in his fourth year, that adviser was suddenly let go, and Eduardo realized too late that he had missed the deadline to apply for a tuition payment plan. Eduardo was forced to take the semester off. Locked out of school, he began working for a landscaping company, where he was paid under the table.

Working full-time in landscaping foreshadowed a life he had long feared, and the extended time away from school took an emotional toll. Eduardo began to question the value of his education and the money that he and others had invested in it. Considering his anticipated graduation, he told me,

> I mean, I'm going to be happy. Obviously, I'm going to be happy. But I feel
> like ... why should I finish if I'm just going to be working the same job when
> I'm through? There's no point in wasting time and wasting people's money.
> I just feel like it's a waste of time because I'm going to be doing the same
> landscaping or construction job that I was doing before, even though I have a
> four-year degree and I have really good English. I really want to finish and be
> educated. That's my goal. But I do question the point. It's very frustrating.

Being in school gave Eduardo direction and a place to belong, but the uncertain payoff caused him anguish. He watched his US citizen peers graduate and acquire upwardly mobile jobs, but he knew that those doors were closed to him. He directly compared himself to them: "You work as hard as they do, and at the end, you just get tossed aside." Eduardo felt powerless to advocate for himself when faced with an overwhelming sense of exclusion. In rare moments when he dared to discuss his ambitions for the future, he vaguely mentioned that he wished to "work in an office" instead of "outside."

With a deep understanding of the social value attached to certain jobs, Eduardo contrasted his opportunities to those of his documented and citizen peers: "I really don't like working outside. I'd rather be inside, without having to get all sunburned and get my hands dirty." Yet Eduardo knew there was no place for him to work inside without proper immigration authorization. He was an outsider without a visa. While he remained in school, he at least had a place to belong on the inside.

When I asked Eduardo at twenty-one what he thought he would be doing in five years, the same question I asked him at seventeen, he told me that he did not remember what he had answered previously and he was sure that his response would be different. He was clearly uncomfortable forecasting his life pathway, and he hesitated, stammering, "I really don't know. I have no idea. I'll hopefully be graduated. I have no idea. I really, I have no plans. That's the thing. I can't make a plan. There's no such thing as a plan. I just have to go with it. Whatever." I reminded him of his very similar answer four years earlier, and he thought back to the time when he received the news that he could not enroll in community college. He responded immediately and emotionally: "There you go. It hasn't changed. It sucks, not knowing. That community college policy, that's the thing that really changed my mind. I was going to go and play soccer and do what I wanted to do. And that just got taken away from me. And that just really sucked. It hurt. It hurt a lot, and then after that I just felt like, I'm not going to plan anything. . . . Because that was a plan. It was such a perfect plan. And it just disappeared." The community college ban and subsequent derailment of Eduardo's college plan was a turning point in his life. It marked the moment when he truly identified as undocumented and felt the sting of his immigration status.

Eduardo's opportunities changed suddenly when President Obama announced DACA in 2012. As he explained, "I'll be able to work. If I were to graduate with a four-year degree and not be able to work, I just . . . [He pauses and changes course.] Now I can actually take advantage of my education. It's a great opportunity, but it's not permanent. The policy is not there forever, so just as soon as it comes in, it could go away. If they take the permit away, I'll just have to deal with it."

After hearing about DACA, Eduardo felt a renewed vigor to graduate. With the money he had saved during his semester away from school plus additional scholarship funds from the LAC fund, he reenrolled in school and began working toward graduation. He knew his life had changed, but he remained guarded in his enthusiasm, having lost opportunities before. Yet for the first time since high school, he dared to make a plan. Before he even received his work authorization, Eduardo had already spoken to a contractor with whom he played pick-up soccer every Sunday about hiring him for a drafting position. As a computer-assisted design major in the Engineering Department at his college, he would be able to directly apply his education to his job. He would also be able to work indoors, which, to Eduardo, signified legitimacy and inclusion.

Eduardo was hopeful, but he continued to struggle to pay his out-of-state tuition even with a reduced course load. Eduardo began working for the contractor, and he loved his job. Moreover, he felt appreciated at work. With a full-time job in his chosen field, he decided to put his education on pause indefinitely. He knew that if he needed to, he would be able to complete his degree in the future, but for now, he was satisfied at work and felt that he was fulfilling his adult responsibilities to earn money and be independent. In spite of his frustration that North Carolina policy continued to bar him access to in-state tuition, he was far more hopeful about his future. Eduardo was lucky to be at a stage in his education where he could use DACA as a springboard to a fulfilling career track with opportunities for growth. But he was one of only a handful of unauthorized immigrant youth in this position. For others who were unable to access private scholarship funds, DACA was far less influential in redirecting their occupational trajectories, at least within the first few years of the policy's implementation. After a few years, however, other DACA beneficiaries managed to maneuver their pathways back toward upwardly mobile career tracks, even as the hostile climate in North Carolina did little to propel them toward advancement.

Slowly Getting Educated

Unlike Eduardo, who focused on work instead of schooling after receiving DACA, other youth who had not managed to enroll in college after high school saw DACA as the impetus to save money and steer themselves back to college. Zaíra, an undocumented immigrant from Guatemala, had struggled in the years after high school. She had hoped and planned to attend a four-year private college, but she was unable to secure a private scholarship. Instead, she worked various jobs in factories and fast-food restaurants and tried to put her dreams of college to the back of her mind. Zaíra migrated from Guatemala to North Carolina with a child smuggler when she was ten, and she began working at twelve when her parents split up. Adapting to life in North Carolina was not easy for Zaíra, but she was happy to be reunited with her family. In Guatemala, she felt unwanted in her aunt's home, and she was not treated well. Unfortunately, her family issues did not cease after reuniting with her parents in North Carolina.

After her father left, Zaíra began working multiple jobs to supplement her mother's income from the chicken-processing plant. Zaíra's mother also left home for stretches of time as she tried to establish new relationships or seek better-paying work in other cities. Amid this stress, Zaíra struggled in school, but she was smart and her teachers kept an eye on her. A teacher offered to take Zaíra in and support her, an arrangement that allowed her to cut back her work hours and concentrate on school. Despite her hard work, Zaíra was unable to secure a college scholarship.

After high school graduation, Zaíra worked various low-paying jobs until she acquired what she described as "really good" false documents. She began a retail job, and she finally felt like a "normal" young adult whose life chances were not determined exclusively by her undocumented immigration status. Her life experience had shown her that she could overcome obstacles, and she no longer felt imprisoned by her immigration status. She explained,

> I feel normal now. I don't actually even feel the need to be a citizen. Before, I was like, I want to so bad to be a citizen and work any job I want, but now I feel like I'm already doing that. I'm getting raises and getting promoted. People don't treat me like I'm any different. I don't love my job, but I feel normal. I don't feel like anyone treats me differently because they don't think that I'm different. I feel accomplished that I could get a job like that. . . . It's not a big deal for other people, but it's a big deal for me. And everyone is so nice, and I've gotten so many job offers out of it. So I feel like I'll always have a job.

Even with her unauthorized status, Zaíra's job allowed her to feel normal. With a steady job and a steady boyfriend, Zaíra felt more stable than she had in years. Nonetheless, she had moments when she doubted her security. She explained, "I'm still thinking of going back to Guatemala when I get depressed or have issues. I went through a lot with my family. Now, if I get married, I might have to go back for a little bit, but I feel at peace with whatever happens. If I were to go back to Guatemala, I also feel like I would be able to come back here. I'm not scared anymore."

Zaíra knew that she would find a way to return to the United States if she were deported or if she needed to return to Guatemala to apply for a fiancé visa. Though she was not afraid of returning to Guatemala, she had grown up in the United States and considered it her home. She had found a way to feel comfortable, and she did not want to return to her country of origin. Prior to the announcement of DACA, at age twenty, she described her journey to accepting her undocumented status: "I don't feel like I'm American because I carry a lot of my Guatemalan culture. But also I've lost a lot of my culture. I'm nothing. I feel like the people over there are a lot more humble. I'm like that too. I'm not ashamed of being from Guatemala or of being undocumented. I used to feel ashamed, but now I'm proud." Zaíra struggled to articulate her identity, even going as far as to say she was "nothing." Yet she also embraced her undocumented status and took pride in this identity. She knew, however, that she could not claim it at work. Zaíra's job at a clothing store allowed her to feel normal. But this security was only temporary.

Zaíra lost her job when her sister posted a message about her twenty-first birthday on her Facebook wall. Everyone at Zaíra's work thought that she was twenty-six, as she maintained a work identity consistent with her false work permit. She recalled the shame she felt when her coworker revealed her secret to her boss: "I just felt so ashamed and humiliated. They all said that I had lied to them, but I never wanted to lie." While Zaíra could proudly proclaim her undocumented identity in private, once she was outed in her workplace, she felt the stigma of her status, and she was reminded of her lack of membership and security.

Zaíra struggled to reconcile her self-image as an honest and industrious worker with her coworkers' perception of her as a liar and a troublemaker. I was with her in the shopping center where she worked when one of her former coworkers teased her, good-naturedly, for being "a rebel." I saw her eyes fall as she withdrew into herself. Though they were not malicious, Zaíra took the jokes about her status to heart. She never considered herself a rebel. She had to work, and the only way for her to access the US labor market was to work under false documents.

After applying for DACA, Zaíra explained how it would feel to finally be able to work legally: "It felt like something fell from the sky. I just couldn't believe it. I was so relieved, and I just felt like, finally, I can do something and I can go back to school. It just feels like all of my dreams are finally opening up to me." For Zaíra, just like many others, DACA gave her a sense of belonging and a way to present herself honestly in all spheres of her life. It also allowed her to dream of a future career that she hesitated to imagine before DACA.

Zaíra did not return to school immediately, but she shifted her career path to move from retail into an entry-level administrative job in a hospital. She was passionate about her new focus and felt happier living openly. DACA gave her a feeling of security that she lacked since arriving in the United States. As an adult with DACA status, she no longer had to rely on help from teachers or mentors, to whom she felt grateful but indebted. After saving money for a year and a half, Zaíra enrolled in a prestigious four-year university and began working toward a degree in nursing. She got certified as a phlebotomist while working at the university hospital attached to her school. She loved the job and was grateful that she could pay reduced tuition as a result of her employment. Nonetheless, she struggled to find the time to work sufficient hours to pay tuition even at reduced rates, let alone find the time to study.

After speaking with several nurses and doctors, Zaíra decided to switch from a bachelor of science in nursing (BSN) program into an associate's program. She felt confident that she had acquired the necessary connections to ensure continued career growth. Zaíra was exhausted from attending school while working full-time, plus overtime, but she was grateful for the opportunity to move forward in her life honestly and independently. Thus, even as Zaíra in some senses found herself taking a step backward, from the BSN program to the associate's program, she ultimately knew that she was on a career path that she could not have accessed prior to DACA. She was excited for the future.

Liminal Legality beyond DACA

Because of its limitations and temporary nature, DACA illustrated what migration scholar Cecilia Menjívar (2006) has described as "liminal legality." Previous research has repeatedly shown that immigrants with liminal legality confront many of the same uncertainty and barriers to upward mobility as their undocumented immigrant peers, even as they have more security and protection from deportation (Abrego and Lakhani 2015; Cebulko 2013, 2014; Menjívar 2006; Menjívar and Abrego 2012). Not quite incorporated, but not entirely excluded, the youth who received DACA inched toward upward mobility as best they could, given the obstacles in their way. Because the president announced DACA to a national audience and opened up the program to hundreds of thousands of beneficiaries at the same time, administrators and officials became more familiar with this liminally legal status. Immigrants with TPS, a lesser-known type of liminal legality, however, struggled to differentiate themselves from both undocumented immigrants and DACA recipients as they navigated various institutions where they were required to provide official documentation. Because most of the administrators and staffers at colleges and in DMV offices in North Carolina had relatively little experience with liminally legal immigrants, they were often unsure of how to address them. When the NCCCS banned undocumented students in 2008, for example, Patricia, an immigrant from Honduras with TPS, witnessed firsthand how her liminally legal status obstructed her pathway to college even when it should not have.

Patricia moved to the United States when she was seven. Hondurans were first granted TPS after Hurricane Mitch devastated the country in 1998, and Patricia and her family were among the estimated sixty-four thousand Honduran beneficiaries of the federal program (Messick and Bergeron 2014). Because of her TPS status, Patricia was able to fly to the United States in an airplane, which she directly compared to her friends' journeys "in a car or walking and suffering a lot." She labeled her airplane journey "a privilege" and felt that her status gave a security and protection not extended to her unauthorized immigrant classmates.

Patricia knew about the struggles her undocumented friends faced, but she never imagined that she would confront the same problems. Because she had TPS, she assumed she would have the same access to college as her citizen peers. She viewed high school as preparation for college, and she felt confident that she would be admitted into one of her top choices. A couple of weeks after graduation, we met up for an interview. Sitting on the bleachers behind the school, Patricia reflected nostalgically on the optimism she had felt earlier in high school:

> Well, when I was in junior year, I was so happy, and I thought that it was going to work. I thought that I was going to get accepted because my grades were perfect. Not the best, but they were good enough for college. And I had done most of my homework. I had applied on time. I had done my SATs. They were on a good grade level. So then came senior year, and that's when I started applying to almost every single college I could think of except community because I never thought of community college as my option.

The one option Patricia never considered soon became her only hope for higher education. After working so hard in high school, Patricia was blindsided by unanticipated barriers obstructing her entrance into college. She explained how deflated she felt on learning that her protected immigration status did little to ease her entrance into college:

> One of my counselors asked me, what was my status, and I told them about TPS, and they were like, "I don't know what that is." And they were like, "You're considered undocumented here, so I don't think you'll be eligible for in-state tuition. So I guess you must look for something smaller if you can't afford it, unless you look for scholarships." . . . So for [colleges], I was still considered undocumented because I didn't have a visa or residence card, or I was not even a citizen. So it was a useless time and effort for me to do everything. Even SATs, AP exams, and getting in extracurricular activities, and all that stuff. It was all useless.

This was the first time that anyone had ever told Patricia that she was undocumented, but it was not the last. Patricia was not undocumented; she had a visa that allowed her to reside and work in the United States. Because the college counselor had more experience dealing with undocumented students, she used the more familiar title to describe Patricia's status. Not wanting to believe her counselor, Patricia continued to apply to colleges just as she planned. She explained her thought process and her subsequent disappointment:

So I'm like, I'll go ahead and still apply for big schools, you know, and I'll apply for scholarships. But then I saw that everything was closing. All the doors that I tried to apply and open, they were closing on me in my face. And I was like, I don't know what I'm gonna do after this. Because I can't apply for scholarships, and I can't apply for a good college that I want, because I'm undocumented and if they do accept me, it's going to be with out-of-state tuition and that's a lot of money. It's more than, probably, what my mom makes in a year. And I don't know how I'm going to pay this. So that's when my faith started fading, pretty much. When I started thinking what am I going to do with my life? My dream has been to go to college and become a doctor or a nurse and help people and be somebody in this life, and now it's just gone. What am I going to do? Am I going to be stuck working in a poultry factory? I don't know. It's just terrible.

Patricia had a very hard time accepting the limitations of her liminally legal status. Her initial instinct was to ignore her college counselor, but she eventually came to terms with her situation. Even when Patricia received her letters of acceptance, she knew that she would not be able to follow her dreams of attending college. Patricia's mother worked in a nearby chicken-processing plant, and her salary was not nearly enough to cover out-of-state tuition at a four-year university.

Patricia began to adopt an undocumented identity that was inconsistent with her previous understanding of her position in the United States. She felt extremely frustrated as she struggled against barriers that seemed to emerge at every turn. Because she could not apply for public financial aid or scholarships, Patricia turned her sights toward community college programs in nursing. She never imagined that the NCCCS ban would apply to her, so she was shocked when the admissions officer at Greenfield Community College told her she was ineligible to apply. When she cried to her parents and teachers about her disappointment, her soccer coach sprang into action to advocate on her behalf. She went with her soccer coach and her father to the admissions office to dispute the decision. She described the visit:

I wanted my dad to be there for him to see that I wanted to become somebody, because he had lost faith in me too. He thought that I was just joking around and that I wasn't doing anything to go to college. And I wanted to show him that it's not me. It's other people closing the doors on me and that I'm trying my best to get in. And so I just took him, and when we went there, coach asked for the college admissions officer. So she was there, and the first thing she told me was the same thing that they had told me a couple of weeks ago—that I had sent my Social Security card and it said for employment use only and that I was not eligible, and that she could get in trouble or get fined if she accepted me because I was supposedly undocumented or "illegal." So then coach was like, it's not true. He said that I was really documented and that I was legally here and that I had the right to go to college and be considered as in-state tuition. And so she sent me to the dean, and there is where we talked and we told her my story. We explained to her what TPS was, and we told her that attorneys and even the person who really is in charge of the community colleges told us that we could have a chance to be there and pay in-state tuition. And she said that she was going to find out about it, and she was going to give me a call, and she was more concerned about my in-state tuition stuff than me being accepted, which means that I have more possibilities to be in there, maybe pay out-of-state, but at least be in it, and that's all I wanted, I guess.

Eventually Patricia got into Greenfield Community College, and with the help of a lawyer, she was able to pay in-state tuition. The costs of attendance were still expensive for Patricia's family, which relied solely on her mother's income after Patricia's father lost his job as a truck driver when his license expired and he could not renew it. Patricia's boyfriend paid the majority of her tuition, and Patricia worked at a local elder-care facility to help when she could. After her first semester, Patricia had to argue her case all over again. Though she succeeded a second time, the constant battle to prove her legitimacy as an authorized resident of North Carolina exhausted Patricia.

Patricia completed her first year of school, but money became tighter when her boyfriend's construction work decreased during the recession. Instead of enrolling in her second year of school and arguing her case for in-state tuition yet again, she worked more hours to build her savings. Her parents were disappointed with her choice and with her decision to marry her boyfriend later that year. They feared her marriage marked the end of her educational ambitions. Indeed, Patricia took a longer break from school after she had a child, but she was determined to complete her education even if it took longer than she initially anticipated.

Patricia eventually found work at a nearby assisted-living facility catering to a wealthier clientele. She appreciated the cleanliness of the facility and the friendliness of her new coworkers. She also enjoyed speaking with the residents of the facility and hearing about their lives. She told me that she met doctors and professors and other people who "inspire me to go back to school and get an education, so I can have a story to tell." She was lucky that her new place of employment sponsored scholarships for its employees. Patricia took advantage of the scholarship program, paid for by the residents of the facility as well as private donors. She enrolled in a community college and earned a certification as a medical technologist, followed by a certification as a licensed practical nurse (LPN). Her new credentials augmented her opportunities and responsibilities and set her on a path toward upward mobility. When I checked back in with her in 2015, she was taking community college classes toward the completion of her nursing degree. After two additional semesters, she would qualify to take the test to become a registered nurse (RN), and she hoped to continue to a BSN on completion of her RN course. Ultimately, her goal was to work as a nurse practitioner in oncology at a hospital, but she knew she had at least ten years ahead of her before that dream would be realized. Still, she remained determined.

With a three-year-old and a new baby, Patricia was also busier than she had ever been. When I pulled up to her home in 2015, I was grateful to find her with a free moment. She opened the door, wearing a knee brace and ready to give me a big hug. Taking multitasking to new heights, she had used her maternity leave to have surgery on an old soccer injury. She mentioned that she was sleep deprived between the recovery, the new baby, and her now three-year-old son, but she was in good spirits. I was struck by how much more mature she appeared than the last time I had seen her just two years ago. When two neighborhood girls stopped by from a neighboring trailer to borrow a movie, she chatted with them about high school and their teachers, whom she of course knew well. Again, I marveled as I recalled talking with Patricia when she was in their shoes years earlier. Looking at Patricia and her younger neighbors, I thought back to how far she had come in achieving the goals she had set for herself in school, in spite of all of the obstacles in her way and the major life changes she had experienced. At times, she admitted, she felt that she took on too much and feared that the stress and sleep deprivation put her health at risk. But she was thankful that she could share child-care responsibilities with her husband, and he paid most of the household bills so that she could pay for her school supplies and costs not covered by scholarship funds.

Although Patricia's path meandered more than she initially hoped, she could envision a way forward. The community college admissions officers initially identified her as "undocumented," but she was not undocumented, and her TPS status gave her options not afforded to her peers. Nonetheless, like DACA, Patricia's liminally legal TPS status did not give the security or access of citizenship. Three years later, when her younger brother Dario was applying to college, he faced the same struggles that she had. In fact, Dario ended up paying three years of out-of-state tuition before finally arguing successfully that he should qualify for in-state tuition in his fourth and final year of college. In the first three years, the administration told him that he did not qualify, and he accepted their response, not wanting to draw too much attention to his status. Luckily for him, he had a private scholarship that funded all four years of his education.

Dario majored in social work and, after college graduation, began a job as a school social worker, serving elementary, middle, and high schools in Allen County. He utilized his bilingual and bicultural skills to connect with youth and their parents. He knew that his language skills and familiarity with the region and its Latino population helped him obtain his job and set him on a path toward career advancement. After one very successful year out of college, Dario learned that he had received a full scholarship to pursue a master's in social work program at one of the state's premier universities. Dario was grateful that he could apply his undergraduate education to his career after school and give back to the community where he had grown up. His job could thus be viewed as a direct return on the investment from his privately funded undergraduate education. But had the college granted Dario in-state tuition initially, it's possible that the money that went to fund Dario's education could have gone to help students like Karla and Dalia, whose funding fell short in their second year of college. With such limited private scholarship funds, only a lucky few were able to access them to work toward upwardly mobile and fulfilling careers.

And even as both Patricia and Dario leveraged their TPS status to acquire work in stable and fulfilling careers with room for growth, their struggles with their immigration status continued to follow them even after they had both finally secured in-state tuition. They knew that very few people in the state had heard about TPS, and they knew that their Honduran heritage and immigration history made them vulnerable to inquiries about their legality. Particularly as state policies became increasingly hostile to unauthorized immigrants, they were forced to repeatedly negotiate their own authorized status when they navigated work, school, and other official business.

Because Patricia needed to renew her TPS visa every eighteen months, her visits to the DMV came just as frequently. Though she typically did not feel subject to racism in her daily life, she made a strong exception when discussing the DMV in Allen Creek. She described the tiresome routines that she endured every time she went to renew her license:

Every single time it's a different excuse they give me. The first time they said my papers were fake, so they threw my papers at me on the desk and told me to go somewhere else. And they told me to be careful because I would could get in trouble. So then I went to [a neighboring town] where they're much nicer. The second year I thought, "Why should I have to drive all this way to go to the DMV when there's a DMV five minutes away?" So I went again to Allen Creek, and it was about a week before my card expired and my license expired. And the guy told me, he threw my papers again, and said, "This card hasn't expired, so you can't renew your license. You have to come after it expires." And I asked, "You want me to drive without my driver's license?" And he said, "Well, I guess." And my license was going to expire on the weekend as well, and so he said, "I guess you have to be careful when you drive here next week." So that same day I went again to [the next town over] and got it without waiting. And then another year, I forget what excuse they gave me, but it frustrates me how they treat us. That's the only place that I can see a little bit of racism.

For Patricia, going to the DMV was humiliating. The agents were not familiar with TPS and thus accused her of having falsified documents. Even when they accepted that the documents were legitimate, she still struggled to have an unremarkable interaction with the DMV workers in Allen Creek. Although she had better luck in the neighboring town, she resented having to drive forty minutes to the DMV when the local DMV was only five minutes from her home.

When DACA beneficiaries were granted access to driver's licenses, matters became even more complicated for Patricia and her family. Unlike DACA licenses, which were marked with the phrase "NO LAWFUL STATUS," licenses for immigrants with TPS were unmarked, in spite of both categories of immigrants holding limited-term permits to reside in the country. Because DACA was a much more high-profile program with far more beneficiaries in North Carolina, however, DMV agents got the two programs confused. Thus, when Patricia's mother went to renew her license, she received a DACA license with the red-lettered markings, incorrectly labeling her as having no lawful status. She called Patricia to tell her that they had changed the license format, and Patricia warned her to return to the DMV to change her license. Not wanting to endure the hassle, however, her mother kept the license. When she was pulled over, the police officer asked to see her immigration documentation, and then admonished her for the inconsistency in her paperwork. She felt intimidated by the interaction and went to replace her license shortly thereafter.

Even at work and school, the frequent renewal process for TPS occasionally caused problems for Patricia and her family members. Patricia described how difficult it was for her to maintain her in-state tuition status each time her TPS lapsed: "It's always a struggle. When I was at [my last] community college, my paperwork was due right in the middle of the semester. When it was time for us to renew, they sent me a letter and said that I was no longer going to be considered in the program because I was going to become, well, my card was going to expire. So I had to show them that I had a six-month extension and have another conversation and basically go through the whole thing again." Patricia had the same issue at work but explained that she was lucky that her place of employment was so understanding. She could show them that she had a six-month extension on the website and keep her job. Her mother, however, worked in far less accommodating conditions at an electronics factory in a city about thirty minutes from her home. When her card expired, she was temporarily let go. Once she received her new TPS card, the company hired her back. Nonetheless, she could not make up the lost wages for the weeks that she was not working.

Common to all of these stories are the inconsistencies that Patricia and her family members faced when dealing with people in administrative positions. Their own access to school, work, and licenses seemed to depend not only on their immigration status but also on the individuals in charge of granting them access to particular resources. Although TPS was not well known, the implementation of DACA increased familiarity with varied immigration statuses among administrators at schools, places of employment, and DMVs throughout the state. Nonetheless, DACA seemed to complicate understandings of TPS at least as much as it helped clarify that immigrants fell into categories that stretched beyond the binary classifications of undocumented versus legal permanent resident.

Inching toward Membership and Mobility through DACA and TPS

For youth who managed to obtain college educations and job training, both DACA and TPS were hugely influential in advancing their career potential and increasing their feelings of accomplishment and security. Yet this forward momentum was often slow and interrupted. For youth who were further along in their college careers, like Eduardo, DACA was especially influential in propelling them toward meaningful and upwardly mobile careers. The work authorization provided through DACA allowed Eduardo to land his dream job, in which he directly applied his computer-assisted design and engineering training from college to his work. He, and his skills, were highly valued by his employer and coworkers, and he finally felt the independence and job satisfaction he had desired for so many years.

Prior to DACA, Eduardo was anxious about graduating from college, as he knew it would signal a movement toward exclusion. He was terrified that he would never be able to apply his education to his work or reap the benefits of his hard work in college. Because his progress through college was hampered by the costs of out-of-state tuition, Eduardo's slow path through college at times made him feel as though he were stalling his entrance into adulthood. He yearned for independence, and he could not help comparing himself to his citizen friends who had already transitioned from college into jobs that remained far out of reach for him. Once he received his work permit through DACA, Eduardo finally made the same leap that his friends had made years before he had. Although he had not, at the time of writing, completed his college degree, he knew that his college credits were not going anywhere. For the time being, he relished living as an independent adult with a full-time, highly skilled job.

At a different life stage, Zaíra saw the work permit garnered through DACA as the motivation she needed to work her way back into school. Without a work permit, she knew that she could not take the exams granting nursing certifications at any level. As a result, she saw no reason to enroll in expensive classes if she could not apply her degree to a meaningful career in the future. Once DACA was put into place, however, she immediately set to work building a pathway back to college. Although it took her a couple of years, she finally got a job in the health industry and began taking classes. She ultimately transferred out of her BSN track to pursue a more affordable associate's degree, but she maintained her ambition to return to the BSN program after two years. Because her goal of becoming a nurse practitioner was directly tied to educational credentials, she could not make the same transition to work that Eduardo had without a college degree. Although she knew that her education would take her far longer to complete than it would for many of her citizen peers, she was proud of her ambition, and she was determined to utilize DACA to build the future of her dreams.

Conclusion

While DACA and TPS helped move beneficiaries of the programs toward incorporation, the youth continued to feel excluded from full membership as they struggled against bureaucratic barriers and gatekeepers who lacked clear understanding of their liminal status. Previous research into liminally legal immigrants has demonstrated that categories of legality stretch beyond the legal-illegal binary through which they are frequently characterized (Menjívar 2006). Kara Cebulko's (2013, 2014) research with liminally legal young Brazilian adults in Massachusetts, for example, illustrates that categories of legality are both hierarchical and fuzzy. She explains that individuals in one category of legality may be at risk of losing their temporary authorization and therefore falling into a less secure undocumented status, lacking work permits and access to driver's licenses. Even within liminally legal categories, differential access to resources revealed gradations in membership between DACA beneficiaries and immigrants with TPS.

Patricia and Dario's experiences as TPS immigrants highlight that DACA, with its differentiated license and out-of-state tuition, maintained barriers for advancement in ways that TPS did not. While TPS beneficiaries had greater access to membership, both they and DACA beneficiaries continued to struggle to differentiate themselves from unauthorized immigrants when navigating the DMV, educational institutions, and the workplace. In other words, although they benefited, to different degrees, from their liminally legal status, they nonetheless had to fight for recognition outside the legal-illegal binary that was more familiar to many in the position of administering resources and benefits. As a result, immigrants with a liminally legal status other than DACA found themselves struggling to access resources and benefits that should have been available to them. While DACA opened doors previously closed to unauthorized immigrants, it complicated matters even further for immigrants with TPS who were often mistakenly grouped in with DACA beneficiaries. Consequently, liminally legal youth, with both DACA and TPS, frequently had to battle against misinformation and bigotry to obtain resources and benefits to which they were entitled.

Regardless of the limitations of TPS and DACA, these liminally legal statuses had big impacts on feelings of belonging and personal accomplishment. Even in the hostile state context of North Carolina, driver's licenses and work permits allowed youth with TPS and DACA status to untether themselves from their parents and provided a glimpse at a pathway to incorporation. DACA beneficiaries were finally able to work openly and honestly, paying into Social Security under their own names. Moreover, they obtained a sense of independence and earned a living doing jobs that they felt proud of. Though DACA and TPS were both imperfect and impermanent solutions, the emotional and material gains that came as a result of acquiring upwardly mobile jobs were notable.

Liminally legal young adults knew that they would continue to face obstacles, but they were hopeful that they would be able to build on the advances they made as a result of DACA and TPS. DACA recipients especially described significant life changes once they gained sufficient academic credentials to access upwardly mobile career paths.

6 Inclusion through Activism

Though DACA was not a cure-all, youth who were granted DACA status celebrated the policy as a step toward inclusion. They saw the policy as a reward for their efforts in school and at work, and, for some, their activism. Though DACA did not grant youth activists everything they asked for, it provided a public acknowledgment that unauthorized immigrant youth were at least partial members of the US population. The new policy also demonstrated that the immigrants' rights youth movement had grown very powerful in a short period of time. Indeed, when President Obama announced DACA, he borrowed language from activists, clearly acknowledging that he had heard their message. He claimed that DACA-eligible youth were "Americans . . . in every single way but one: on paper." Knowing that this claim would highlight the injustice of their situation, youth activists had strategically crafted this message to garner sympathy and political support.

Youth activists revolutionized the immigrants' rights movements, as many came out of the shadows, proudly proclaiming their undocumented status and leveraging their vulnerability as a human rights argument for inclusion in the country they knew best. They were dedicated, passionate, institutionally connected, and media savvy, and they formed a powerful political force. Unauthorized youth activists relied on their peers, whom they met though well-organized campaigns and on social media, to form supportive communities of resistance. For those who took part in the movement, it offered a space of belonging and a sense of comfort in being able to take ownership over their undocumented identities.

The undocumented youth movement followed a long tradition of social movements that galvanized participants based on their shared struggles and identities. Previous research demonstrates that social movements effectively utilize collective identities to mobilize individuals and to redefine the cultural meaning of these identities (Polletta and Jasper 2001). Accordingly, the immigrants' rights movements relied on undocumented youths' shared identities and experiences to unite and mobilize this community and transform the label "illegal." Highlighting their innocence, aspirations, and allegiance to their country of residence, DREAMers were careful to craft an activist strategy that appealed to the sympathies and logic of American voters. They announced their undocumented status to erase the stigma from the term and to garner support. By highlighting their ambition and social position as students and young people, they targeted a "niche opening," or strategic angle, in the political climate (Coutin 1998; Nicholls 2013). They used this niche opening to garner recognition and compassion, and they were immensely successful. The movement, however, did not appeal to all undocumented immigrant youth.

While youth activists leveraged their undocumented status as a means to inclusion, their less involved or apolitical peers could not use the same tactics to find a sense of membership among their peers in school or at work. Additionally, some undocumented youth felt alienated by the movement. These youth were unwilling to embrace a public undocumented identity consistent with the activists' message. For example, undocumented youth in Allen Creek who did not view themselves as model students or leaders did not necessarily see a place for themselves within the movement. After years of witnessing government inaction, some also saw the movement as futile. In contrast to youth activists who proudly and loudly claimed their undocumented identities to gain a sense of belonging, other youth continued to feel excluded from the country and the movement.

Activism as a Means to Inclusion

Youth leaders in the immigrants' rights movement gained visibility during marches that took place in cities throughout the United States in 2006. These demonstrations were a response to the proposed Border Protection, Antiterrorism, and Illegal Immigration Control Act of 2005, which included a measure that would have redefined misdemeanor illegal entry into the United States as a felony. The bill ultimately failed to pass in the Senate, but the threat of further criminalization mobilized hundreds of thousands to come out in support of the approximately eleven million undocumented immigrants who were at risk of being pushed further into the margins of society.

During the 2006 demonstrations, large numbers of undocumented immigrants began to announce themselves as contributing members of society and participants in the polity. Youth and young adults stepped forward as leaders within the immigrants' rights movement, spearheading the DREAMer movement (Bada et al. 2010; Gonzales 2008; Nicholls 2013). Utilizing tactics from past successful social movements and human rights campaigns, they held mock college classes and graduations, occupied senators' offices, marched to Washington, and went on hunger strikes as they campaigned vociferously for their own inclusion. By embracing a collective identity as undocumented Americans, they were better able to recruit others who shared the same life experiences and confronted the same obstacles. They thus found a sense of community that helped propel the DREAMer movement forward.

The immigrants' rights movement of the early 2000s differed from previous movements that stressed legal precedents and contexts. For example, previous movements challenged the language of illegality, choosing instead to highlight more sympathetic labels like "refugees" or "asylum seekers" (Coutin 2005). Stop-gap policies that opened up areas of protection for certain migrant groups, such as refugees or TPS migrants, offered alternative labels to subgroups of liminally legal immigrants. Policies in more welcoming states such as California also facilitated alternative labels for undocumented youth in those states. After undocumented students in California gained access to in-state college tuition through Assembly Bill 540 in 2001, they were able to identify publicly as "AB 540 students" rather than the more stigmatized identity of undocumented or illegal immigrants (Abrego 2008). Though some researchers suggest that similar transformative labels such as "DACAmented" are now available to youth with DACA status (Gonzales, Terriquez, and Ruszczyk 2014), the DREAMer movement may have removed some of the stigma from the "undocumented" label by allowing youth to boldly assert their undocumented identities, particularly in locales where institutional or legislative policies offer them some degree of protection.

For some undocumented immigrant youth, activist movements themselves became spaces of inclusion and belonging. Embracing strategies from the lesbian, gay, bisexual, transgender, queer (LGBTQ) rights movement, unauthorized immigrant activists proudly announced their undocumented immigration status and demanded respect as fellow humans and members of the polity (Nicholls 2013; Seif 2014; Terriquez 2015; White 2014). Indeed, many of the leaders of the DREAM movement identified as gay, lesbian, bisexual, transgender, and/or queer, and they formed intersectional identities as "undocuqueer" individuals who were "out" about both their immigration status and their sexual orientation (Nicholls 2013; Seif 2014; Terriquez 2015). Though the DREAM movement was not generally seen as an LGBTQ rights movement, the strategy of "coming out" emboldened the immigrants' rights movement by tying its demands to a broader human rights narrative. Powerfully capturing the message of the undocuqueer movement, artist Julio Salgado (2012) created an undocuqueer series of portraits in which he depicted unauthorized youth alongside quotations of self-acceptance, pride, and empowerment. In his self-portrait, he paints himself wearing a badge stating "undocumented and unafraid" next to a quotation that reads, "I am undocuqueer. I don't choose my identities. But I choose to use my identities to empower myself." Like Salgado, the youth involved in the immigrants' rights movement appropriated the "outsider" label imposed on them as a means to empowerment and membership (Nicholls 2013; Vargas 2012). They announced their presence loudly, provided each other with a community of mutual support, and demanded rights.

Highlighting their innocence, ambitions, and allegiance to their country of residence, DREAMers tried to craft a collective identity that redefined unauthorized immigrants from criminals to hardworking, ambitious students. To persuade Washington policy makers to recognize their plight and authorize their presence, DREAMers pointed to their achievements in school and their contributions to their communities, purposefully demonstrating assimilation and highlighting their American identities (Nicholls 2013). As English-speaking, US-educated youth who had been brought to the United States by their parents, the DREAMers were in a unique position to garner widespread sympathy.

As the DREAM movement gained momentum, publicity surrounding DREAMers became increasingly high profile. The June 25, 2012, cover of *Time* magazine showed the faces of about thirty young undocumented immigrants along with undocumented journalist Jose Antonio Vargas. They all stood proudly under a bold headline stating, "WE ARE AMERICANS.*" The asterisk directed the readers' attention to the bottom of the cover where subtler lettering read, "Just not legally." Within the magazine, the article highlighted DREAMers who came out publicly, refusing the isolation of a life in the shadows. The DREAMers in the article aspired to careers as social workers, doctors, tattoo artists, and dancers. They were a diverse group, but they were all engaged and motivated. The article used names, faces, and stories to personalize the DREAMers' shared plight and to argue that this group of individuals was deserving of naturalization. The final line of the article asked the reader, "When will you realize that we are one of you?"

The strong social networks of DREAMers allowed these youth to feel safe and empowered coming out of the shadows. But not all youth could identify with the DREAMer narrative, and many were uninterested in joining the movement. Coming out was harder for undocumented youth who did not fit neatly into the rhetoric of achievement. Some undocumented youth who were unengaged in school or who had trouble with the law did not see themselves reflected in the DREAMer movement. Unauthorized immigrant youth who did not have impressive academic credentials were as "American" as their DREAMer peers, yet these young people were not used as the face of the immigrants' rights youth movement. Indeed, even within the movement, some youth felt alienated by the DREAMer narrative and criticized it for distinguishing between deserving, college-bound youth and their less-deserving parents or peers who lacked educational access (Nicholls and Fiorito 2015; J. Perez 2014). Many undocumented youth who were not activists found themselves frustrated by the sense that they could not live up to the "perfect DREAMer" narrative. Not only did they feel alienated from their country of residence; they also felt excluded from the movement that was supposed to fight for their membership (Lauby 2016). Attachment to the collective "undocumented American" identity was most accessible to youth who fit the "perfect DREAMer" narrative.

Asserting Membership through Activism

Like adolescents throughout the United States, few teenagers and young adults in Allen Creek were politically active, and few youth that I interviewed recognized the DREAM Act by name. Some Latino youth who were involved with the town's Latino Outreach Center's youth group, however, became involved in activism under the mentorship of the center's Latino administrators. These youth vigorously campaigned for immigrants' rights, and youth incorporation in particular. They rejected their classification as outsiders and nonmembers and argued that their participation in their school and community was evidence of their attachment to the United States and their de facto membership in the nation.

Gabriela, an undocumented Mexican immigrant who arrived in the United States at age three, joined the immigrants' rights movement and came out publicly as an undocumented immigrant during a 2006 immigrants' rights march when she was sixteen years old.

Gabriela remembered the Allen Creek immigrants' rights march on May 1, 2006, as a pivotal life event:

I was the one in charge of getting the students out of high school to march all the way to the Latino Outreach Center to meet there. And so with the help of the principal we did that. . . . Our mission was to make the people get the idea of passing the DREAM Act because that has to do with us. So we had to go up there and say something. [The leaders of the Latino Outreach Center] told me that my dad was out there, and he was so proud, and I was like, "Whoa, my dad?!" And they were like, "Yeah. We could just see it in his face. . . . " I just got up there, and I think it was the coolest day. There was a whole bunch of people, and everybody was looking at you and listening. I thought it was so cool. And then we saw the Ku Klux Klan over there in the corner [laughs], and I was like, "Whoa, are they gonna kill all of us right now, hang us?" But I think it was a good experience. It didn't work, right, because then they started doing the, checking for licenses and everything, so I think it was a bad idea.

Gabriela recalled the immigrants' rights march with nostalgia and pride, but also regret. The march symbolized her emergence as a leader in the community, among her peers and even within her own family. But Gabriela also felt that her activism hurt the immigrant community. She noted the Klan presence at the rally, and she also noted heightened police targeting of immigrants after the march. She believed that the national demonstrations of 2006 contributed to the increased scrutiny of immigrants in her community and throughout North Carolina.

She felt guilty about participating in the demonstrations: "If we wouldn't have ever done that much of a big deal about it, things would have been different. Now, families are getting separated, people are getting deported. . . . We're at risk, you know? At first I was like, yeah it's gonna be good, it's gonna be good, but then now that I think about it, I'm like no, we shouldn't have done that."

Gabriela believed that the immigrants' rights demonstrations had backfired, and she became discouraged. She withdrew from activism and shied away from the spotlight after graduating from high school in 2008. At seventeen years old, she moved in with her boyfriend, much to the disappointment of her parents. She stopped participating in the Latino Outreach Center youth group, and she gave up a four-year scholarship to a private university. She had a difficult time imagining how she could go from living with her boyfriend to living in a college dormitory, and she knew her immigration status would constrain her job opportunities after college. She struggled with her decision, acutely aware of what she was giving up, but she ultimately chose to work and focus on her relationship rather than go away to college. Instead of participating in the national activist movement, she watched from the sidelines as other DREAMers took center stage in the immigrants' rights movement in 2010.

Since the marches of 2006, DREAMers have continued to build support. They hoped that their efforts would finally be rewarded when the House passed the DREAM Act in 2010. When it went up for a vote in the Senate in December 2010, however, they were forced to face crushing disappointment again. Although the vote was 55–41 in favor of the bill, the bill required sixty senators to vote in favor of the measure for it to advance. North Carolina senator Kay Hagan was one of only five Democratic senators to vote against the bill. In a political climate where even Democratic North Carolina legislators were voting against efforts to open up opportunities for immigrant youth, it was no wonder that Gabriela felt discouraged.

Though Gabriela stepped away from her leadership positions and activism, other Latinos in the community emerged as leaders within and beyond the community of Allen Creek. Mariano, an undocumented immigrant from Guatemala, was also part of the Latino Outreach Center youth group. Two years younger than Gabriela, Mariano was not initially attracted to leadership. He was soft-spoken and shy but eager to participate in activities through the Latino Outreach Center, his church, and school.

Mariano first became involved in activism through his participation in the Latino Outreach Center. Bridging his activism and academic pursuits, he decided to do his high school senior project on the proposed DREAM Act. A teacher contacted a former county commissioner to act as his external (non-school) mentor, and he then connected him to the county's Democratic Society. Mariano delivered a polished presentation about the DREAM Act at one of the society's meetings, personalizing the proposed bill by telling them about a friend who would benefit from the act. He recounted his presentation:

> I explained that my friend did really well in high school and that a lot of the kids that would benefit have really good grades, and some won't be able to go to college because of their immigration status, and it's not fair. Well, that's my opinion, that it's not fair to keep some very talented students from contributing to society just because they don't have proper documentation. I told them that they should support the DREAM Act because one of the things that this country is known for is human rights, but how can we be known for that if we don't do that in our own country?

The Democratic Society members were very encouraging of Mariano, and he felt energized after the presentation. He also felt empowered to use his voice and, eventually, his own story to advocate for himself and his peers.

Activism was healing for Mariano. During Mariano's first year of high school, he made the near-impossible decision to remain in the United States instead of choosing to return to Guatemala with his parents. Mariano's father had received an order of deportation in the 1990s, but he was not a priority for removal. As state-level enforcement increased, however, he became nervous that ICE would track him down and did not want to suffer the indignity of deportation. Leaving was not easy, however. Mariano's father had an accident while working a construction job, and he sustained debilitating injuries. He had a lot of complications and felt that the doctors whom he saw did not treat him with respect. He endured chronic pain and at times feared the worst. He wanted to see his parents, his other children, and his homeland before he died, so he decided to return to Guatemala. Mariano talked about how his father made the decision to return to Guatemala: "He was scared that [ICE] might come knocking at our house. And he really didn't want that. He'd prefer that he go himself than people kick him out." Even though Mariano was heartbroken to see his parents leave, he understood their motivation for returning the way they did.

He was only fifteen years old when his parents left for Guatemala, and he was conflicted about his decision to remain in the United States without them:

> I mean, I really wanted to go back with them, because I didn't want to separate from my family and my little sister, but at the same time, I also wanted to continue studying here. One of the reasons I didn't want to go back was because I really didn't know the culture over there. I really don't have any memories of Guatemala. My mom really wanted me to go back, but I felt that I belonged here. And I felt that if I did go back, the things that I know here, I might not be able to apply back there. And whenever I asked my brothers if I should go back or not, they said that I probably shouldn't because there wouldn't be as many opportunities. . . . And also, back then, there was all this talk about the immigration reform around 2007, and I was very hopeful. Like, what if I leave and the next year, they're going to give everyone papers? I decided that I'd rather stay another year and maybe get the papers and go visit them. And that didn't happen, but I'm still here.

Mariano's decision to remain in the United States was motivated by a multitude of factors. He could scarcely remember Guatemala, and he was nervous about how he would adapt to his country of origin. He also thought that there were more opportunities in the United States than in Guatemala. Mariano's family was from a very small town where very few people were educated beyond the primary school level. He wanted to remain in the United States to continue studying. Finally, Mariano was just starting to learn about immigration reform, and due to his own connections to the topic, his interest in activism began to pique. He saw that his opportunities were potentially on the verge of expanding, and he was hopeful for the DREAM Act in 2007. Like the 2010 vote, however, the 2007 vote in the Senate had also failed to reach the required number of supporters to overcome a filibuster. Despite this disappointment, Mariano remained confident in his decision to stay, and he became increasingly involved in activism.

Separated from his parents, Mariano moved in with his older brother. But he never felt quite at home there. He was searching for a place to belong, and activism offered him the community that he yearned for. His talk about the DREAM Act during his senior year was his first major step toward a career in activism. Mariano's political involvement steadily grew after this initial entrée into lobbying local politicians. In 2009, he attended a meeting with Reform Immigration for America at a nearby high school and then traveled to Washington, D.C., with the group to lobby for the DREAM Act. Mariano was motivated by the power of the movement and the people he met.

When Mariano was admitted to a prestigious four-year university with a guaranteed four-year private scholarship, he decided to defer for a year to continue to lobby in Washington, D.C. He knew that he was lucky to have the scholarship, but he also saw that his best friends from high school faced limited opportunities after graduation. Mariano's friends had not excelled academically, and they were far less politically involved. He mentioned them by name as he explained why he decided to defer his scholarship. He felt he owed it to them to advocate on their behalf. He also knew that delaying his college career would guarantee him at least one more year of institutional connectedness before he was forced to confront the full impact of his own undocumented status. Finally, Mariano's involvement in the immigrants' rights movement gave him unique insights into the political process.

He knew that state-level political movements were constraining opportunities for immigrants, but he also saw support building for the DREAM Act in Washington, D.C. He highlighted the importance of timing when explaining his decision to lobby instead of beginning college: "It was during a time that I knew that immigration was going to be a hot topic and it was around the time that Arizona passed SB 1070 as well as the DREAM movement was starting to build momentum. So it was really exciting, and I knew that there was probably going to be a vote later that year." Just as Mariano's hope for the DREAM Act had encouraged him to remain in the United States in 2007, this same hope influenced his decision to defer college for one year. Moreover, political movements toward more restrictions at the state level indicated to him that the friction between hostile states and a powerful immigrants' rights movement would soon push definitive political action at the federal level. He wanted to have a say in the outcome.

In 2009, Mariano joined the United We Dream campaign. After some initial training, he moved to Washington, D.C., where he worked as an intern and lobbied Senator Kay Hagan nearly every Wednesday morning at 8:00 a.m. for a full year. Though she rarely gave him an audience, she and her staff began to recognize him. Mariano felt effective as a consistent presence in her office and as a part of a larger movement.

As Mariano immersed himself in immigration activism in Washington, he began to gain a national reputation as a youth leader in the movement and as a member of the undocuqueer movement. He wrote op-ed articles for national online publications and was featured in two high-profile popular press publications. Inspired by Jose Antonio Vargas, journalist and author of the groundbreaking *Time* magazine article, as well as other LGBTQ youth leaders whom he knew personally in the movement, Mariano felt empowered to come out as both undocumented and gay. He identified his sexual orientation as key to his activist identity. He told me, "Once I came out as undocumented, I realized that I was still hiding part of myself, and it was really important to me to be honest about all of who I was." Mariano's bond with his fellow activists and his identity as an undocumented immigrant empowered him to reveal his sexual orientation and specifically adopt this intersectional identity as central to his activism.

When I asked how he felt about all of the public attention he received, Mariano said that his connections to other activists made him feel protected even if revealing himself publicly made him vulnerable. He stated, "I think that if anything happened . . . I'd have a good network of people that would have my back." Mariano's connection to others in the social movement bolstered his resolve to continue his activism and helped him maintain a sense of agency over his life even as he faced crushing disappointments each time immigration reform failed to pass in Congress. Thinking back to when the DREAM Act failed again in 2010, he recalled his heartbreak but also the powerful feelings of connectedness to his fellow activists. He felt that the bond that he shared with his peers helped protect him from the pain of disappointment: "I remember when the vote was finally announced that it didn't pass, we all started crying in the gallery. And we all left and congregated in the main floor, and we made a huge circle and we had our arms around everyone. And we just started chanting, 'We are the DREAMers. The mighty mighty DREAMers.' And we were crying and chanting at the same time. And security told us that if we didn't stop, they were going to arrest all of us, but we kept on doing it and it was really powerful."

Mariano was the most politically active of all of the youth in this study, and between his activism and his enrollment in college on a guaranteed four-year private scholarship, he was also the most institutionally connected. He found a sense of belonging in a community where he was one of many other individuals who shared his status, his experience, and his passion. Mariano was thus able to claim his undocumented status loudly and proudly in ways that his peers who were less involved in the movement were not.

He was also able to celebrate DACA as a direct result of his own efforts. Yet the implementation of DACA revealed to him that he was not as secure in his out and proud undocumented identity as he had previously claimed. When he discussed the license that he would get after receiving DACA, he said,

> I think it's going to be really powerful. I mean, I do have a sense of an identity, but this is going to make it much more official. I think that it's going to make me, I'm going to actually have a face in terms of . . . [pauses] I don't know what I'm trying to say. I think it's just going to be really powerful to have an ID that says my name and says who I am and that I can use for basically anything. Obviously, if they were to reverse it, I know how to survive, but this just makes it so much more official.

Mariano felt that the license was both practically and symbolically important and that DACA would allow him to live an open and unshadowed life. DACA was an opportunity for Mariano to claim his identity publicly and have it officially recognized. It was what he and his activist peers had been fighting for over so many years, and it gave him a huge sense of relief. He knew, however, that the policy was tenuous. He had adapted to life as an undocumented immigrant and no longer saw papers as necessary for his survival. Yet the driver's license served as a powerful symbol of legitimacy and membership.

Alienated from Activism

Undocumented youth who moved from high school into work or college settings had less freedom to publicly proclaim an undocumented identity, as doing so could jeopardize their security and set them apart from their peers. Despite the high-profile momentum of DREAMer activism, most unauthorized immigrant youth were only peripherally aware of the movement. Furthermore, many unauthorized immigrants were embedded in school, work, or social environments where their peers were uninformed about the DREAMer movement and the obstacles facing unauthorized youth and DACA beneficiaries. Surrounded by peers who did not share an undocumented identity, they could not leverage their unauthorized status as a means to membership within their intimate social circles. They also had fewer opportunities to explore their binational identities or embrace their biculturalism as an asset.

Clearly drawing on his connections to activism, Mariano described his identity: "I definitely consider myself a part of two different countries, but I think, ultimately I realize, that I'm part of this. . . . It may sound cheesy, but I'm a global citizen." Borrowing language from his activist circles, Mariano emphasized his belonging not simply as an American but as a global citizen. Unlike Mariano, most unauthorized immigrant youth were unable to find membership in activism or global citizenship. In stark contrast to Mariano, Zaíra described her own national identity as "I'm nothing."

Zaíra admired the activist work of both Gabriela and Mariano while they were all in high school, but she had never participated in any immigrants' rights movements herself. She knew that joining a public activist movement could jeopardize her job. She thought that she would perhaps have been more involved in the movement had she gotten a scholarship and been able to enroll in college immediately after high school, but she was not that fortunate. Even after receiving temporary authorization through DACA, Zaíra was unable to fully shake the sting of her undocumented status. Because Zaíra primarily interacted with US citizens in both her work and social spheres, she could not claim membership as an undocumented immigrant, or even as "DACAmented." Unlike Mariano, who found himself surrounded by other unauthorized activists and therefore in the position of discussing his immigration background as part of his daily work routine, Zaíra's work environment did not offer her this opportunity.

Other youth simply did not see a place for themselves within the movement. When I asked Alonso if he ever did any activist work with his friend Mariano, he replied, "No, well, [Mariano] is really good at that because he did it in high school, and he did really well in high school. And now he's in college, so I don't really talk to him that much anymore. I never really did that stuff." Alonso would occasionally ask Mariano about how policy shifts would change his opportunities, but he never saw activism as a potential calling or space of belonging for himself. He did not have good grades in high school and never went to college. As the Latino Outreach Center youth group in Allen Creek was only for high school students, Alonso also lost that connection to activism once he graduated from high school. For Alonso, activism was reserved for youth like Mariano.

Similarly, Soraya, Zaíra's sister, who also did not excel academically in high school, said that she was reluctant to join clubs because, in her mind, clubs were reserved for people with good grades. She chose not to get involved in the DREAM movement because she did not envision herself going to college. From what little she knew about the DREAM Act, she thought it was a "good thing" since immigrants in her position "didn't do anything wrong," but she did not feel compelled to learn more. Gustavo, another undocumented immigrant from Mexico, had a similar response to Soraya's when I asked him about the DREAM Act. He said, "Isn't that for people with good grades?" For many youth, the DREAM Act was something only vaguely familiar and not applicable to them.

After high school, most unauthorized youth and DACA recipients in this study found themselves surrounded by documented or citizen peers who lacked an understanding of the policies and pressures surrounding the immigrant community in North Carolina. Youth who were engaged in activist circles had the most access to spaces of membership for undocumented immigrants. They could bond with other youth who faced the same obstacles and challenges as they did, and they could use their collective identities and experiences to advocate for their own rights. Thus, empowerment by appropriation of pejorative labels of illegality or by embracing an exclusionary status as a tool of resistance was most possible for youth who devoted themselves primarily to activism and were therefore surrounded by peers who understood their struggles. For youth whose parents expected them to work and contribute to household expenses after high school, and for youth who lacked the grades or connections to gain both admission and scholarships to college, activism was not a viable path to inclusion and membership. Unauthorized youth in college were also not necessarily inclined to join activist movements.

When I asked Eduardo about the DREAM movement in 2012, prior to the implementation of DACA, he voiced his frustration with the lack of government action but also with the activists rallying for the DREAM Act:

> I mean, those groups, you know on Facebook and stuff, or on the news, that say "Believe," you know, you see posters, and I was like, "Believe?" I mean, that thing has been going on for so long. Who are you supposed to believe in? I used to think like that, and believe, especially when Obama came in. And now, I just

focus on doing whatever I can do right now. The DREAM Act has been going on for so long, and it just gets your hopes up and then you get disappointed. I don't believe. I don't even pay attention to it, period. You know on Facebook when they say to call your representative, they're not going to listen to it. They're just going to hear some kid on the phone. It won't mean anything.

Disheartened by the government's delay in implementing immigration reform and disillusioned by the failure of the Obama administration to improve his opportunities, Eduardo had given up hope in the political process. He could not bring himself to pay attention to activist groups or to participate in a movement that he felt was a lost cause. Eduardo chose instead to focus on his school work and doing what he could to help his family. Even after DACA, he still worried that a new administration could reverse the decision. His frustration and mistrust of the system stayed with him, and sadly, his fears came to pass when the Trump administration rescinded DACA.

Like Eduardo, most unauthorized youth preferred to see themselves simply as students and residents trying to go through daily life like their peers and neighbors. They did not feel the need to proclaim an American identity or the desire to publicly proclaim their undocumented immigration status. They had grown tired of hoping for change, and they had lost faith in politicians who did little to improve their opportunities.

After the implementation of DACA, however, some youth felt emboldened to become more involved in the political process. After Dalia gained legal presence, she went with her father to a protest at the state capitol where she joined other demonstrators arguing that DACA beneficiaries deserved access to in-state tuition and driver's licenses. She was encouraged by DACA, and she felt secure enough to demand that her state representatives recognize her rights. Her efforts, however, were not rewarded, as the out-of-state tuition policy remained firmly in place. Dalia felt that DACA was a step in the right direction, but she still could not afford out-of-state tuition as a full-time student. She kept up with news about North Carolina immigration policies, but she did not engage in much activism after attending the protest. She chose instead to focus on working and saving money for community college where tuition was more affordable. Zaíra also attended a protest march after the inauguration of President Trump. Fearful that Trump would overturn DACA and furious at the anti-immigrant rhetoric of the Trump campaign, she felt compelled to do everything in her power to maintain her newfound security. Yet she continued to center the majority of her focus on work and school, and she did not primarily identify as an activist.

Conclusion

Only two of the undocumented study participants, Gabriela and Mariano, found a sense of belonging through activism. Viewing activist organizations as one tectonic plate among many layered contexts, activism offered involved youth a sense of belonging and empowerment even as hostility at the state and federal levels grew. In this pluralistic model of incorporation, youth could acknowledge the exclusionary forces within institutions and governments while simultaneously resisting these forces and creating their own spaces of belonging. Among their peers, they could resist the labels being placed on them as undeserving, illegal, and dangerous.

Though activism was a powerful agent of inclusion, of the youth in this study, only Mariano ultimately maintained an activist or organizer identity. Gabriela left the movement, in part for personal reasons, but also because she became frustrated by the lack of political action at the federal level and the backlash against immigration at the state level in North Carolina. Similarly, Dalia ended her brief flirtation with activism when she saw that the protest she attended failed to incite policy change. Thus, while activism could shelter youth from exclusionary landscapes, the protective benefits of activism often could not withstand the pressures of increasingly hostile social climates at the state and federal levels. Facing disappointment after disappointment some youth became disheartened and apolitical. The political backlash at the state level and the inaction at the federal level diminished the appeal of activism for many.

Most undocumented youth chose never to join the DREAM movement. Some did not feel comfortable as leaders or activists, and others did not see themselves represented in the DREAMer narrative. Though some unauthorized youth in this study fit the "perfect DREAMer" mold, many were frustrated by unresponsive or hostile politicians. Moreover, most were embedded in environments where they lacked ties to a substantial number of unauthorized peers, and they therefore struggled to attach to a collective undocumented identity.

The narrative emerging from the DREAMer movement did not necessarily reach work and school environments where unauthorized youth found themselves surrounded by documented or citizen coworkers and peers. Even after DACA, immigrant youth remained in environments where their peers had a limited understanding of the political obstacles they faced. In North Carolina, where most immigrant youth were unable to attend college due to the high costs of tuition, they were even less likely to be connected to politically active and engaged peer networks. Instead, they were more often surrounded by peers and coworkers with little knowledge of the pressures they confronted. Consequently, while identity-based social movements acted as a mechanism of inclusion for some, other youth who could plainly identify with the struggles identified by DREAMer activists were unable to find membership in the movement.

Conclusion

Instead of experiencing incorporation as a linear process moving gradually toward full membership or increasingly further into the margins, immigrant youth in Allen Creek, North Carolina, experienced varying levels of membership and exclusion within different institutional and political contexts simultaneously. Their experiences did not fit neatly into existing theories of "straight line" assimilation (Gans 1973, viii; Gordon 1964; Warner and Srole 1945) or even "segmented assimilation" (Portes and Zhou 1993; Portes and Rumbaut 2001; Rumbaut 2005). Much like an M. C. Escher staircase, leading both up and down in noncontiguous and disjointed pathways, the incorporation of immigrant youth in North Carolina was interruptive and confusing. As policies at the institutional, local, state and federal levels shifted past each other in opposite directions, immigrant youth were thrust off course as their plans collapsed around them, and they struggled to regain their footing.

At the federal level, DACA marked a key turning point in the lives of previously unauthorized immigrant youth, but the subsequent resistance at the state and local levels curtailed the benefits of DACA. After DACA, youth in North Carolina clearly saw the ways that the state stymied their opportunities for incorporation even as the federal government moved to expand their rights. Of course, the state response to DACA was not the first time that the political climate in the state had overtly labeled unauthorized immigrants as unwanted outsiders. The community college bans, the early statewide adoption of Secure Communities in 2011,[1] and the proliferation of 287(g) throughout various counties in North Carolina all preceded the state resistance to DACA and contributed to increasing feelings of exclusion among Latino youth.

The shifting policies forced immigrant youth in North Carolina to navigate their pathways into early adulthood while on very unstable footing. These overlapping contexts, depicted in the applied tectonic incorporation model shown in Figure C.1, destabilized youth, causing some individuals to backslide or lose their footing completely, while others moved precariously toward upward mobility. As illustrated in the model, unauthorized immigrant youth experienced movements toward incorporation and membership in some spheres of life while simultaneously getting propelled toward exclusion in others.

The uneven political landscapes at the local, state, and federal levels caused immigrant youth to experience a disjointed sense of membership. Although they felt strong attachments to their school, community, and even their home state, they also understood that they were unwanted by many. As the social and legislative climate in North Carolina became increasingly hostile to unauthorized immigrants, immigrant youth were forced to seek structures of support and spaces of belonging in either smaller social networks of friends and family or in larger national activist movements. Moreover, because of racialized ethnic discrimination, assumptions about immigration status and intimate connections to unauthorized immigrants, second-generation Latinos also faced exclusion in their home state in spite of their citizenship.

Membership Obstructed and Facilitated

Though immigration to North Carolina had slowed since the 1990s and early 2000s, Latinos in the state continued to be regarded as newcomers. Mounting anti-immigrant enforcement in the state targeted unauthorized immigrants, but citizen, liminally legal, and unauthorized Latinos all described heightened anxiety as a result of the hostile climate. With approximately 43 percent of the state's immigrant population made up of unauthorized immigrants in 2014, North Carolina had the second-highest percentage of unauthorized immigrants in the country (Pew Research Center 2016). As the vast majority of immigrants in North Carolina were Latino, Latinos throughout the state faced a widespread expectation of illegality, regardless of immigration status. And while Latinos in general feared racial profiling and harassment, unauthorized immigrants in the state were of course most limited due to restrictive policies and at greatest risk due to heightened local enforcement.

In Allen Creek, unauthorized immigrant youth could find spaces of membership in school and forge close relationships with their teachers. But as high school graduation approached, they began to doubt the benefits of their education. They knew that their opportunities would be very different from the

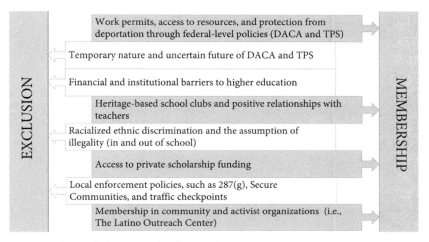

Figure C.1. Tectonic incorporation in practice.

opportunities of their documented peers, and they struggled to come to terms with the barriers obstructing their paths to college and the labor market. As anti-immigrant policies in the state and region increased, they became acutely aware of the hostile environments in which they were embedded.

Although the youth in this study increasingly felt like outsiders in the United States and in their home state of North Carolina, most could not imagine returning to a country they left behind so many years ago. Like Eduardo said, he had no connection to his native Mexico, and he could not envision himself going back there, but the political backlash in the state and country also prevented him from dreaming about a future in the United States. As unauthorized youth traversed the early stages of adulthood, they realized that they faced a dual exclusion from two nation-states: legally in one and socially in the other. In other words, undocumented immigrant youth experienced a sense of subtractive transnationalism as they inhabited a space in between two nations without full membership in either. However, unauthorized immigrants' sense of belonging changed over time, depending on the ways that policies shifted around them.

The vast majority of the youth that I interviewed expressed a deep appreciation for North Carolina. Indeed, as a transplant from the northeastern United States, I came to appreciate North Carolina far more once I began my research and started to see the state through their eyes. Though they complained about small-town boredom and gossip, they also spoke at length about how much they loved the trees, rivers, and landscapes surrounding them. They loved seeing animals and farmlands as they drove around, and they noted how different North Carolina was from the urban areas where many had lived before Allen Creek. Like Vicente noted, "I was used to hearing police cars at night, not hearing the crickets. I actually never heard a cricket before I moved to North Carolina. . . . I've grown to love North Carolina. . . . I've become very country." They appreciated the tranquility of their surroundings. Moreover, they enjoyed being part of a small, yet diverse community and feeling like their teachers truly cared about and watched over them. Though two returned to their countries of origin, and a few more moved to other states, most could not imagine leaving. For them, North Carolina was home. And while they were acutely aware of the mounting anti-immigrant legislation in the state, most felt reasonably comfortable while growing up and going to school in Allen Creek.

Because the 1982 Supreme Court Decision of *Plyler v. Doe* granted some protection to unauthorized immigrant children and youth in primary and secondary school, the lives of undocumented youth tended to be more secure at younger ages. Once youth transitioned into the early stages of adulthood, their feelings of exclusion magnified as they saw their opportunities shift in response to political transitions at local, state, and federal levels. For youth in North Carolina and other states responding to recent immigrant population booms, political restrictions seemed to mount exponentially in the first two decades of the 2000s.

Even as policies inched in a slightly more inclusive direction at the national level with the implementation of DACA, state policies in North Carolina pushed back against this perceived overreach at the federal level. For many, this state-level pushback felt like a betrayal as politicians in their home state aggressively lobbied against federal actions, instead of merely acting in concert with exclusionary measures at the federal level. Policies impeding opportunities for unauthorized young immigrants reminded youth that even after they had gained "legal presence," they retained "unlawful status." In other words, they remained national outsiders, and, perhaps more pointedly, they were excluded from membership in the state they considered their home.

Undocumented immigrant youth in North Carolina saw their peers in other states granted opportunities denied to them, and they felt a deepening sting of rejection. In contrast, youth in more hospitable states were aware of the exclusionary policies in more hostile states and consequently felt enhanced state loyalty when comparing their home states to more hostile states like Arizona and North Carolina (Cebulko and Silver 2016). In other words, state policies reverberated outward, affecting the ways in which immigrants experienced feelings of belonging or exclusion in their home states.

Exclusion and Racialized Ethnicity

Unauthorized youth who transitioned out of high school in the early 2000s confronted an unstable political landscape in which they struggled to make plans or find a sense of security. And while the increasingly hostile context of reception was particularly difficult for young adults without immigration authorization, their documented and citizen peers were not immune to the repercussions of the reactive political atmosphere either. Latino youth in Allen Creek worried about their unauthorized family members, and they knew that they too were vulnerable to discrimination and police surveillance because of their racialized ethnicity.

Like previous research in new immigrant destinations has found, Latinos in Allen Creek stood out from the rest of the population and consequently faced the "impossibility of anonymity" (Schmalzbauer 2014, 51). Both citizen and unauthorized immigrant Latinos commented that appearing Latino resulted in more frequent interactions with police officers while driving than one would expect. And while Latino youth tended to link surveillance, and particularly checkpoints, to a belief that police were checking immigration status, similar perceptions of police harassment in the black community highlighted how relationships between police and communities of color were strained more generally.

Perceptions of racism extended beyond the police, and youth of color also discussed incidents where they felt discrimination from people within the community. Both black and Latino youth talked about avoiding one gas station and particular restaurants that were known to be overtly racist. Moreover, both groups discussed discrimination from white parents who did not want their children engaging in romantic relationships with their black or brown classmates. While Latinos and blacks had to contend with similar racial discrimination from police and some community members who disliked that their community was becoming increasingly less white, Latinos also discussed unique experiences with discrimination.

Latino youth noted hostile stares and recalled getting chastised for speaking Spanish in stores or public spaces. Similarly, youth spoke about community members and even a teacher leveling insults about "working in the chicken plant," a euphemism for underachieving and doing "immigrant work," at all Latinos regardless of immigration status. Indeed, there was a widespread assumption that most Latinos in Allen Creek were also undocumented, or "illegal" immigrants. Regardless of their citizenship status and country of birth, many of the US-born Latino youth in this study had to navigate around the expectation of illegality even as they did not face the same barriers as their unauthorized peers.

Where possible, Latino youth took actions to combat stereotypes that others had of them, but they also maintained connections to their heritage cultures and were proud to speak Spanish. Sada explained how her attitude about discriminatory treatment had changed as she got older. She described how she felt surveilled and unwelcome by people in and around her community:

> It's different stares that you get just because [of] the color of your skin, and it's like, why? I mean, way before DACA, I would get comments like, "In this country you can't speak Spanish. You speak English." And I'm like, "Why so much anger?" People at Walmart would say that when I was talking with my sister or my friends. At first when I was younger, I wouldn't say anything because my parents taught me to be polite to people older than me, but then it gets to a point where I'm like I'm not going to keep my mouth shut anymore. Now I'll say something to shut them up.

Sada described what previous research has termed "hypervisibility" and "hyperaudibilty" (Maldonado 2014, 1928) in Allen Creek. As a teenager, she had quietly received the racism leveled at her. As she got older, however, and particularly after acquiring increased security with DACA, she resisted discriminatory treatment. She corrected store clerks who told her that her DACA-specific driver's license was illegitimate, and she stood up to people who told her to speak English.

Though Sada linked some of her experiences with discrimination to her unauthorized status, she also emphasized that her appearance and her linguistic practices marked her as distinct. For these reasons, citizen Latinos in Allen Creek were not immune to discrimination either. Sadly, their experiences as unequal citizens are hardly new or unique. Indeed, citizenship in the United States has always included gradations in membership, with disfavored groups reaping unequal privileges from citizenship (Román 2010). Too frequently, these gradations in membership hinge on race and racialized ethnicities. As the political landscape shifted increasingly toward exclusion at the both the state and, approaching the 2016 election, federal levels, both citizen and immigrant Latinos felt increasingly vulnerable.

Multilayered Contexts of Reception

To be sure, federal contexts influenced feelings of membership among immigrant youth, but the more proximate local and state contexts arguably had
more immediate impacts on them. The small-town environment of Allen
Creek affected youth and young adults in the town both positively and nega-
tively. In spite of experiences with racism, the community generally facilitated
opportunities for youth to form supportive and beneficial relationships with
teachers; coaches; AVID, AIM, and LAC leaders and mentors; immigrant advocates in the Latino Outreach Center; and other community adults with whom
the youth interacted in their neighborhoods, through their parents' jobs, or
through school-related projects. Moreover, the demographic makeup of the
school allowed black, white, and Latino students to feel represented as no one
group was overwhelmed by the others.

Although Latino students benefited from membership in ethnicity-based
clubs both within the school and in the community-based Latino Outreach
Center, they struggled to overcome stereotypes and surmount institutional
policies restricting their mobility. Young Latino students would speak in frustration about how community members expected them to achieve little beyond
work at a chicken plant or in landscaping. Moreover, young Latino men, in
particular, strove to distance themselves from stereotypes of Latino thugs or
gangsters. Because the community and school were so small, however, young
Latinos were often able to combat stereotypes as teachers and other community
adults came to know them as individuals. While unauthorized Latino youth
could challenge stereotypes and hence affect the social climate in school and in
the small community of Allen Creek, they were less able to overcome obstacles
at the state and national levels. In other words, undocumented youth could access membership at a local level, even as they could not entirely avoid discrimination. But they continued to struggle against the larger landscape of exclusion
where their individual identities were overwhelmed by a cloak of illegality.

Without federal immigration reform, and particularly without the passage
of the DREAM Act, unauthorized immigrant youths' life pathways remained
vulnerable to the constantly shifting political climate. Some adolescents saw
their college plans derailed after the NCCCS prohibited admission to unauthorized immigrants in 2008. Others were forced to drop out of school when
their scholarship funds were insufficient to continue to fund their educations
at prohibitively expensive out-of-state rates. Even after DACA, beneficiaries in
North Carolina were ineligible for in-state tuition and were, for a time, prohibited driver's licenses. Although they celebrated DACA as a step in the right di-

rection, many expressed feelings of confusion and frustration on hearing about the various ways that the state government and public institutions continued to impede their opportunities and limit their access to resources.

Furthermore, DACA was not universally available to the youth within the study. Two study participants who would have been eligible to apply had returned to their countries of origin before DACA was enacted, largely out of frustration with the increasingly hostile political climate in North Carolina. I lost contact with one, but the other, Luis, watched with very mixed feelings from Mexico as he saw policies that he had long given up on come to fruition. Displaying his Southern roots by quoting a country music song, he explained his mixed feelings about watching DACA from Mexico: "I couldn't really think about it for that long. I wish I had stayed longer, but I realized that if I had stayed, I wouldn't have what I have now. It reminded me of Garth Brooks's 'Unanswered Prayers.' I think about my wife and my kids, and I 'thank God for unanswered prayers.'" Luis had started a family in Mexico and was thankful that he had met his wife and had two beautiful children. Nonetheless, he knew that his life could have been very different had he remained in the United States, where had had lived since he was four, and acquired DACA protection.

Two other young men were ineligible to apply because of DUI arrests. They were acutely aware of the grave price of their adolescent mistakes, and they took full responsibility for their actions. Despite their limited opportunities for regularization and advancement within North Carolina, neither planned to return to their country of origin. Both had US-born children whom they planned to raise in the same country and community in which they themselves had spent their teenage and early adult years. Having established roots in Allen Creek, they were excited to watch their children flourish there and, as one of them told me, not make the same mistakes that he had.

Finally, many within the study had older siblings who were ineligible for DACA because they were older than the thirty-year-old age limit. Thus, families with children of varying statuses gained even more variety when some became eligible for DACA and others did not. In these families, DACA beneficiaries continued to worry about family members who remained on the margins, without any protection from deportation.

Even for beneficiaries, DACA did little to upend social stigma and suspicion. DACA was not well understood by institutional gatekeepers in North Carolina or by the black and white citizens alongside whom many DACA beneficiaries worked. Consequently, many beneficiaries continued to feel like outsiders even after acquiring legal presence. They spoke in frustration about social segregation, sustained police surveillance, and continuing political efforts to maintain their exclusion, illustrating how they continued to be marked with assumptions of illegality and criminality.

Just as DACA was not sufficient to remove the stigma associated with unauthorized immigration status, neither could it illuminate a clear pathway into college or a career. Immigration status, financial limitations, and family pressures complicated the transition out of high school even for the highest-achieving unauthorized immigrant youth. For adolescents who were less academic, college was even further out of reach. Without in-state tuition or access to financial assistance, many DACA beneficiaries remained stuck in jobs with very little opportunity for advancement. Nonetheless, for those lucky enough to qualify for DACA, they felt a great sense of relief from the more acute threat of deportation, particularly while driving.

Furthermore, DACA facilitated a movement from exclusion to at least partial inclusion, especially for beneficiaries who managed to obtain college educations. Several of the respondents in the study found more stable work after receiving DACA status, and a few returned to college, at least part-time, after working and saving money for out-of-state tuition. For these DACA beneficiaries, the ability to work in jobs with potential for growth and without hiding their identities was invaluable. Nonetheless, DACA beneficiaries knew that there was no guarantee that the policy would be renewed indefinitely. They worried that their newfound security could be revoked as soon as political tides shifted in Washington. With the election of President Trump, this fear magnified exponentially.

Looking toward the Future after Trump

As Donald Trump gained traction in the presidential primaries, his bombastic speeches on immigration made immigrant youth increasingly apprehensive. As noted in Chapter 5, Sada worried that the next president would overturn DACA and use the data gathered from DACA to enact a mass deportation of all DACA beneficiaries on file. Sada's fear conveyed a sense of chronic underlying anxiety that she linked to DACA. Although Sada discussed remarkable changes in her level of comfort working and driving after DACA, she worried that her name, address, and fingerprints were on file with the government. Before Sada applied for DACA, she explained how nervous the application made her but eventually decided that she would gamble her future in order to reap the benefits of policy. She explained, "I just put it in God's hand and whatever happens happens." Sada's fear that DACA was, in her words, "a setup" began to creep up again as she awaited the outcome of the 2016 election.

When President Trump took office in January 2017, he quickly followed through on many of his campaign promises surrounding immigration. He instituted a travel ban for seven predominantly Muslim nations, he announced plans to begin building a wall on the US-Mexico border, and he signed Executive Order 13768, stating that undocumented immigrants convicted of any offense, or believed to have committed a criminal offense, would be a priority for deportation. The executive order, moreover, expanded the power of ICE agents by stating that all persons who, "in the judgment of an immigration officer . . . pose a risk to public safety or national security" would be considered a priority for deportation. Following the signing of this executive order, high-profile raids in at least eleven states, both old and new immigrant destinations, resulted in the arrest of more than six hundred immigrants in early February 2017 (Robbins and Dickerson 2017). North Carolina was one of the eleven states targeted in the raids.

Though spokespersons for ICE maintained that these "targeted enforcement operations" were consistent with enforcement efforts carried out under the Obama administration, immigrant communities throughout the country were on high alert. Indeed, deportations had peaked under President Obama. And while the deportation raids kicking off Trump's presidency may well have been a continuation of Obama-era enforcement tactics, the vastly expanded deportation priorities, coupled with President Trump's anti-immigrant rhetoric, signaled a shift toward more draconian and indiscriminate enforcement tactics.

The enforcement focus of the new administration in Washington sent shockwaves through immigrant communities in both hostile and more welcoming states. And while immigrants and allied organizations throughout the nation were anxious about the impacts of a Trump presidency, immigrants in states where local law enforcement had agreed to cooperate with federal mandates on immigration were arguably at highest risk of deportation. Memos signed in February 2017 by John F. Kelly, the secretary of Homeland Security, indicated a renewed focus on expanding and reinvigorating 287(g) policies to deputize local police to enforce immigration law (White House Office of the Press Secretary 2017). In 2016, North Carolina led the nation in 287(g) partnerships, and the administrative shift suggested that more partnerships between local police and ICE would emerge in 2017. Indeed, several news sources warned of a substantial increase in the use of 287(g), particularly in red states (Kulish et al. 2017; Nakamura 2017; New York Times Editorial Board 2017). The New York Times Editorial Board also suggested that governors and state legislatures in conservative states, emboldened by Trump's tough stance against un-authorized immigrants, would also roll back in-state tuition policies and other pro-immigrant protections.

If the discretionary memos move forward in their current iterations, the federal enforcement shift would be particularly dangerous for unauthorized immigrants in states with hostile legislative stances on unauthorized immigrants, as these states would be better able to leverage federal policies to enforce immigration law at the local level. Moreover, state actions implemented under federal policies are better protected from judicial challenges based on preemption. In his analysis of the interplay of federal and state immigration enforcement, legal scholar Hiroshi Motomura (2014) points out that independent state actions, such as Arizona's SB 1070 and Alabama's HB 56, were both largely dismantled because they differed from federal discretionary enforcement and were thus preempted by federal law. In other words, the state acts would have allowed police and other officials in those states to enforce immigration law in a manner that would have been inconsistent with federal enforcement priorities. When state and local enforcements are sanctioned through federal policies, such as 287(g), however, preemptory challenges are far less likely to emerge.

Thus, immigrants in hostile states would be at greater risk of detention and deportation due to higher rates of participation in the 287(g) program. Additionally, legal advocates would be less able to challenge the constitutionality of those programs, as they would comply with federal enforcement standards in spite of ample evidence that they rely on racial profiling (American Civil Liberties Union and the Rights Working Group 2009; Coleman 2012; Shahshahani 2010; Weisman, Headen, and Parker 2009). However, even in cities like Los Angeles and Boston, where mayors and police chiefs have vowed not to cooperate with Trump's mass deportation directives, state officials can do only so much to shelter immigrants from independent actions by ICE agents. The memos from the Department of Homeland Security also indicated plans to hire ten thousand additional ICE agents and crack down on sanctuary jurisdictions, thus drastically expanding enforcement capabilities throughout the interior of the United States.

Though the February 2017 memos did not lay out plans for DACA, the program remained a focus of officials and legislators at both the state and federal levels. When Attorney General Jeff Sessions announced the termination of DACA on September 5, 2017, beneficiaries throughout the country were heartbroken but not shocked. The rescission was merely the latest tidal change in a constantly churning sea of political shifts. The end of the policy was announced after ten state attorneys general, largely from Southern states, threatened to sue the administration if they did not rescind DACA. When the Trump administration ended the program, the tectonic plates at both the state and federal levels shifted immigrant youth suddenly toward exclusion. The termination of DACA illustrated how hostile climates at the state level can reverberate upward, particularly when the federal administration is sympathetic to the anti-immigrant policies in these states.

Despite the state's history of anti-immigrant policies, North Carolina officials' responses to the Trump administration's actions surrounding DACA varied. The North Carolina attorney general was not among the attorneys general from the ten states that had originally threatened to sue if the Trump administration did not rescind DACA, and he joined a lawsuit with attorneys general from fourteen other states and Washington, D.C., to protect DACA beneficiaries after Sessions announced the termination of the policy. Other North Carolina senators publicly expressed sympathy for the beneficiaries but supported ending the program in favor of implementing legislative reforms to extend benefits and security to the DREAMers (Blythe 2017).

Though President Trump publicly urged Congress to pass legislation addressing the DACA beneficiaries within the six-month lag period leading up to the expiration of the policy, the immigration reforms that the White House proposed to Congress suggested vastly expanding enforcement, decreasing protections for vulnerable immigrant groups such as unaccompanied minors and asylum seekers, and decreasing legal immigration (Meckler 2017). DREAMer activists emphatically refused to be used as a bargaining chip in immigration reform negotiations and urged Democrats to deny any plan that proposed harsh anti-immigration measure in exchange for their protection (O'Keefe 2017). DACA beneficiaries throughout the country worried about their parents, siblings, and loved ones, and they were particularly fearful that measures implemented to extend their own protections would further undermine the dignity of other immigrants. They also worried about their own futures under President Trump. Like Zaíra said, "I still have hope that it will work out, but we are on the loop, like a game. Nothing is certain. It's on my thoughts every day. What is next, what will happen today? Not only to me, but my family, my community, my people. And I'm ready to fight back." Trump's presidency had resulted in widespread anxiety among immigrants, and youth with provisional statuses like DACA felt acutely unsteady and insecure. Yet youth like Zaíra also felt a renewed sense of urgency to resist and reassert their positions as members of the United States.

Policy Recommendations

Acknowledging that unauthorized immigrant youth who grew up in the United States are likely to remain in the United States, it makes sense to examine which policies and practices are most successful in promoting their incorporation. Indeed, doing so extends the discussion surrounding the 1982 *Plyler v. Doe* decision. When Justice Brennan delivered the opinion of the court, he warned that children without education would "become permanently locked into the lowest socio-economic class."[2] He thus argued that the *Plyler v. Doe* decision would help prevent the creation of an underclass of residents for the benefit of both the children and the country. The decision publicly acknowledged the presence of unauthorized immigrants and furthermore provided some degree of protection to them.

Like *Plyler v. Doe*, a variety of federal and state priority enforcement measures and integration policies, including DACA, acknowledge that a sector of the population at any given time comprises unauthorized immigrants. Legal scholars have argued that these long-term unauthorized immigrants should thus be regarded as "Americans in waiting" (Motomura 2006, 2014) due to their political engagement, acknowledged personhood rights, long-term residence, and identity (Bosniak 2006, 2007). In some ways, policies such as the right to primary and secondary education, in-state tuition, temporary protection from deportation, and access to work permits and driver's licenses provide pathways to membership and incorporation. Yet these policies fall far short of ensuring that unauthorized immigrant youth will be able to surmount the substantial financial and social obstacles in front of them. Mechanisms to help unauthorized youth access legal permanent residence and citizenship, in conjunction with concerted efforts to dismantle systematic racism in institutions such as schools, police forces, and ICE, are all necessary to facilitate pathways to membership and mobility. In the absence of these sweeping and admittedly challenging reforms, schools, community centers, activist organizations, and additional legislation must all work cooperatively to promote the incorporation of immigrant youth in their communities. To that end, a multipronged approach to incorporation is the best strategy to reach the widest population.

Because schools are the most universally utilized youth-centered institutions, they are a good place to start in terms of reaching youth and attempting to engage them in positive, school-based activities. In Allen Creek, youth benefited immensely from heritage-based clubs that provided youth from immigrant families with a safe space to discuss common issues. Clubs that linked ethnic background to academic coursework were doubly effective, as the youth in these clubs could specifically link their ethnic identities to their academic achievements. These clubs offered youth a space to belong and directly facilitated engagement in school and relationships with teachers and mentors. Moreover, teachers supported the clubs as they felt they increased the number of focused students in their classrooms. They were well aware that, due to immigration status and financial pressures, many of their students would have a difficult time accessing college. They worried that students that did not see the purpose of high school would disrupt class lectures and discussions. Teachers felt that the clubs promoted a model of school engagement.

Although school curriculum and extracurricular programs focused on ethnic heritage and current events facing immigrants seem like feasible programs to implement, programs like these have been under attack even in areas like Tucson, Arizona, where data clearly illustrate their success in retaining students and promoting college (Delgado 2013). Programs focusing on ethnic histories and targeted social studies topics should be encouraged and not discouraged. Students benefit from these programs as they become excited about school and forge close relationships with invested teachers.

Additionally, when clubs offer links to private scholarships and expose students to nearby colleges, students who had previously thought of college as unattainable begin to envision ways to extend their educations beyond high school. Even students who are unable to cross the bridge from high school to college can benefit from participation in clubs and extracurricular activities. School clubs and sports teams help provide students with purpose and peer groups that make school meaningful for them.

For students less inclined to participate in school-based programs, community-based programs offer another important resource for immigrant youth and children of immigrants. In Allen Creek, for example, newer immigrants were less involved in school programs than many of their peers who had arrived at younger ages. The churches and outreach organizations in the community offered additional spaces for youth to belong. The Latino Outreach Center was a primary resource for immigrant and second-generation youth in town. They felt comfortable going there after school, where they could speak in Spanish, interact with Latino staff, work on their homework, and plan events that would cater to the Latino community in town. Although public transportation was not available in the town, the center was walking distance from the school. Thus, youth could travel there safely without worrying about being pulled over. Moreover, the Outreach Center partnered with other nonprofit organizations throughout the nation to organize trips, conferences, radio shows, and events. Participating youth thereby gained invaluable opportunities to attend leadership summits, join activist movements, and travel to nearby states and Washington, D.C. The Latino Outreach Center recruited participants by connecting with the high school and local churches. By reaching youth in places where they were already present, the center was effective in recruiting a small but loyal group of teenagers.

Although small nonprofit centers can be difficult to fund, particularly in small towns and rural areas (Snavely and Tracy 2000), they provide crucial services to clients and have intimate knowledge of the needs of the communities where they are located. Government and private organizations should increase efforts to increase contributions toward these organizations. Moreover, local nonprofits should collaborate to offer local populations the most comprehensive services. In Allen Creek, the Latino Outreach Center worked with local food banks, pro bono lawyers, mental health organizations, dental clinics, family services organizations, the local school system, and local churches, as well as the national AmeriCorps program to provide its clients with a variety of goods and services. Effective partnerships among local organizations can maximize services while minimizing overhead costs.

Beyond schools and community outreach centers, activist organizations can also offer youth safe spaces in which they can vent their frustrations and work together to better their own life chances. Students who became involved in activism flourished in these roles and saw themselves emerge as leaders and spokespersons for their communities in ways that they did not imagine were possible prior to their engagement in activism. Moreover, they forged connections to peers facing the same pressures and obstacles, and they found comfort and empowerment through their collaborative efforts to argue for their own recognition and inclusion.

Although activist organizations were extremely powerful for the youth who joined the movements, most unauthorized immigrant youth do not join activist movements. Like most teenagers, they are not necessarily interested in politics. Moreover, many have pressing obligations to work and family, and others do not feel as though their own narratives are captured by the DREAMer movement. Finally, not all youth are comfortable with the idea of coming out publicly or participating in disruptive demonstrations. As immigrant rights activist movements evolve, they will surely continue to expand their narratives to include more immigrant youth who may not fit within the perfect DREAMer mold. Schools, churches, and community organizations should also offer youth more opportunities to critically engage with their communities and express

and showcase their beliefs through the arts and in written dialogues. By expanding activism to community organizations in which youth already participate, and by promoting various types of activism, more unauthorized youth
will find opportunities to take ownership of their status and become more civically engaged.

Programs for youth are highly effective, and efforts to engage youth in community projects and positive peer networks should not end in high school.
Schools and community organizations offer crucial support to youth while
they are enrolled in high school, but most unauthorized immigrant youth report a marked increase in feelings of isolation and exclusion after high school
graduation. Programs to maintain connections to alumni of schools and
community-based youth groups can both protect and empower youth entering the early stages of adulthood. Engaging recent high school graduates as
peer mentors or apprentice leaders in youth programs will allow unauthorized
immigrant young adults, and particularly those who are unable to access college, to maintain ties to organizations that promote their professional development and personal growth. If young unauthorized immigrants continue to
feel a sense of membership in their communities as a result of sustained ties to
mentors and community organizations, they will be less likely to feel isolated,
frustrated, and depressed.

While local organizations can promote civic engagement through their programs and outreach efforts, they are limited in their abilities to comprehensively
address the incorporation of immigrant youth without parallel governmental
actions increasing opportunities for immigrant youth. DACA was the most influential factor in increasing feelings of membership and security for the unauthorized youth in this study. Although not all of the youth were able to redirect
their life pathways as a result of DACA, they all noted feelings of freedom that
came with being able to work and drive with valid documentation. Moreover,
they were thrilled that they could decrease their dependence on their parents
for financial resources and their citizen siblings and friends for rides. Policies
like DACA allow immigrants to come out of the shadows and find a sense of
autonomy and security. Nonetheless, state policies limited the reach of DACA
and prevented youth from achieving a full sense of membership in their home
state of North Carolina. And the temporary nature of DACA demonstrated
how fleeting these feelings of security and membership were when the Trump
administration ended the program.

Comprehensive and uniform legislation is necessary for immigrant youth
to carve out spaces of membership and achieve upward mobility. Moreover,

documents that authorized residents are given should not mark them as obvious national outsiders. Licenses without marks of distinction would protect license holders from discriminatory treatment from police, store clerks, bouncers, and other residents during routine interactions requiring identification documents.

Furthermore, if immigrant youth are to be given a fair shot at achieving upward mobility, additional legislation building on *Plyler v. Doe* must be passed to address present-day economic realities. Investment in elementary and secondary education will do little to guarantee economic security without parallel legislation opening up access to higher education and the labor market. Temporary authorization programs, such as DACA and DAPA, would be far more effective if they were made permanent. Additionally, youth with diplomas from public high schools would benefit from access to in-state tuition and financial aid in all states. As current policies stand, unauthorized immigrant youth and youth with DACA status in states with more hostile contexts have far fewer opportunities to access higher education and, by extension, upwardly mobile jobs than their peers in more welcoming states. By limiting access to education, US federal and state policies also limit the development and potential contributions of unauthorized youth and DACA beneficiaries.

Policies and practices facilitating the integration of immigrant youth in tertiary schools as well as in the labor market would open up opportunities for youth to make economic, civic, social, and artistic contributions to the country in which they were raised. Indeed, one study out of the North American Integration and Development Center at UCLA estimates that granting authorization and pathway to citizenship via the DREAM Act would garner between 1.4 and 3.6 trillion dollars in income for DREAM Act beneficiaries over a forty-year period (Ojeda and Takash 2010). In addition to the tax and Social Security contributions from newly authorized workers in upwardly mobile jobs, regularized 1.5-generation immigrants would generate economic growth through job creation. Estimates based on the American Community Survey suggest that DREAMers would add 1.4 million new jobs and $329 billion to the US economy by 2030 (Guzmán and Jara 2012). Immigrant youth have bicultural and bilingual capital, and they can draw on multiple cultural and linguistic frames as they approach challenges on the job. Their transnational perspectives and bilingual skills position 1.5-generation immigrants to compete and create in the global labor market.

Looking beyond the substantial economic benefits of permanently authorizing young immigrants who grew up in the United States, the social and cultural benefits are also ample. Youth who have overcome substantial obstacles to find a sense of belonging are poised to act as mentors to their younger counterparts. They can draw on their own experiences to help their younger peers avoid or cope with the isolation and exclusion that comes with being labeled an outsider. Moreover, young mentors and activists can act as role models to encourage their younger peers to become more civically and socially engaged. Young activists have done a remarkable job in developing the tools to advocate for themselves, and they are well positioned to teach the next generation of immigrant and second-generation youth to invest in themselves and in their communities. Finally, more accommodating policies would recognize the dignity of immigrant youth and young adults.

Once public officials begin to recognize immigrant youth as a resource to invest in rather than a threat or burden to be dealt with, the walls of exclusion that have long stifled the growth of so many will begin to crumble. If DACA was not enough to change the perception of Latinos as outsiders, perhaps time will. Latino immigration to North Carolina had slowed substantially in the second decade of the 2000s, and the established Latino community was steadily planting roots. As the 1.5-generation youth in Allen Creek grew up and had children, they began to form multigenerational North Carolina families. The children of the youth who participated in this study will be dually advantaged by having citizenship and the guidance of parents who traversed the US school system. Even if their children continue to confront discrimination, these new North Carolinians will, at the very least, face a very different legal situation than many of their unauthorized immigrant parents and grandparents.

It remains to be seen if the social climate within hostile states like North Carolina will adapt to promote the successful incorporation of immigrants and their US-born children or if state legislators, emboldened by the Trump administration, will move toward even less accommodating policies that threaten young unauthorized immigrants and immigrant families. As anti-immigrant activist movements gain momentum, so too do movements of resistance. Unauthorized youth and DACA beneficiaries are at the forefront of these movements of resistance, and the vast majority of these youth and young adults will remain in the states in which they were raised, where they continue to contribute to the communities, states, and country they know as home.

Notes

Introduction

1. To protect the anonymity of the individuals in this study, the name of the research site and all research participants are pseudonyms. When it does not affect the relationships I describe between community members, I also occasionally change small biographical details for certain individuals who would otherwise be identifiable by their jobs and particular characteristics. I consulted study participants to ensure that these minor changes felt close to their identities and roles. The names of political officials have not been changed, unless they were government officials local to the research site, in which case I either replaced names with pseudonyms or did not use a name at all. While I did not change the names of major universities, I changed the names of smaller colleges and community colleges close to the primary research site.

2. Throughout the book I use "undocumented" and "unauthorized" to describe the statuses of immigrants without authorization to reside in the United States. "Second-generation" immigrants refer to individuals who were born in the United States to at least one foreign-born immigrant parent. I use the term "1.5-generation" immigrants to refer to individuals who were born outside the United States but migrated or were brought to the United States before the age of fourteen. Three of the 1.5-generation youth in the study had TPS, but the remaining twenty lacked immigration authorization. Finally, when I discuss "children of immigrants," I am referring to first-, second-, and 1.5-generation immigrants, regardless of immigration status.

3. AVID (Advancement via Individual Determination) is an educational program designed to propel students in the academic middle toward four-year college. For more information on the program, which is available at schools in forty-five states, see www.avid.org.

4. Elements of Alabama's HB 56 were repealed or permanently blocked in a settle-

159

ment after several lawsuits were filed by the US Department of Justice and a coalition of civil rights groups.

5. Development, Relief, and Education for Alien Minors Act, S.B. 1291, 107th Cong. (2001).

6. According to US Citizenship and Immigration Services, "The Secretary of Homeland Security may designate a foreign country for TPS due to conditions in the country that temporarily prevent the country's nationals from returning safely, or in certain circumstances, where the country is unable to handle the return of its nationals adequately. USCIS may grant TPS to eligible nationals of certain countries (or parts of countries), who are already in the United States. Eligible individuals without nationality who last resided in the designated country may also be granted TPS." See http://www.uscis.gov/humanitarian/temporary-protected-status-deferred-enforced-departure/temporary-protected-status.

Chapter 1

1. "Obama on Scotus Immigration Ruling," *The Hill*, June 23, 2016, http://origin-nyi.thehill.com/blogs/pundits-blog/immigration/284656-transcript-obama-on-scotus-immigration-ruling?amp.

2. Virginia led the nation in 287(g) policies at the time of the initial 2007–11 study period. Participation in the program in states throughout the nation declined after much criticism about widespread racial profiling (American Civil Liberties Union and the Rights Working Group 2009; Coleman 2012; Shahshahani 2010). However, North Carolina continued its use of 287(g), and with five active memorandums of agreement in 2016, North Carolina replaced Virginia for first place, leading the nation in participation in the program at the time of this writing.

3. Plyler v. Doe, 457 U.S. 202, 207 (1982).

4. Republican representatives introduced a bill titled "An Act to Prohibit Illegal Aliens from Attending North Carolina Community Colleges and Appropriating Funds for the Verification of Prospective Students' Immigration Status." A joint resolution to consider an act titled "An Act Prohibiting Illegal Aliens from Attending North Carolina Community Colleges and Universities" was introduced in the same session.

5. The 2008 memorandum from the NCCCS titled "Unrestricted Admission of Undocumented or Illegal Immigrants" stated, "Federal Law, 8 USC Section 1621 makes most undocumented or illegal aliens ineligible for most state or local public benefits. Post-secondary education is one of those benefits that undocumented or illegal aliens are not eligible to receive."

6. Letter to Thomas J. Ziko, North Carolina special deputy attorney general, from Jim Pendergraph, Immigration and Customs Enforcement, July 8, 2008 (online site discontinued).

Chapter 2

1. The mission of the North Carolina Migrant Education Program (MEP) is to help migrant students and youth meet high academic challenges by overcoming the obstacles created by frequent moves, educational disruption, cultural and language differences, and health-related problems. The MEP is federally funded as part of the Elementary and Secondary Education Act and is regulated by Title I, Part C., US Department of Education, last modified September 15, 2004, http://www.ed.gov/policy/elsec/leg/esea02/pg8.html.

Chapter 4

1. After Antonin Scalia died in February 2016, the Supreme Court lost a tie-breaking vote in cases that tended to split along ideological or political lines.

2. Plyler v. Doe, 229.

3. Ibid., 220.

Conclusion

1. Secure Communities is a DHS program that relies on partnerships with state jails to identify immigrants eligible for deportation.

2. Plyler v. Doe, quoting from 458 F.Supp. 569, 577 E.D. Tex. (1978).

References

Abrego, Leisy J. 2006. "'I Can't Go to College Because I Don't Have Papers': Incorporation Patterns of Latino Undocumented Youth." *Latino Studies* 4 (3): 212–31. https://link.springer.com/article/10.1057/palgrave.lst.8600200.

———. 2008. "Legitimacy, Social Identity, and the Mobilization of Law: The Effects of Assembly Bill 540 on Undocumented Students in California." *Law and Social Inquiry* 33 (3): 709–34.

Abrego, Leisy J., and Sarah M. Lakhani. 2015. "Incomplete Inclusion: Legal Violence and Immigrants in Liminal Legal Statuses." *Law and Policy* 37 (4): 265–93. http://onlinelibrary.wiley.com/doi/10.1111/lapo.12039/full.

Agius Vallejo, Jody. 2012. *Barrios to Burbs: The Making of the Mexican-American Middle Class.* Stanford, CA: Stanford University Press.

Alba, Richard D., and Nancy Foner. 2015. *Strangers No More: Immigration and the Challenges of Integration in North America and Western Europe.* Princeton, NJ: Princeton University Press.

Alba, Richard D., and Victor Nee. 2003. *Remaking the American Mainstream: Assimilation and Contemporary Immigration.* Cambridge, MA: Harvard University Press.

American Civil Liberties Union and the Rights Working Group. 2009. *The Persistence of Racial and Ethnic Profiling in the United States,* June 30. https://www.aclu.org/sites/default/files/pdfs/humanrights/cerd_finalreport.pdf.

Anderson, Benedict. 1983. *Imagined Communities: Reflections on the Origin and Spread of Nationalism.* London: Verso.

Aranda, Elizabeth, Cecilia Menjívar, and Katharine M. Donato. 2014. "The Spillover Consequences of an Enforcement-First U.S. Immigration Regime." *American Behavioral Scientist* 58 (13): 1687–95. http://journals.sagepub.com/doi/abs/10.1177/0002764214537264.

Aranda, Elizabeth, and Elizabeth Vaquera. 2015. "Racism, the Immigration Enforcement

Regime, and the Implications for Racial Inequality in the Lives of Undocumented Young Adults." *Sociology of Race and Ethnicity* 1 (1): 88–104. http://journals.sagepub.com/doi/abs/10.1177/2332649214551097.

Arellano, Daniel A. 2012. "Keep Dreaming: Deferred Action and the Limits of Executive Power." *Arizona Law Review* 54 (4): 1139–56.

Armenta, Amada. 2016. "Between Public Service and Social Control: Policing Dilemmas in the Era of Immigration Enforcement." *Social Problems* 63 (1): 111–26. http://doi.org/10.1093/socpro/spv024..

———. 2017. *Protect, Serve, and Deport: The Rise of Policing as Immigration Enforcement.* Oakland: University of California Press. https://doi.org/10.1525/luminos.33.

Bada, Xóchitl, Jonathan Fox, Robert Donnelly, and Andrew Seele. 2010. *Context Matters: Latino Immigrant Civic Engagement in Nine U.S. Cities.* Washington, DC: Woodrow Wilson International Center for Scholars. https://www.wilsoncenter.org/sites/default/files/Context%20Matters.pdf.

Batalova, Jeanne, Sarah Hooker, and Randy Capps. 2014. *DACA at the Two-Year Mark: A National and State Profile of Youth Eligible and Applying for Deferred Action.* Washington, DC: Migration Policy Institute. http://www.migrationpolicy.org/sites/default/files/publications/DACA-Report-2014-FINALWEB.pdf.

Bean, Frank D., Susan K. Brown, and James D. Bachmeier. 2015. *Parents without Papers: The Progress and Pitfalls of Mexican-American Integration.* New York: Russell Sage Foundation.

Behnke, Andrew O., Laura M. Gonzalez, and Ronald B. Cox. 2010. "Latino Students in New Arrival States: Factors and Services to Prevent Youth from Dropping Out." *Hispanic Journal of Behavioral Sciences* 32 (3): 385–409. http://journals.sagepub.com/doi/abs/10.1177/0739986310374025.

Bejarano, Cynthia L. 2005. *¿Qué Onda? Urban Youth Culture and Border Identity.* Tucson: University of Arizona Press.

Benjamin-Alvarado, Jonathan, Louis DeSipio, and Celeste Montoya. 2009. "Latino Mobilization in New Immigrant Destinations: The Anti-H.R. 4437 Protest in Nebraska's Cities." *Urban Affairs Review* 44 (5): 718–35.

Bettie, Julie. 2003. *Women without Class: Girls, Race, and Identity.* Berkeley: University of California Press.

Blythe, Anne. 2017. "DACA Recipients Rally in NC: 'We Were Not Born Illegal. . . . We Are Here to Stay.'" *Raleigh News and Observer*, September 5. http://www.newsobserver.com/news/politics-government/state-politics/article171357787.html.

Bohon, Stephanie A., Heather Macpherson, and Jorge H. Atiles. 2005. "Educational Barriers for New Latinos in Georgia." *Journal of Latinos and Education* 4 (1): 43–58. http://www.tandfonline.com/doi/abs/10.1207/s1532771xjle0401_4.

Bonilla-Silva, Eduardo. 2003. *Racism without Racists: Color-Blind Racism and the Persistence of Racial Inequality in the United States.* Lanham, MD: Rowman and Littlefield.

Bonilla-Silva, E., and Tyrone A. Forman. 2000. "'I Am Not a Racist but . . .': Mapping

White College Students' Racial Ideology in the USA." *Discourse and Society* 11 (1): 50–85.

Bosniak, Linda. 2006. *The Citizen and the Alien: Dilemmas of Contemporary Membership*. Princeton, NJ: Princeton University Press.

———. 2007. "Being Here: Ethical Territoriality and the Rights of Immigrants." *Theoretical Inquiries in Law* 8 (2): 389–410.

Brettell, Caroline B., and Faith G. Nibbs. 2011. "Immigrant Suburban Settlement and the 'Threat' to Middle Class Status and Identity: The Case of Farmers Branch, Texas." *International Migration* 49 (1): 1–30. http://onlinelibrary.wiley.com/doi/10.1111/j.1468-2435.2010.00611.x/full.

Brown, Hana E. 2013. "Race, Legality, and the Social Policy Consequences of Anti-immigration Mobilization." *American Sociological Review* 78 (2): 290–314. http://journals.sagepub.com/doi/abs/10.1177/0003122413476712.

Brubaker, Rogers. 2010. "Migration, Membership, and the Modern Nation-State: Internal and External Dimensions of the Politics of Belonging." *Journal of Interdisciplinary History* 41 (1): 61–78.

Capps, Randy, Marc R. Rosenblum, Muzaffar Chishti, and Cristina Rodríguez. 2011. *Delegation and Divergence: A Study of 287 (g) State and Local Immigration Enforcement*. Washington, DC: Migration Policy Institute. http://www.migrationpolicy.org/research/delegation-and-divergence-287g-state-and-local-immigration-enforcement.

Cebulko, Kara B. 2013. *Documented, Undocumented, and Something Else: The Incorporation of Children of Brazilian Immigrants*. El Paso, TX: LFB Scholarly Publishing.

———. 2014. "Documented, Undocumented, and Liminally Legal: Legal Status during the Transition to Adulthood for 1.5-Generation Brazilian Immigrants." *Sociological Quarterly* 55 (1): 143–67.

———. 2017. "Privileged, but Excluded: Intersecting Inequalities among 1.5-Generation Brazilians in Massachusetts." Paper presented at the annual meeting of the American Sociological Association, Montreal, Quebec, Canada, August 12–15.

Cebulko, Kara B., and Alexis Silver. 2016. "Navigating DACA in Hospitable and Hostile States: State Responses and Access to Membership in the Wake of Deferred Action for Childhood Arrivals." *American Behavioral Scientist* 60 (13): 1553–74. http://journals.sagepub.com/doi/pdf/10.1177/0002764216664942.

Chavez, Leo R. 2008. *The Latino Threat: Constructing Immigrants, Citizens, and the Nation*. Stanford, CA: Stanford University Press.

Chavous, Tabbye M., Debra Hilkene Bernat, Karen Schmeelk-Cone, Cleopatra H. Caldwell, Laura Kohn-Wood, and Marc A. Zimmerman. 2003. "Racial Identity and Academic Attainment among African American Adolescents." *Child Development* 74 (4): 1076–90. http://onlinelibrary.wiley.com/doi/10.1111/1467-8624.00593/abstract.

Ciscel, David H., Barbara Ellen Smith, and Marcela Mendoza. 2003. "Ghosts in the Global Machine: New Immigrants and the Redefinition of Work." *Journal of Economic Issues* 37 (2): 333–41.

Clotfelter, Charles T., Helen F. Ladd, and Jacob L. Vigdor. 2012. "New Destinations, New Trajectories? The Educational Progress of Hispanic Youth in North Carolina." *Child Development* 83 (5): 1608–22. http://onlinelibrary.wiley.com/doi/10.1111/j.1467-8624.2012.01797.x/abstract.

Coleman, Mathew. 2009. "What Counts as the Politics and Practice of Security, and Where? Devolution and Immigrant Insecurity after 9/11." *Annals of the Association of American Geographers* 99 (5): 904–13.

———. 2012. "The 'Local' Migration State: The Site-Specific Devolution of Immigration Enforcement in the U.S. South." *Law and Policy* 34 (2): 159–90. http://dx.doi.org/10.1111/j.1467-9930.2011.00358.x.

Coleman, Mathew, and Austin Kocher. 2011. "Detention, Deportation, Devolution and Immigrant Incapacitation in the US, Post 9/11." *Geographical Journal* 177 (3): 228–37. http://onlinelibrary.wiley.com/doi/10.1111/j.1475-4959.2011.00424.x/abstract.

Collins, Kristin. 2007. "Sheriffs Help Feds Deport Illegal Aliens." *Raleigh News and Observer*, April 22, A1.

———. 2008a. "Mom Arrested, Kids Left on I-85: Abandoned by Fellow Immigrant." *Raleigh News and Observer*, July 23, A1.

———. 2008b. "Tolerance Wears Thin." *Raleigh News and Observer*, September 7, A1.

Cortina, Regina. 2008. "Latinos and Educational Policy in the Global American South." *Latino Research Review* 6 (3): 93–104.

Coutin, Susan B. 1998. "From Refugees to Immigrants: The Legalization Strategies of Salvadoran Immigrants and Activists." *International Migration Review* 32 (4): 901–25.

———. 2005. "Contesting Criminality: Illegal Immigration and the Spatialization of Legality." *Theoretical Criminology* 9 (1): 5–33.

Cuadros, Paul. 2006. *A Home on the Field: How One Championship Team Inspires Hope for the Revival of Small Town America*. New York: HarperCollins Publishers.

De Genova, Nicholas. 2002. "Migrant 'Illegality' and Deportability in Everyday Life." *Annual Review of Anthropology* 31 (1): 419–47.

———. 2010. "The Deportation Regime: Sovereignty, Space, and the Freedom of Movement." In *The Deportation Regime: Sovereignty, Space, and the Freedom of Movement*, edited by Nicholas De Genova and Nathalie Peutz, 33–65. Durham, NC: Duke University Press.

Deeb-Sossa, Natalia, and Jennifer Bickham Mendez. 2008. "Enforcing Borders in the Nuevo South: Gender and Migration in Williamsburg, Virginia, and the Research Triangle, North Carolina." *Gender and Society* 22 (5): 613–38.

Delgado, Richard. 2013. "Precious Knowledge: State Bans on Ethnic Studies, Book Traffickers (Librotraficantes), and a New Type of Race Trial." *North Carolina Law Review* 91:1513–54. http://ssrn.com/abstract=2274898.

Donato, Katharine M., and Leslie Ann Rodríguez. 2014. "Police Arrests in a Time of Uncertainty: The Impact of 287(g) on Arrests in a New Immigrant Gateway."

American Behavioral Scientist 58 (13): 1696–1722. http://journals.sagepub.com/doi/abs/10.1177/0002764214537265.

Dreby, Joanna. 2015. *Everyday Illegal: When Policies Undermine Immigrant Families.* Oakland: University of California Press.

Ebert, Kim, and Sarah M. Ovink. 2014. "Anti-immigrant Ordinances and Discrimination in New and Established Destinations." *American Behavioral Scientist* 58 (13): 1784–1804. http://journals.sagepub.com/doi/abs/10.1177/0002764214537267.

Ellis, Mark, and Gunnar Almgren. 2009. "Local Contexts of Immigrant and Second-Generation Integration in the United States." *Journal of Ethnic and Migration Studies* 35 (7): 1059–76.

Ellis, Mark, Richard Wright, and Matthew Townley. 2016. "State-Scale Immigration Enforcement and Latino Interstate Migration in the United States." *Annals of the American Association of Geographers* 106 (4): 891–908. http://www.tandfonline.com/doi/abs/10.1080/24694452.2015.1135725.

Ennis, Sharon R., Merarys Ríos-Vargas, and Nora G. Albert. 2011. *The Hispanic Population: 2010.* 2010 *Census Briefs.* Washington, DC: United States Census Bureau. http://www.census.gov/prod/cen2010/briefs/c2010br-04.pdf.

Enriquez, Laura E. 2017. "A 'Master Status' or the 'Final Straw'? Assessing the Role of Immigration Status in Latino Undocumented Youths' Pathways out of School." *Journal of Ethnic and Migration Studies* 43 (9): 1526–43. http://www.tandfonline.com/doi/abs/10.1080/1369183X.2016.1235483.

Esbenshade, Jill, and Barbara Obzurt. 2008. "Local Immigration Regulation: A Problematic Trend in Public Policy." *Harvard Journal of Hispanic Policy* 20:33–47.

Feliciano, Cynthia. 2001. "The Benefits of Biculturalism: Exposure to Immigrant Culture and Dropping out of School among Asian and Latino Youths." *Social Science Quarterly* 82 (4): 865–79.

———. 2009. "Education and Ethnic Identity Formation among Children of Latin American and Caribbean Immigrants." *Sociological Perspectives* 52 (2): 135–58.

———. 2012. "The Female Educational Advantage among Adolescent Children of Immigrants." *Youth and Society* 44 (3): 431–49.

Feliciano, Cynthia, and Rubén Rumbaut. 2005. "Gendered Paths: Educational and Occupational Expectations and Outcomes among Adult Children of Immigrants." *Ethnic and Racial Studies* 28 (6): 1087–1118.

Flores, René D. 2014. "In the Eye of the Storm: How Did Hazleton's Restrictive Immigration Ordinance Affect Local Interethnic Relations?" *American Behavioral Scientist* 58 (13): 1743–63.

Fortuny, Karina. 2010. *Children of Immigrants: 2008 State Trends Update. Brief 17.* Washington, DC: Urban Institute. http://www.urban.org/UploadedPDF/412212-children-of-immigrants.pdf.

Frederickson, Caroline, Joanne Lin, Mónica M. Ramírez, and Reginald T. Shuford. 2009. *Examining 287(g): The Role of State and Local Enforcement in Immigration Law.*

American Civil Liberties Union. https://www.aclu.org/files/images/asset_upload_file717_39062.pdf.

Fuligni, Andrew J., Melissa Witkow, and Carla Garcia. 2005. "Ethnic Identity and the Academic Adjustment of Adolescents from Mexican, Chinese, and European Backgrounds." *Developmental Psychology* 41 (5): 799–811. http://psycnet.apa.org/buy/2005-11023-009.

Furuseth, Owen J., and Heather A. Smith. 2010. "Localized Immigration Policy: The View from Charlotte, North Carolina, a New Immigrant Gateway." In *Taking Local Control: Immigration Policy Activism in U.S. Cities and States*, edited by Monica W. Varsanyi, 173–92. Stanford, CA: Stanford University Press.

Gallagher, Charles. 2003. "Color-Blind Privilege: The Social and Political Functions of Erasing the Color Line in Post Race America." *Race, Gender and Class* 10 (4): 22–37.

Gans, Herbert J. 1973. 'Foreword.' In *Ethnic Identity and Assimilation: The Polish-American Community*, by Neil C. Sandberg. New York: Praeger Publishers.

———. 1992. "Comment: Ethnic Invention and Acculturation, a Bumpy-Line Approach." *Journal of American Ethnic History* 12 (1): 42–53.

General Assembly of North Carolina. 2013. *An Act Prohibiting Illegal Aliens from Attending North Carolina Community Colleges and Universities*. North Carolina House Bill 218, March 5. http://www.ncleg.net/Sessions/2013/Bills/House/PDF/H218v1.pdf.

Gibson, Margaret A., Livier F. Bejínez, Nicole Hidalgo, and Cony Rolón. 2004. "Belonging and School Participation: Lessons from a Migrant Student Club." In *School Connections: U.S.-Mexican Youth, Peers, and School Achievement*, edited by Margaret A. Gibson, Patricia C. Gándara, and Jill P. Koyama, 129–49. London: Teachers College Press.

Gilbert, Liette. 2009. "Immigration as Local Politics: Re-bordering Immigration and Multiculturalism through Deterrence and Incapacitation." *International Journal of Urban and Regional Research* 33 (1): 26–42.

Gill, Hannah E. 2010. *The Latino Migration Experience in North Carolina: New Roots in the Old North State*. Chapel Hill: University of North Carolina Press.

Gleeson, Shannon, and Roberto G. Gonzales. 2012. "When Do Papers Matter? An Institutional Analysis of Undocumented Life in the United States." *International Migration* 50 (4): 1–19.

Golash-Boza, Tanya. 2015. *Deported: Immigrant Policing, Disposable Labor and Global Capitalism*. New York: New York University Press.

Gonzales, Roberto G. 2008. "Left Out but Not Shut Down: Political Activism and the Undocumented Latino Student Movement." *Northwestern Journal of Law and Social Policy* 3 (2): 219–39.

———. 2011. "Learning to Be Illegal: Undocumented Youth and Shifting Legal Contexts in the Transition to Adulthood." *American Sociological Review* 76 (4): 602–19.

———. 2016. *Lives in Limbo: Undocumented and Coming of Age in America*. Oakland: University of California Press.

Gonzales, Roberto G., and Leo R. Chavez. 2012. "Awakening to a Nightmare." *Current Anthropology* 53 (3): 255–81. https://www.jstor.org/stable/10.1086/665414?seq=1#page_scan_tab_contents.

Gonzales, Roberto G., and Veronica Terriquez. 2013. *How DACA Is Impacting the Lives of Those Who Are Now DACAmented: Preliminary Findings from the National UnDACAmented Research Project.* Washington, DC: Immigration Policy Center. https://www.americanimmigrationcouncil.org/sites/default/files/research/daca_final_ipc_csii_1.pdf.

Gonzales, Roberto G., Veronica Terriquez, and Stephen P. Ruszczyk. 2014. "Becoming DACAmented: Assessing the Short-Term Benefits of Deferred Action for Childhood Arrivals (DACA)." *American Behavioral Scientist* 58 (14): 1852–72. http://journals.sagepub.com/doi/abs/10.1177/0002764214550288.

Gonzalez, Jennifer. 2009. "North Carolina Community Colleges to Resume Enrolling Illegal Immigrants." *Chronicle of Higher Education*, September 18. http://chronicle.com/article/North-Carolina-Community/48518/.

Gordon, Milton M. 1964. *Assimilation in American Life: The Role of Race, Religion and National Origin.* Oxford: Oxford University Press.

Griffith, David. 2008. "New Midwesterners, New Southerners: Immigration Experiences in Four Rural American Settings." In *New Faces in New Places: The Changing Geography of American Immigration*, edited by Douglas S. Massey, 179–210. New York: Russell Sage Foundation.

Grusky, David B., Bruce Western, and Christopher Wimmer. 2011. *The Great Recession.* New York: Russell Sage Foundation.

Guzmán, Juan Carlos, and Raúl C. Jara. 2012. *The Economic Benefits of Passing the DREAM Act.* Washington, DC: Center for American Progress. https://www.americanprogress.org/wp-content/uploads/2012/09/DREAMEcon-7.pdf.

Haddix, Lindsay. 2008. "Immigration and Crime in North Carolina: Beyond the Rhetoric." Master's thesis, University of North Carolina at Chapel Hill. https://cdr.lib.unc.edu/indexablecontent/uuid:24ffb9f4-82a0-4a72-985f-4d7566bb72fa.

Hagan, Jacqueline M. 1994. *Deciding to Be Legal: A Maya Community in Houston.* Philadelphia: Temple University Press.

———. 1998. "Social Networks, Gender, and Immigrant Incorporation: Resources and Constraints." *American Sociological Review* 63 (1): 55–67.

Hagan, Jacqueline M., Rubén Hernández-León, and Jean-Luc Demonsant. 2015. *Skills of the "Unskilled": Work and Mobility among Mexican Migrants.* Oakland: University of California Press.

Hagan, Jacqueline M., Nichola Lowe, and Christian Quingla. 2011. "Skills on the Move: Rethinking the Relationship between Human Capital and Immigrant Economic Mobility." *Work and Occupations* 38 (2): 149–78. https://www.ncbi.nlm.nih.gov/pmc/articles/PMC3658444/.

Hagan, Jacqueline M., Nestor Rodriguez, and Brianna Castro. 2011. "Social Effects of

Mass Deportations by the United States Government, 2000–10." *Ethnic and Racial Studies* 34 (8): 1374–91. http://doi.org/10.1080/01419870.2011.575233.

Hernández-León, Rubén, and Victor Zúñiga. 2000. "'Making Carpet by the Mile': The Emergence of a Mexican Immigrant Community in an Industrial Region of the U.S. Historic South." *Social Science Quarterly* 81 (1): 49–66.

———. 2005. "Appalachia Meets Aztlán: Mexican Immigration and Intergroup Relations in Dalton, Georgia." In *New Destinations: Mexican Immigration in the United States*, edited by Victor Zúñiga and Rubén Hernández-Leon, 244–74. New York: Russell Sage Foundation.

Hipsman, Faye, Bárbara Gómez-Aguiñaga, and Randy Capps. 2016. *DACA at Four: Participation in the Deferred Action Program and Impacts on Recipients*. Washington, DC: Migration Policy Institute. https://www.migrationpolicy.org/research/daca-four-participation-deferred-action-program-and-impacts-recipients.

Jones, Jennifer A. 2012. "Blacks May Be Second Class, but They Can't Make Them Leave: Mexican Racial Formation and Immigrant Status in Winston-Salem." *Latino Studies* 10 (1–2): 60–80. https://www.researchgate.net/publication/263328292_Blacks_may_be_second_class_but_they_can%27t_make_them_leave_Mexican_racial_formation_and_immigrant_status_in_Winston-Salem.

Kandel, William, and Emilio A. Parrado. 2004. "Hispanics in the American South and the Transformation of the Poultry Industry." In *Hispanic Spaces, Latino Places: Community and Cultural Diversity in Contemporary America*, edited by Daniel D. Arreola, 255–76. Austin: University of Texas Press.

———. 2005. "Restructuring of the U.S. Meat Processing Industry and New Hispanic Migrant Destinations." *Population and Development Review* 31 (3): 447–71. http://onlinelibrary.wiley.com/doi/10.1111/j.1728-4457.2005.00079.x/abstract.

———. 2006. "Hispanic Population Growth and Public School Response in Two New South Immigrant Destinations." In *The New South: Latinos and the Transformation of Place*, edited by Heather A. Smith and Owen J. Furuseth, 111–34. Aldershot, UK: Ashgate Press.

Kanstroom, Daniel. 2007. *Deportation Nation: Outsiders in American History*. Cambridge, MA: Harvard University Press.

———. 2012. *Aftermath: Deportation Law and the New American*. New York: Oxford University Press.

Kao, Grace, and Jennifer Thompson. 2003. "Racial and Ethnic Stratification in Educational Achievement and Attainment." *Annual Review of Sociology* 29:417–42.

Kao, Grace, Elizabeth Vaquera, and Kimberly Goyette. 2013. *Education and Immigration*. Cambridge: Polity Press.

Kasinitz, Philip. 2008. "Becoming American, Becoming Minority, Getting Ahead: The Role of Racial and Ethnic Status in the Upward Mobility of the Children of Immigrants." *Annals of the American Academy of Political and Social Science* 620 (1): 253–69.

Kasinitz, Philip, John H. Mollenkopf, Mary C. Waters, and Jennifer Holdaway. 2008. *Inheriting the City: The Children of Immigrants Come of Age*. New York: Russell Sage Foundation.

Kibria, Nazli. 2002. "Of Blood, Belonging, and Homeland Trips: Transnationalism and Identity among Second-Generation Chinese and Korean Americans." In *The Changing Face of Home: The Transnational Lives of the Second Generation*, edited by Peggy Levitt and Mary C. Waters, 295–311. New York: Russell Sage Foundation.

Kochhar Rakesh, Roberto Suro, and Sonya Tafoya. 2005. "The New Latino South: The Context and Consequence of Rapid Population Growth." Paper presented at the Immigration to New Settlement Areas Conference, Pew Hispanic Research Center, Washington, DC, July 26. http://www.pewhispanic.org/2005/07/26/the-new-latino-south/.

Krogstad, Jens M., and Ana Gonzalez-Barrera. 2014. *If Original DACA Program Is a Guide, Many Eligible Immigrants Will Apply for Deportation Relief*. Washington, DC: Pew Research Center. http://www.pewresearch.org/fact-tank/2014/12/05/if-original-daca-program-is-a-guide-many-eligible-immigrants-will-apply-for-deportation-relief/.

Kulish, Nicholas, Vivian Yee, Caitlin Dickerson, Liz Robbins, Fernanda Santos, and Jennifer Medina. 2017. "Trump's Immigration Policies Expanded." *New York Times*, February 21. https://www.nytimes.com/2017/02/21/us/trump-immigration-policies-deportation.html.

Lacy, Elaine, and Mary E. Odem. 2009. "Popular Attitudes and Public Policies: Southern Responses to Latino Immigration." In *Latino Immigrants and the Transformation of the U.S. South*, edited by Mary E. Odem and Elaine Lacy, 143–64. Athens: University of Georgia Press.

Lauby, Fanny. 2016. "Leaving the 'Perfect DREAMer' Behind? Narratives and Mobilization in Immigration Reform." *Social Movement Studies* 15 (4): 374–87. http://www.tandfonline.com/doi/abs/10.1080/14742837.2016.1149461.

Lee, John B., Ellen Frishberg, Gina M. Shkodriani, Stanley A. Freeman, Alice M. Maginnis, and Sharon H. Bob. 2009. *Study on the Admission of Undocumented Students into the North Carolina Community College System*. Bethesda, MD: JBL Associates Inc. and Powers, Pyles, Sutter and Verville PC. http://www.webcitation.org/66JPnJ5Si.

Leerkes, Arjen, Mark Leach, and James Bachmeier. 2012. "Borders behind the Border: An Exploration of State-Level Differences in Migration Control and Their Effects on US Migration Patterns." *Journal of Ethnic and Migration Studies* 38 (1): 111–29. http://www.tandfonline.com/doi/abs/10.1080/1369183X.2012.640023.

Levitt, Peggy, and Mary C. Waters. 2002. *The Changing Face of Home: The Transnational Lives of the Second Generation*. New York: Russell Sage Foundation.

López, Janet Kier. 2007. "'We Asked for Workers and They Sent Us People': A Critical Race Theory and Latino Critical Theory Ethnography Exploring College-Ready Undocumented High School Immigrants in North Carolina." PhD. diss., University of North Carolina at Chapel Hill. https://cdr.lib.unc.edu/indexablecontent/uuid:c6ea154f-db55-47c5-9b5a-f94d71ea9909.

Lopez, Nancy. 2002. "Race-Gender Experiences and Schooling: Second-Generation Dominican, West Indian, and Haitian Youth in New York City." *Race, Ethnicity & Education* 5 (1): 67–89. https://doi.org/10.1080/13613320120117207.

———. 2003. *Hopeful Girls, Troubled Boys: Race and Gender Disparity in Urban Education.* New York: Routledge.

López-Sanders, Laura. 2009. *Trapped at the Bottom: Racialized and Gendered Labor Queues in New Latino Destinations.* Center for Comparative Immigration Studies Working Paper No. 176, San Diego, CA. http://ccis.ucsd.edu/_files/wp176.pdf.

Maldonado, Marta Maria. 2014. "Latino Incorporation and Racialized Border Politics in the Heartland: Interior Enforcement and Policeability in an English-Only State." *American Behavioral Scientist* 58 (14): 1927–45. http://journals.sagepub.com/doi/abs/10.1177/0002764214550292.

Marrow, Helen B. 2009. "New Immigrant Destinations and the American Colour Line." *Ethnic and Racial Studies* 32 (6): 1037–57. http://www.tandfonline.com/doi/abs/10.1080/01419870902853224.

———. 2011. *New Destination Dreaming: Immigration, Race, and Legal Status in the Rural American South.* Stanford, CA: Stanford University Press.

———. 2017. "The Difference a Decade of Enforcement Makes: Hispanic Racial Incorporation and Changing Intergroup Relations in the American South's Black Belt (2003–16)." In *The Politics of New Immigrant Destinations: Transatlantic Perspectives,* edited by Stefanie Chambers, Diana Evans, Anthony Messina, and Abigail Fisher Williamson, 102–20. Philadelphia: Temple University Press.

Martinez, Lisa M. 2008. "The Individual and Contextual Determinants of Protest among Latinos." *Mobilization* 13 (2): 189–204.

Massey, Douglas S., and Chiara Capoferro. 2008. "The Geographic Diversification of American Immigration." In *New Faces in New Places: The Changing Geography of American Immigration,* edited by Douglas S. Massey, 25–50. New York: Russell Sage Foundation.

Meckler, Laura. 2017. "White House Sends Congress Plans for Immigration Enforcement." *Wall Street Journal,* October 8. https://www.wsj.com/articles/white-house-sends-congress-plans-for-immigration-enforcement-1507505814.

Menjívar, Cecilia. 2006. "Liminal Legality: Salvadoran and Guatemalan Immigrants' Lives in the United States." *American Journal of Sociology* 111 (4): 999–1037.

Menjívar, Cecilia, and Leisy J. Abrego. 2012. "Legal Violence: Immigration Law and the Lives of Central American Immigrants." *American Journal of Sociology* 117 (5): 1380–1421.

Messick, Madeleine, and Claire Bergeron. 2014. *Temporary Protected Status in the United States: A Grant of Humanitarian Relief That Is Less Than Permanent.* Washington,

DC: Migration Policy Institute. http://www.migrationpolicy.org/article/temporary-protected-status-united-states-grant-humanitarian-relief-less-permanent.

Mohl, Raymond A. 2003. "Globalization, Latinization, and the Nuevo New South." *Journal of American Ethnic History* 22 (4): 31–66.

Morales, P. Zitlali, Tina M. Trujillo, and René E. Kissell. 2016. "Educational Policy and Latin@ Youth." In *Educational Policies and Youth in the 21st Century: Problems, Potential, and Progress*, edited by Sharon L. Nichols, 3–22. Charlotte, NC: Information Age Publishing.

Motomura, Hiroshi. 2006. *Americans in Waiting: The Lost Story of Immigration and Citizenship in the United States*. New York: Oxford University Press.

———. 2014. *Immigration outside the Law*. New York: Oxford University Press.

Nakamura, David. 2017. "Trump Administration Moving Quickly to Build Up Nationwide Deportation Force." *Washington Post*, April 12. https://www.washingtonpost.com/politics/trump-administration-moving-quickly-to-build-up-nationwide-deportation-force/2017/04/12/7a7f59c2-1f87-11e7-be2a-3a1fb24d4671_story.html?utm_term=.5c5099c085b0.

Napolitano, Janet. 2012. *Memorandum Exercising Prosecutorial Discretion with Respect to Individuals Who Came to the United States as Children*. Washington, DC: US Department of Homeland Security, June 15. https://www.dhs.gov/xlibrary/assets/s1-exercising-prosecutorial-discretion-individuals-who-came-to-us-as-children.pdf.

National Conference of State Legislatures. 2014. *Undocumented Student Tuition: State Action*. Washington, DC. http://www.ncsl.org/issues-research/educ/undocumented-student-tuition-state-action.aspx.

———. 2015. *Tuition Benefits for Immigrants*. Washington, DC. http://www.ncsl.org/documents/immig/InStateTuition_july212015.pdf.

National Immigration Law Center. 2013. *Are Individuals Granted Deferred Action under the Deferred Action for Childhood Arrivals (DACA) Policy Eligible for State Driver's Licenses?* Washington, DC. https://www.nilc.org/wp-content/uploads/2016/06/DACA-and-drivers-licenses-2013-06-19.pdf..

New York Times Editorial Board. 2017. "Breaking the Anti-immigrant Fever." *New York Times*, February 18. https://www.nytimes.com/2017/02/18/opinion/sunday/breaking-the-anti-immigrant-fever.html?_r=0.

Nicholls, Walter J. 2013. *The DREAMers: How the Undocumented Youth Movement Transformed the Immigrant Rights Debate*. Stanford, CA: Stanford University Press.

Nicholls, Walter J., and Tara Fiorito. 2015. "Dreamers Unbound: Immigrant Youth Mobilizing." *New Labor Forum* 24 (1): 86–92.

North Carolina Community College System. 2008. *Memorandum: Unrestricted Admission of Undocumented or Illegal Immigrants*. http://www.nccommunitycolleges.edu/sites/default/files/numbered-memos/cc08-114.pdf.

———. 2009. *Memorandum: Important Administrative Code Information: Proposed*

Changes in the Administrative Code. http://www.nccommunitycolleges.edu/sites/default/files/numbered-memos/cc09-033.pdf.

———. 2013. *Memorandum: Deferred Action for Childhood Arrivals ("DACA") Classification and Eligibility for Community College Tuition Exceptions.* https://uncw.edu/centrohispano/documents/DACA-and-CC-Tuition-Exceptions-FINAL-12SEP13.pdf.

North Carolina Department of Transportation. 2013. "Driver License Process for DACA Applicants." https://apps.ncdot.gov/newsreleases/Image.ashx?id=2154.

Ochoa, Gilda L. 2013. *Academic Profiling: Latinos, Asian Americans, and the Achievement Gap.* Minneapolis: University of Minnesota Press.

Ojeda, Raul H., and Paule C. Takash. 2010. *No DREAMers Left Behind: The Economic Potential of DREAM Act Beneficiaries.* Los Angeles: North American Integration and Development Center, University of California, Los Angeles. http://cccie.org/reports/no-dreamers-left-behind-economic-potential-dream-act-beneficiaries/.

O'Keefe, Ed. 2017. "Nancy Pelosi Confronted by Immigrants Rights Protesters about Her DACA Talks with Trump." *Washington Post*, September 18. https://www.washingtonpost.com/news/powerpost/wp/2017/09/18/nancy-pelosi-confronted-by-daca-recipients-protesting-her-agreement-with-trump/?utm_term=.f5495deda36a.

Okamoto, Dina, and Kim Ebert. 2010. "Beyond the Ballot: Immigrant Collective Action in Gateways and New Destinations in the United States." *Social Problems* 57 (4): 529–58. https://www.researchgate.net/publication/228350604_Beyond_the_Ballot_Immigrant_Collective_Action_in_Gateways_and_New_Destinations_in_the_United_States.

Olivas, Michael A. 2007. "Immigration-Related State and Local Ordinances: Preemption, Prejudice, and the Proper Role for Enforcement." *University of Chicago Legal Forum* 1:27–56.

———. 2012. *No Undocumented Child Left Behind: "Plyler v. Doe" and the Education of Undocumented Schoolchildren.* New York: New York University Press.

Oyserman, Daphna, Kathy Harrison, and Deborah Bybee. 2001. "Can Racial Identity Be Promotive of Academic Efficacy?" *International Journal of Behavioral Development* 25 (4): 379–85. http://journals.sagepub.com/doi/10.1080/01650250042000401.

Parrado, Emilio A., and William Kandel. 2008. "New Hispanic Migrant Destinations: A Tale of Two Industries." In *New Faces in New Places: The Changing Geography of American Immigration,* edited by Douglas S. Massey, 99–123. New York: Russell Sage Foundation.

Passel, Jeffrey, and D'Vera Cohn. 2009. *A Portrait of Unauthorized Immigrants in the United States.* Washington, DC: Pew Hispanic Center. http://www.pewhispanic.org/2009/04/14/a-portrait-of-unauthorized-immigrants-in-the-united-states/.

Passel, Jeffrey, D'Vera Cohn, and Mark H. Lopez. 2011. *Hispanics Account for More Than Half of the Nation's Growth in Past Decade.* Washington, DC: Pew Hispanic Center. http://www.pewhispanic.org/2011/03/24/hispanics-account-for-more-than-half-of-nations-growth-in-past-decade/.

Patel, Leigh. 2013. *Youth Held at the Border: Immigration, Education, and the Politics of Inclusion.* New York: Teachers College Press.

Perez, William. 2009. *We Are Americans: Undocumented Students Pursuing the American Dream.* Sterling, VA: Stylus.

———. 2014. "Challenging the 'DREAMer' Narrative." *Huffington Post, The Blog,* November   16.   http://www.huffingtonpost.com/jonathan-perez/challenging-the-dreamerna_b_6163008.html.

Perreira, Krista M., Andrew Fuligni, and Stephanie Potochnick. 2010. "Fitting In: The Roles of Social Acceptance and Discrimination in Shaping the Academic Motivations of Latino Youth in the U.S. Southeast." *Journal of Social Issues* 66 (1): 131–53.

Pew Research Center. 2016. *U.S. Unauthorized Immigrant Population, by State, 2014.* http://www.pewhispanic.org/interactives/unauthorized-immigrants/.

Pham, Huyen. 2004. "The Inherent Flaws in the Inherent Authority Position: Why Inviting Local Enforcement of Immigration Laws Violates the Constitution." *Florida State University Law Review* 31:965–1003.

Polletta, Francesca, and James M. Jasper. 2001. "Collective Identity and Social Movements." *Annual Review of Sociology* 27:283–305.

Portes, Alejandro, and Rubén G. Rumbaut. 2001. *Legacies: The Story of the Immigrant Second Generation.* Berkeley: University of California Press.

Portes, Alejandro, and Min Zhou. 1993. "The New Second Generation: Segmented Assimilation and Its Variants." *Annals of the American Academy of Political and Social Science* 530 (1): 74–96. https://web.stanford.edu/group/scspi/_media/pdf/Classic_Media/Portes_Zhou_93_Immigration.pdf.

Potochnick, Stephanie, Krista M. Perreira, and Andrew Fuligni. 2012. "Fitting In: The Roles of Social Acceptance and Discrimination in Shaping the Daily Psychological Well-Being of Latino Youth." *Social Science Quarterly* 93 (1): 173–90. http://onlinelibrary.wiley.com/doi/10.1111/j.1540-6237.2011.00830.x/abstract.

Ramakrishnan, S. Karthick, and Tom T. Wong. 2010. "Partisanship, Not Spanish: Explaining Municipal Ordinances Affecting Undocumented Immigrants." In *Taking Local Control: Immigration Policy Activism in U.S. Cities and States,* edited by Monica W. Varsanyi, 73–96. Stanford, CA: Stanford University Press.

Redden, Elizabeth. 2008. "For the Undocumented: To Admit or Not to Admit?" *Inside Higher Ed,* August 18. https://www.insidehighered.com/news/2008/08/18/immigrants..

Ribas, Vanesa. 2016. *On the Line: Slaughterhouse Lives and the Making of the New South.* Oakland: University of California Press.

Rincón, Alejandra. 2008. *Undocumented Immigrants and Higher Education: Sí Se Puede.* New York: LFB Scholarly Publishing.

Rios, Victor M. 2011. *Punished: Policing the Lives of Black and Latino Boys.* New York: New York University Press.

Robbins, Liz, and Caitlin Dickerson. 2017. "Immigration Agents Arrest 600 People across U.S. in One Week." *New York Times*, February 12. https://www.nytimes. com/2017/02/12/nyregion/immigration-arrests-sanctuary-city.html?_r=0.

Rodriguez, Cristina M., Muzaffar Chishti, and Kimberly Nortman. 2010. "Legal Limits of Immigration Federalism." In *Taking Local Control: Immigration Policy Activism in U.S. Cities and States*, edited by Monica W. Varsanyi, 31–50. Stanford, CA: Stanford University Press.

Román, Ediberto. 2010. *Citizenship and Its Exclusions: A Classical, Constitutional, and Critical Race Critique*. New York: New York University Press.

Romero, Mary. 2006. "Racial Profiling and Immigration Law Enforcement: Rounding Up of Usual Suspects in the Latino Community." *Critical Sociology* 32 (2): 447–73. http://doi.org/10.1163/156916306777835376.

Rumbaut, Rubén G. 2005. "Turning Points in the Transition to Adulthood: Determinants of Educational Attainment, Incarceration, and Early Childbearing among Children of Immigrants." *Ethnic and Racial Studies* 28 (6): 1041–86. http://www.tandfonline.com/doi/abs/10.1080/01419870500224349.

Rumbaut, Rubén G., and Alejandro Portes. 2001. *Ethnicities: Children of Immigrants in America*. Berkeley: University of California Press.

Russell, Alene. 2011. *State Policies regarding Undocumented Students: A Narrative of Unresolved Issues, Ongoing Debates, and Missed Opportunities*. Washington, DC: American Association of State Colleges and Universities. http://www.aascu.org/up- loadedFiles/AASCU/Content/Root/PolicyAndAdvocacy/PolicyPublications/PM_ UndocumentedStudents-March2011.pdf.

Salgado, Julio. 2012. *I Am Undocuqueer!* http://juliosalgadoart.com/search/ I+am+undocuqueer.

Schmalzbauer, Leah. 2009. "Gender on a New Frontier: Mexican Migration in the Rural Mountain West." *Gender and Society* 23 (6): 747–67.

———. 2014. *The Last Best Place? Gender, Family, and Migration in the New West*. Stanford, CA: Stanford University Press.

Seif, Hinda. 2014. "'Coming out of the Shadows' and 'Undocuqueer': Undocumented Immigrants Transforming Sexuality Discourse and Activism." *Journal of Language and Sexuality* 3 (1): 87–120. https://www.researchgate.net/publication/262872097_ Coming_out_of_the_shadows_and_undocuqueer_Undocumented_immigrants_ transforming_sexuality_discourse_and_activism.

Shahshahani, Azadeh. 2010. *The Persistence of Racial Profiling in Gwinnett: Time for Accountability, Transparency, and an End to 287(g)*. https://www.acluga.org/sites/de- fault/files/gwinnett_racial_profiling_report_1.pdf.

Silver, Alexis M. 2012. "Aging into Exclusion and Social Transparency: Transitions to Adulthood for Undocumented Immigrant Youth." *Latino Studies* 10 (4): 499–522.

———. 2015. "Clubs of Culture and Capital: Immigrant and Second-Generation Incorporation in a New Destination School." *Ethnic and Racial Studies* 38 (5): 824–40. http://www.tandfonline.com/doi/abs/10.1080/01419870.2014.941892.

————. 2017. "No Place like Home: From High School Graduation to Deportation." In *Forced Out and Fenced In: Immigration Tales from the Field*, edited by Tanya M. Golash-Boza, 193–202. Oxford: Oxford University Press.

Singer, Audrey, Nicole P. Svajlenka, and Jill H. Wilson. 2015. *Local Insights from DACA for Implementing Future Programs for Unauthorized Immigrants.* Washington, DC: Brookings Metropolitan Policy Program. https://www.brookings.edu/wp-content/uploads/2016/06/BMPP_Srvy_DACAImmigration_June3b.pdf.

Smith, Barbara E. 2001. *The New Latino South.* Memphis, TN: Center for Research on Women. http://www.intergroupresources.com/rc/The%20New%20Latino%20South%20An%20Introduction.pdf.

Smith, Heather A., and Owen J. Furuseth. 2006. *Latinos in the New South: Transformations of Place.* Burlington, VT: Ashgate.

Smith, Robert C. 2002. "Gender, Ethnicity and Race in School and Work Outcomes of Second Generation Mexican Americans." In *Latinos Remaking America*, edited by Marcelo M. Suárez-Orozco and Mariela M. Páez, 110–25. Berkeley: University of California Press.

————. 2006. *Mexican New York: Transnational Lives of New Immigrants.* Berkeley: University of California Press.

————. 2014. "Black Mexicans, Conjunctural Ethnicity, and Operating Identities: Long-Term Ethnographic Analysis." *American Sociological Review* 79 (3): 517–48. http://journals.sagepub.com/doi/abs/10.1177/0003122414529585.

Snavely, Keith, and Martin B. Tracy. 2000. "Collaboration among Rural Nonprofit Organizations." *Nonprofit Management and Leadership* 11 (2): 145–65. http://doi.org/10.1002/nml.11202..

Sohoni, Deenesh, and Jennifer Bickham Mendez. 2014. "Defining Immigrant Newcomers in New Destinations: Symbolic Boundaries in Williamsburg, Virginia." *Ethnic and Racial Studies* 37 (3): 496–516. http://www.tandfonline.com/doi/abs/10.1080/01419870.2012.716521?journalCode=rers20.

Stanton-Salazar, Ricardo D. 2001. *Manufacturing Hope and Despair: The School and Kin Support Networks of U.S.-Mexican Youth.* New York: Teachers College Press.

Striffler, Steve. 2005. *Chicken: The Dangerous Transformation of America's Favorite Food.* New Haven, CT: Yale University Press.

Stuesse, Angela. 2016. *Scratching Out a Living: Latinos, Race, and Work in the Deep South.* Oakland: University of California Press.

Stumpf, Juliet. 2006. "The Crimmigration Crisis: Immigrants, Crime, and Sovereign Power." *American University Law Review* 56 (2): 367–419.

Suárez-Orozco, Carola. 2008. *Learning a New Land: Immigrant Students in American Society.* Cambridge, MA: Belknap Press of Harvard University Press.

Suárez-Orozco, Carola, Desirée B. Qin, and Ramona F. Amthor. 2008. "Adolescents from Immigrant Families: Relationships and Adaptation in School." In *Adolescents at*

School: Perspectives on Youth, Identity, and Education, edited by Michael Sadowski, 51–69. Cambridge, MA: Harvard Education Press.

Suárez-Orozco, Carola, and Marcelo M. Suárez-Orozco. 2001. *Children of Immigration.* Cambridge, MA: Harvard University Press.

Szkupinski Quiroga, Seline, Dulce M. Medina, and Jennifer Glick. 2014. "In the Belly of the Beast: Effects of Anti-immigration Policy on Latino Community Members." *American Behavioral Scientist* 58 (13): 1723–42. http://journals.sagepub.com/doi/abs/10.1177/0002764214537270.

Tatum, Beverly D. 1997. *"Why Are All the Black Kids Sitting Together in the Cafeteria?" and Other Conversations about Race.* New York: Basic Books.

Telles, Edward Eric, and Vilma Ortiz. 2008. *Generations of Exclusion: Mexican Americans, Assimilation, and Race.* New York: Russell Sage Foundation.

Terriquez, Veronica. 2014. "Trapped in the Working Class? Prospects for the Intergenerational (Im)Mobility of Latino Youth." *Sociological Inquiry* 84 (3): 382–411. http://onlinelibrary.wiley.com/doi/10.1111/soin.12042/abstract.

———. 2015. "Intersectional Mobilization, Social Movement Spillover, and Queer Youth Leadership in the Immigrant Rights Movement." *Social Problems* 62 (3): 343–62. https://academic.oup.com/socpro/article/62/3/343/1638996/Intersectional-Mobilization-Social-Movement.

Torres, Rebecca M., E. Jeffrey Popke, and Holly M. Hapke. 2006. "The South's Silent Bargain: Rural Restructuring, Latino Labor, and the Ambiguities of Migrant Experience." In *Latinos in the New South: Transformation of Place,* edited by Heather A. Smith and Owen J. Furuseth, 37–67. Burlington, VT: Ashgate.

Tran, Van C., and Nicol M. Valdez. 2015. "Second-Generation Decline or Advantage? Latino Assimilation in the Aftermath of the Great Recession." *International Migration Review* 51 (1): 155–90. http://onlinelibrary.wiley.com/doi/10.1111/imre.12192/abstract.

Tyson, Karolyn. 2011. *Integration Interrupted: Tracking, Black Students, and Acting White after Brown.* New York: Oxford University Press.

US Citizenship and Immigration Services. 2016. *Number of I-821D, Consideration of Deferred Action for Childhood Arrivals by Fiscal Year, Quarter, Intake, Biometrics and Case Status: 2012–2016.* June 30. https://www.uscis.gov/sites/default/files/USCIS/Resources/Reports%20and%20Studies/Immigration%20Forms%20Data/All%20Form%20Types/DACA/daca_performancedata_fy2016_qtr3.pdf.

US Department of Homeland Security. 2017. "Rescission of Memorandum Providing for Deferred Action for Parents of Americans and Lawful Permanent Residents ('DAPA')." June 15. https://www.dhs.gov/news/2017/06/15/rescission-memorandum-providing-deferred-action-parents-americans-and-lawful.

US Department of Justice. 2017. "Attorney General Sessions Delivers Remarks on Justice." September 5. https://www.justice.gov/opa/speech/attorney-general-sessions-delivers-remarks-daca.

Valdez, Inés. 2016. "Punishment, Race, and the Organization of U.S. Immigration Exclusion." *Political Research Quarterly* 69 (4): 640–54. https://papers.ssrn.com/sol3/papers.cfm?abstract_id=2941180.

Valenzuela, Angela. 1999. *Subtractive Schooling: U.S.-Mexican Youth and the Politics of Caring.* Albany: State University of New York Press.

———. 2005. *Leaving Children Behind: How "Texas-Style" Accountability Fails Latino Youth.* Albany: State University of New York Press.

Vargas, José A. 2012. "Not Legal, Not Leaving." *Time*, June 25, 34–44.

Varsanyi, Monica W. 2010. *Taking Local Control: Immigration Policy Activism in U.S. Cities and States.* Stanford, CA: Stanford University Press.

Varsanyi, Monica W., Paul G. Lewis, Doris M. Provine, and Scott Decker. 2012. "A Multilayered Jurisdictional Patchwork: Immigration Federalism in the United States." *Law and Policy* 34 (2): 139–58.

Waldinger, Roger D. 2003. *How the Other Half Works: Immigration and the Social Organization of Labor.* Berkeley: University of California Press.

Warner, W. Lloyd, and Leo Srole. 1945. *The Social Systems of American Ethnic Groups.* New Haven, CT: Yale University Press.

Waters, Mary. 1996. "The Intersection of Gender, Race, and Ethnicity in Identity Development of Caribbean American Teens." In *Urban Girls: Resisting Stereotypes, Creating Identities*, edited by Bonnie Leadbeater and Niobe Way, 65–84. New York: New York University Press.

Weissman, Deborah M., Rebecca C. Headen, and Katherine L. Parker. 2009. *The Policies and Politics of Local Immigration Enforcement Laws: 287(g) Program in North Carolina.* Chapel Hill: Immigration and Human Rights Policy Clinic, University of North Carolina. http://www.law.unc.edu/documents/clinicalprograms/287gpolicyreview.pdf.

White House Office of the Press Secretary. 2012. "Remarks by the President on Immigration." June 15. https://www.whitehouse.gov/the-press-office/2012/06/15/remarks-president-immigration.

———. 2017. "Executive Order: Enhancing Public Safety in the Interior of the United States." January 25. https://www.whitehouse.gov/the-press-office/2017/01/25/presidential-executive-order-enhancing-public-safety-interior-united.

White, Melissa Autumn. 2014. "Documenting the Undocumented: Toward a Queer Politics of No Borders." *Sexualities* 17 (8): 976–97. http://journals.sagepub.com/doi/abs/10.1177/1363460714552263.

Wimmer, Andreas. 2008. "The Making and Unmaking of Ethnic Boundaries: A Multilevel Process Theory." *American Journal of Sociology* 113 (4): 970–1022. http://www.journals.uchicago.edu/doi/abs/10.1086/522803.

———. 2013. *Ethnic Boundary Making: Institutions, Power, Networks.* New York: Oxford University Press.

Winders, Jamie. 2007. "Bringing Back the (B)order: Post-9/11 Politics of Immigration,

Borders, and Belonging in the Contemporary US South." *Antipode* 39 (5): 920–42. http://onlinelibrary.wiley.com/doi/10.1111/j.1467-8330.2007.00563.x/abstract.

Wishnie, Michael J. 2001. "Laboratories of Bigotry? Devolution of the Immigration Power, Equal Protection and Federalism." *New York University Law Review* 76:493–569.

Wolf, Diane L. 2002. "There's No Place like 'Home': Emotional Transnationalism and the Struggles of Second-Generation Filipinos." In *The Changing Face of Home: The Transnational Lives of the Second Generation*, edited by Peggy Levitt and Mary C. Waters, 255–94. New York: Russell Sage Foundation.

Yablon-Zug, Marcia A., and Danielle R. Holley-Walker. 2009. "Not Very Collegial: Exploring Bans on Undocumented Immigrant Admissions to State Colleges and Universities." *Charleston Law Review* 3:101–17. http://scholarcommons.sc.edu/cgi/viewcontent.cgi?article=1836&context=law_facpub.

Zatz, Marjorie S., and Nancy Rodriguez. 2015. *Dreams and Nightmares: Immigration Policy, Youth, and Families*. Oakland: University of California Press.

Index